D0378811

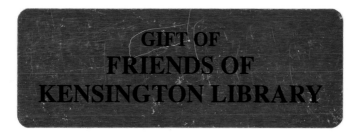

THE
OTHER
8
HOURS

ALSO BY ROBERT PAGLIARINI

THE SIX-DAY FINANCIAL MAKEOVER

ROBERT PAGLIARINI

THE OTHER 8 HOURS

MAXIMIZE YOUR FREE TIME
TO CREATE NEW WEALTH & PURPOSE

WITHDRAWN

ST. MARTIN'S PRESS ≈ NEW YORK

www.stmartins.com

Book design by Mspace/Maura Fadden Rosenthal

Library of Congress Cataloging-in-Publication Data

Pagliarini, Robert.
    The other 8 hours : maximize your free time to create new wealth & purpose / Robert Pagliarini.—1st ed.
                p. cm.
    Includes index.
    ISBN 978-0-312-57135-1
  1. Time management.   2. Finance, Personal.   I. Title.
    HD69.T54P34 2010
    650.1'1—dc22

                                                    2009033515

First Edition: January 2010

10 9 8 7 6 5 4 3 2 1

To my two favorite gals . . . Elizabeth Pagliarini and
Alexandra "Bean" Pagliarini.
I love you both so much. I am blessed to have you in my life.

CONTENTS

ACKNOWLEDGMENTS

I hope John Murphy doesn't read this. He's the director of publicity at my publisher, St. Martin's Press. I know he knows I think he's fabulous, but if he really knew how grateful I am for his tireless efforts, his encouragement, and his friendship, it would just go to his head. John has been my #1 fan since I met him in an elevator in 2005. He's pushed and fought (and probably annoyed many a producer) to get me in the door. He's the best friend and supporter a guy could ask for. Thank you for everything, John! You are the BEST.

Here's how lucky I am . . . I was able to work with two amazing editors at St. Martin's Press. Thank you first to David Moldawer. He immediately got *the other 8 hours* and helped me refine and define what makes a Cre8tor different from a creator. David, it was an honor to work with you for those first few weeks, and I wish you continued success at your new firm.

I was then fortunate to work closely with Kathy Huck. She is a fantastic editor. She was the yin to my yang. She kept me in check and helped set the tone for the book. She was patient and thoughtful. She understands that writers pour their hearts into their work and was always considerate enough to say, "What if you tried this?" instead of saying, "This is crap—need to rework." Kathy, thank you for telling me what I needed to hear in the way I needed to hear it. That's a gift. I look forward to working with you again!

Thanks to the following experts who answered the question, What one thing should readers do with their other 8 hours that will have the greatest positive impact on their lives? Leo Babauta, Kim Barnouin, Seth Godin, Sonja Lyubomirsky, Merlin Mann, Michael Michalowicz, Gretchen Rubin, Tim Sanders, and Twyla Tharp.

Thank you to all those who shared their AnOther 8 Success stories: Dr. Susan Biali, Michael Brooke, Gabrielle de Cuir, Todd Defren, Mindee Doney, Allison Hagendorf, Cheryl Haggard, Samantha Hahn, Miriam Hughes, Ryan Kappel, Michael Khalili, Nick Loper, Charla Muller, Drew Oliver, Darren Rowse, Stefan Rudnicki, John Schulte, and Eric Stephens.

Thank you to everyone at *20/20*, *Dr. Phil*, and *Good Morning America* (and to Chris Cuomo, the only guy in the country who can say my last name better than I can!). You've all been so supportive and gracious. I've loved being part of the team.

There are few things more satisfying to me than sitting down at my computer, feeling a warm summer breeze, cranking up some loud music, and writing. Thanks to the following bands for providing me energy and inspiration: Guns N' Roses (*Chinese Democracy* rocks!), Coldplay, Incubus, Nirvana, Pearl Jam, and Sugarland ("Something More" is the theme song for this book).

As always, thank you to my team at Dupree Miller & Associates. My superagent, "Miller, Jan Miller," and Nena Madonia are full of energy and passion. Thank you for pushing me to write the best book I can and for your years of support and encouragement.

A special thank you to my sister, Cathy Pagliarini. Those long phone calls on the road from LA provided some important clarification and inspiration for the book. Thanks to Mike Millar for his friendship and seemingly never-ending help with the subtitle. Thanks to Simon Anthony for his review and tips for writing a screenplay. And thanks to Barrett Yeretsian for his insight into the Music Cre8tor Channel.

Words cannot express the gratitude I have for having two amazing women in my life . . . my wife, Elizabeth Pagliarini, and my daughter, Alexandra "Bean" Pagliarini. A lot of wives are supportive, but my wife has gone one step further. Many years ago she saw something in me that I didn't see in myself. She believed in me and has inspired me to not settle and to keep reaching. Confidence is like a little seed. With a little caring and support it can turn into a massive and strong tree. Elizabeth helped plant that first seed. Thank you. I'll love you forever.

I was born on October 5, 2005—at least that's what it feels like. The minute my daughter was born I was a new man. She has brought joy that is indescribable. She is the prettiest girl in the world, and I am so proud to be her daddy. Bean, a few years from now you'll be able to read about how much I love you, but I hope there isn't a day that goes by that you don't know this already.

Lastly, thank you to God and his son, Jesus. Encourage all of us to spend some of the other 8 hours growing closer to you.

INTRODUCTION

Do you have a "gap" between where you are and where you'd like to be? Maybe you have a mortgage you can't afford, credit card debt you can't get rid of, twenty pounds you can't seem to lose, kids who are asleep before you get home every night, or a gnawing feeling that life is passing you by. If so, what's the solution? Is it to sleep more? To work longer hours?

This book is about the 8 hours in the day when you are not working or sleeping. This "free" time is the most valuable resource you have to achieve your ideal life. Think about it. You lose 8 hours to sleep and you sell (at least) 8 hours to your job. That leaves just 8 more. What are you doing during the other 8 hours, and, more importantly, what are the other 8 hours doing for you?

Look around. Anyone who is successful and lives a rich and meaningful life has used the other 8 hours. They've probably never even heard of this concept, but don't kid yourself. They instinctively know this is the real "secret" to success and fulfillment. Day in and day out, while others squander this time, they have invested it.

How you spend the other 8 hours determines where you are in life, your happiness, your weight, your level of debt, the satisfaction you have with your relationships, the car you drive, the languages you speak, your love life, your education, the places you travel, your bank account balance, and just about everything else that is important to you.

It doesn't really matter where your gaps are because the solution is the same. The only way to radically improve your life and your financial situation is to do something with the other 8 hours. This book will show you how to close the gaps in your life by investing the other 8 hours in yourself. It's about resurrecting the goals and dreams you once had, creating new opportunities, and reclaiming your life.

Are you nervous? A little worried? Don't let the title scare you. *The Other 8 Hours* is not about cramming more into an already overscheduled day—a full calendar doesn't equal a full life. *The Other 8 Hours* is about focusing on those activities that are most important and getting you closer to living your ideal life. And, look at it this way, you're a natural. Unless you're reading this while sleeping or working (tsk, tsk), you're already using your free time to improve yourself and your life.

The promise of *The Other 8 Hours* is to help you get more time, get more money, and get a life. The book is divided into four sections:

- **Get a Clue.** Think free time is free? It's not. This section lays the groundwork for why life begins at 5:00 PM and why we desperately need the other 8 hours to escape from the Living Dead and the Dead Broke.

- **Get More Time.** Chances are you are overworked, overscheduled, and overstressed. There's too much to do and not enough time. You might feel pulled in a hundred different directions and have little hope of relief. If you'd be happy with just 8 minutes of free time, this section will show you how to create hours of additional free time each day so you can pursue those things that bring you closer to reaching your goals and provide happiness and meaning to your life.

- **Get More Money.** There are a zillion strategies to help you *improve* your financial situation by cutting back on morning lattes, saving a little bit more each month, and investing in your 401(k). The problem with such traditional financial strategies is that the advice always comes down to cutting your expenses and saving money. This is a tried-and-true strategy, but for a lot of hardworking people who are already in debt and/or have already slashed expenses to the bone, it's not enough.

  Traditional financial advice can also leave a lot of people frustrated and bored. "Cancel your cable TV subscription and bring a sack lunch to work, and in fifty years you might have enough money to retire." Yippee. Whoo-hoo. It's no wonder so few people follow the traditional advice. *The Other 8 Hours* introduces some new, unconventional strategies. It's a book for the next level. Call it financial planning, version 2.0.

- **Get a Life.** *The Other 8 Hours* is more than a whole new way to "get rich," it also provides a blueprint for how to "get a life." After talking to hundreds of people, a common theme began to emerge as I listened to the same cries for help.

"I feel like there's got to be something more. I feel like I've wasted the last ten years of my life. There's just no way to get ahead. Everyone around me is doing something with their lives, and I'm just existing. I have no options and no way to change my life. I feel empty."

These are real feelings by real people and millions around the world share those feelings—maybe your neighbor, your hair stylist, the guy at the grocery store, your attorney, your spouse, even you.

The Other 8 Hours will help you find your "pulse" and show you specifically how to use the other 8 hours to get a life.

The Other 8 Hours is a book about life and money, but it's also a message of hope. No matter who you are, where you live, how much debt you are in, or your level of education, you can invest in the other 8 hours and create a better life for yourself.

Maybe you're not convinced. Before you can use the other 8 hours to create new wealth and purpose, you have to recognize the importance of the other 8 hours. That's the goal of the first section of the book—Get a Clue.

GET A CLUE

I don't know when it happened, but the rules for getting ahead have changed and nobody got the memo. We plugged into a belief system that promised our hard work would enable us to pay our bills, send our kids to college, enjoy retirement, and live a balanced life with time for our family and friends. How's that working so far?

We've had to run faster and faster just to stay in place. Job security is an oxymoron. Rising expenses and high debt levels weigh us down. Taxes and inflation take a huge bite out of our ability to save for our future. Our solution? Cram more into our already overscheduled calendars without determining how or if these commitments and responsibilities are getting us closer to our ideal life.

This solution is clearly not working. We're overextended and overstressed. We aren't any closer to achieving our goals because we have been chipping away at the one thing that can give us more meaning and income—the other 8 hours.

But before you can use the other 8 hours to close your gaps and achieve your ideal life, you first must recognize the power of your free time. Here are a few things this section will teach you:

- Almost everything important you've ever experienced occurred during the other 8 hours.

- The time you sleep and work helps you survive, but the other 8 hours can help you thrive.

- The problems with the traditional approach to work, saving, and investing.

- Why it has become harder to get ahead.

- Why the other 8 hours is the answer to closing our gaps, improving financial security, and living a more meaningful life.

We spend the first quarter of our lives learning and growing, but then something happens and we stop investing in ourselves. This section is your wake-up call to the challenges we face if we don't use the other 8 hours.

CHAPTER ONE

LIFE BEGINS AT 5:00 PM

The Other 8 Hours Determine
Your Happiness and Net Worth

Six years ago, Mark and Sarah were on a cruise ship touring the South Pacific when a violent tropical storm damaged the ship's hull. Several passengers were knocked overboard and into the dark, churning waters nearly fifty feet below. Mark and Sarah were two of the passengers who plunged into the cold waters that night. They frantically grabbed pieces of debris and hung on tight—doing whatever they could to keep their head above water.

The next morning, Mark washed up onto a small and uninhabited island. Sarah washed up onto a neighboring island, also uninhabited, about two miles from Mark.

After the initial shock of the situation wore away, fear and anxiety overcame them. They knew that it would not be easy. They would have to work hard to build a shelter, pick fruits, locate fresh water, and fish for food. The first few days were scary and difficult, but they both managed to build makeshift shelters to protect them from the rain and sun. They found freshwater streams deeper into the islands and plenty of fruits and nuts. As the days turned into weeks, they even got good at trapping crabs and spearing fish.

In the late afternoons, Mark had some time to relax after a hard day's work. He'd climb to his favorite bluff and watch the waves crash against rocks. As the sun set and the stars lit up the sky, he'd dream of galaxies far away and pray that he'd be rescued soon.

Sarah struggled to survive each day, too. Like Mark, her day began when the sun came up. Chopping wood, climbing trees for fruit, picking nuts and berries, fishing, and getting water kept her busy. At the end of her daily routine, she'd long to relax on the beach, but she knew she wanted more than just to survive. Sarah wanted to get off the island.

Each afternoon, Sarah spent a couple of additional hours gathering and storing wood. She tested nearly every type of vegetation on the island to see which produced the darkest and thickest smoke. She collected rocks of all sizes and used them to spell "H E L P" in gigantic letters on the beach in four areas around the island. Sarah also dug fire pits on the beach in several areas where she kept a large supply of dry wood and special vegetation.

Because it rained often, Sarah found it necessary to continuously replace wet wood and vegetation with dry supplies. Her rock signs around the island also needed care and attention. Not wanting to place her fate in the hands of a rescue team that might never come, Sarah started building a raft out of bamboo and vines—a little bit each day.

Of course, she'd relax as well. Her favorite time of day was sunset. Sarah would take a handful of nuts and berries she'd picked earlier in the day down to the beach and sit under her favorite palm tree. She'd daydream about her family and how wonderful a big piece of her mother's special chocolate cake would taste. During these daydreams, she'd also spend a few minutes going over her rescue plan.

Day after day, without any fanfare or recognition, Mark and Sarah did what they needed to do to survive. After several noneventful weeks, that day finally came. Sarah was picking fruit near the beach and Mark was trapping crabs when they both—almost at the same time—saw a small plane in the distance.

Sarah jumped into action. She ran to the small fire and used it to light the large pile of wood. She dumped the vegetation on it and used her homemade tiki torch to light the other stacks of wood on fire. She then ran back to add more wood and vegetation to the fire. Huge plumes of smoke rose into the air and filled the sky above her island.

Meanwhile, Mark was frantic. He ran around trying to figure out what to do. He fumbled, trying to light a fire, and once he had one lit, he was disappointed that it produced very little visible smoke. He sprinted into the jungle and grabbed any kind of vegetation he could find to throw on the fire. Unfortunately, the vegetation he used quickly suffocated the fire and Mark wasted several precious minutes trying to light another one. Each time he threw new vegetation on the fire to create more smoke, the fire would die and he would waste time trying to restart it.

The plane turned and started heading toward the islands. As it got closer, Mark realized it was not flying toward him but was headed several miles off course. The plane circled Sarah's island and touched down a hundred yards offshore. Two rescuers jumped out of the plane and started paddling toward her in a raft. As they got closer, she looked around her island one last time and dove into the ocean and swam toward the raft. Minutes later, Sarah was airborne. The pilot asked her if there were any other survivors and Sarah told them that she had been alone.

Desperate to get their attention, Mark resorted to running up and down the beach waving his arms in the air and screaming in desperation. As the plane flew out of sight, Mark realized that he had missed his chance.

Mark survived. He survived the fifty-foot plunge into the water, lived through the violent storm, made it to dry land, built a shelter, and found food and water. Sarah also survived. She did what was necessary to make it each day, but she had a bigger plan—she wanted a better life. She wanted to see her family again, to taste chocolate, and to read a love story. She wanted to hug her friends and hear the sounds of her church choir. She wanted to pet her dog, attend a play, and grow old with her husband. She needed to survive on the island, but she made the decision that surviving was just not enough.

Mark and Sarah's lessons aren't reserved for castaways on remote islands. Their story is played out every day around the globe—in small towns and in big cities, in diners and in corner offices, and for those working for minimum wage and those pursuing advanced degrees.

If you feel like you are stranded on an island of monotony, unpaid bills, and forgotten dreams, or if you find yourself daydreaming of a different life but have no idea how to achieve it, there is only one solution. . . .

THE OTHER 8 HOURS

Your day doesn't start when you crawl out of bed. Your day—and even your life—doesn't really start until 5:00 PM. What you've done with your time after 5:00 PM last week, last month, and last year has determined where you are today. How you use the other 8 hours today, tomorrow, and next year will determine your future—they are your only hope to radically improve your life. The 8 hours you sleep are lost. The 8 hours you sell for a paycheck are gone. What you have—really, all you have—are the other 8 hours. Life not only happens in those the other 8 hours, but life *is* the other 8 hours.

Where you work, the size of your paycheck, the amount of debt you have, what you weigh, the number of people you can count on to help you in an emergency, your connection to God, the relationship you have with your spouse and children, and just about everything else that is meaningful to you is the result of how you've used the other 8 hours.

Look at each of the areas below to see the profound effect the other 8 hours has had:

FAMILY

Even if you met your partner/spouse at work (I did), you needed to put time and energy into your relationship after work if you wanted it to grow and mature. The dates you went on, long walks, and falling in love all occurred during the other 8 hours. Even the disagreements and arguments that make you the couple you are today occurred after 5:00 PM.

If you have children, surely their conception and maybe their birth occurred during the other 8 hours. All of the diapers you changed, Elmo you watched, and homework you've helped complete—all of the things you did to build connections with your children today—wouldn't have happened if it were not for the other 8 hours.

The reason my daughter runs up and hugs me when I come home from work is because of the other 8 hours I've "invested" in her (then again, it's probably the M&Ms I bribed her with).

The love your spouse and children feel toward you—and, yes, the abscence of love—is entirely the result of how you have spent the other 8 hours. The connection you feel toward your siblings and parents is based largely on what you've done during the other 8 hours. If you invested them wisely, you probably have some good relationships. If you didn't, you probably don't.

RELATIONSHIPS

The nine-to-five working hours are a great time to meet people and develop friendships. I met most of my nonchildhood friends while working. It's no surprise. We come into contact with more people for

OTHER 8 EXPERT

Leo Babauta is one cool cat. He is the author of the bestselling book *The Power of Less,* and the popular and enlightening Zen Habits blog (zenhabits.com). Here's how he answered the question, What one thing should readers do with their other 8 hours that will have the greatest positive impact on their lives?

Pursue your passion. Find out what you're most passionate about, and pursue it with everything you have. That might mean doing something with your children, or it might mean creating something brilliant or starting a new enterprise. It might take some experimenting to figure out what you love, but it's worth the effort to find it. Once you've found that passion, really pour your soul into it. Clear away everything else to make space for this, and really focus on it until the world around you disappears. If possible, start to make money from it so that you can eventually quit your day job and make a living doing what you love.

longer periods during working hours than we do at any other time of the day. But to convert your work relationships into real friendships, you have to spend some of your other 8 hours hanging out with and getting to know those people on a different level. It's one thing to chat around the water cooler about the latest *American Idol* contestant to be voted off or to relive Sunday's big game in the lunchroom, but it's an entirely different thing to share a drink or dinner with someone and really get to know him. Your close friends—regardless of where you met them—became your friends during the other 8 hours.

PHYSICAL HEALTH

The notch you use in your belt, how out of breath you feel after climbing a flight of stairs, and how comfortable you are in a bathing suit are almost entirely dependent on how you have used the other 8 hours. What you choose to eat for breakfast, dinner, dessert, and snacks is usually determined during the other 8 hours. If you've chosen wisely, it shows. Do you exercise? If so, when? While you sleep? No. While you work? No. During the other 8 hours? Yup.

PERSONAL GROWTH

This category includes your hobbies, educational pursuits, travel, reading, art, and other activities that you find enriching and are passionate about. One of my hobbies is Brazilian Jiu Jitsu and mixed martial arts. I'm not very good, but I enjoy it and I'm better than when I started. I also enjoy learning Spanish (even though those verbs confuse me). Another of my favorite pastimes? Reading. My clients wouldn't appreciate it, and I wouldn't be very successful if I spent my hours between nine and five practicing Jiu Jitsu, learning Spanish, and reading books. No, I can only do these things that I love and am passionate about—these things that help define me as a person—during the other 8 hours.

SPIRITUALITY

Your spirituality and faith should follow you wherever you go—during work and during the other 8 hours. But, unless your nine-to-five job is in ministry, chances are your spiritual growth and deepest connection to God occur during church/temple, small group meetings, Bible study, chanting, volunteering, meditation, or whatever.

FINANCIAL HEALTH

Surely your financial health is the direct result of the hours between nine and five. It is during this time that you work and earn a paycheck. Your paycheck determines your financial health, right? Not so fast. Obviously your working hours play a significant role in your finances, but you might be surprised at the role the other 8 hours play in the size of your bank account.

Your financial health is determined by just two things . . . your income and your expenses. That's it. No more, no less. Your income is based on what you do for a living and how well you do it. The best snow-cone maker in the world may make a fine snow cone, but her choice of occupation limits her financial success. Likewise, a brain surgeon who botches every surgery isn't going to be financially successful either.

What you do for a living is based on hundreds of factors . . . where you grew up, your intelligence, your parents' encouragement, your personality, your interests, chance, etc. What you do for a living is also determined partly by whether or not you graduated from high school, spent the extra years getting an advanced degree, took online courses or night classes to earn an important industry designation; by how hard you studied, and your personal network of friends and acquaintances. It is these factors—those that you can control—that have a huge impact on what you do between the hours of nine and five. And guess what? All of these other factors are the direct result of how you have spent the other 8 hours.

So the other 8 hours have a huge impact on our income, but what about the other half of the financial health equation . . . our expenses? You guessed it. Your expenses are the result of the decisions you make during the other 8 hours. How much you choose to spend on rent, the type of car you drive, the clothes you buy, the entertainment you experience, and the toys you purchase aren't decisions you usually make while you are working, and they definitely aren't decisions you make while sleeping. Every single one of these spending decisions—and thousands of others, both big and small—occurs during the other 8 hours.

Still aren't convinced? I need you to buy into just how important the other 8 hours are. If you read this book with the same skepticism you have when you read those tabloid headlines in line at the grocery, it's not going to work. Go ahead. Drink the Kool-Aid. Because once you do—once you realize the power the other 8 hours *has had* on your life—you will respect and appreciate the power that the other 8 hours *can have* on your life.

To prove just how important the other 8 hours have been in your life, take this quiz . . .

Directions: After each question, put a checkmark in the "sleeping" box if the event occurred while you were sleeping, a checkmark in the "working" box if it occurred while you were working, and a checkmark in the "Other 8" box if the event occurred in the other 8 hours.

Meaningful Moments in Your Life	Sleeping	Working	Other 8
1. When did you meet the love of your life?			
2. When did you have your first child (please note, office stairwell fans, the question is when did you *have*, not conceive, your first child)?			
3. When did your most emotionally painful experience occur?			
4. When did you see the most spectacular sunset you've ever seen?			
5. When do you feel the most intellectually alive and excited about your future?			
6. When do you participate in your favorite hobby?			

Meaningful Moments in Your Life	Sleeping	Working	Other 8
7. When was the first time you saw your child walk?			
8. Think about your favorite movie of all time. When was the first time you watched it?			
9. When did you meet your best friend?			
10. When was the last time you could hardly catch your breath because of your excitement?			
11. When was your most profound spiritual moment?			
12. When did the most rewarding physical thing you've ever done occur?			
13. If you could relive one event from your past, when would it occur?			
14. When do you find you feel the most sure and confident?			
15. If you had one year left to live, what would you spend the majority of your time doing?			
TOTAL			

Now add the checkmarks in each column. Do you notice anything? I've done this exercise with a whole lot of folks and the results are almost always the same.

Sleeping: Necessary and feels great, but doesn't provide much "life" to life. Most likely, you don't have a single checkmark in this column.

Working: Also necessary and can feel rewarding, but it is typically something you must do and not something you love to do. Most people have between one and three checkmarks in this column.

Other 8: Surprise! The majority of the most important events in your life don't occur while you sleep or work . . . they occur during the other 8 hours.

While it's true that I created the quiz to convince you of the significance of the other 8 hours, I think it is still a valuable illustration. Prove it to yourself by thinking about the most meaningful events and memories in your own life. When did they occur?

IT CUTS BOTH WAYS

Time has no conscience, and the other 8 hours are indifferent. They can be invested or wasted. The other 8 hours can improve every aspect of your life, but you must do something valuable with them. If you waste the other 8 hours, they can't help you. The clock ticks. Seconds, minutes, and hours pass, regardless of what you do.

Your finances, your job responsibilities, your relationship with your parents or spouse, your health, and even your quality of life and level of happiness are either getting better or getting worse. Life and all of the things in it are moving forward, progressing, and advancing or falling behind, stagnating, and dying. Is your net worth growing or shrinking? Are you moving up in the company or down? Are you getting closer to your boyfriend or moving farther away from him? Are you getting into shape or losing the battle of the bulge?

If you don't invest the other 8 hours in the areas of your life that are important to you, those areas will shrivel up and waste away (unless you're talking about weight, and in that circumstance, neglect tends to have the opposite effect). How many friendships have you had that disappeared because you didn't put the time into them? Have you grown apart from a spouse or significant other? Have you lost touch with your faith? Have you felt shocked after stepping on the bathroom scale? Have you ever wondered where the last year, or five or ten years, have gone? Do you get sick of coming up with reasons for why you didn't start a business or take that trip? The reason for all of these shortfalls can be traced to how you failed to invest the other 8 hours into these areas of your life.

Still not convinced that life starts after 5:00 PM? Talk to someone who has completely wasted the other 8 hours for several years (or decades). You'll see pain, frustration, anger, and despair. You'll hear about

ANOTHER 8-HOUR SUCCESS

What do you do if you spent your whole life studying for and becoming something you don't love? Would you give it all up on a whim so you could start over doing something you love? Of course you wouldn't. You'd do the smart and strategic thing, just like Dr. Susan Biali did, and transition gradually.

Dr. Biali worked in emergency medicine and then as a general practitioner, but found herself growing more and more depressed. During a trip to Cuba, she signed up for a salsa class. It was then that she remembered that as a kid she had always wanted to learn to dance. When she returned home, she continued taking dance classes during her free time and found that dancing gave her more joy than "doctoring."

Instead of immediately quitting her lucrative medical practice, she used the other 8 hours to find meaning and passion in dance. While working as a full-time physician, she commuted every few weeks from Vancouver to Mexico to further her dance studies. It was also during her free time on a trip to Italy that she began writing about her travels. A major newspaper in her area loved her article and put it on the front page with her picture. From there, she started to write various travel and health articles, while still working as a full-time physician.

Today she is a professional flamenco dancer and is married to a professional dancer and instructor. She has two columns in national magazines and is writing her first book, *Your Prescription for Life*. She speaks professionally about her life experience of going from a depressed physician to a happy writer, speaker, and professional dancer. Her advice to others who feel trapped in unfulfilling jobs? "Give dreams a top priority in your life," she insists.

Oh, and that career that made her so depressed? She quit last year.

how life is unfair and that having the "good" life is hopeless. If you sleep 8, work 8, and waste 8, at the very best, you'll manage to survive, much like Mark has on his lonely island.

Each of us is given the other 8 hours (some more, some less). It's up to us to use this time as wisely as possible. If you have a plan for your day after 5:00 PM and actually do something with this time, there is very little in life you can't accomplish or achieve. Those who invest the other 8 hours achieve and experience the most from life. Those who waste the other 8 hours feel stagnant and unfulfilled, and they are the subject of the next chapter . . .

CHAPTER TWO

THE LIVING DEAD AND
THE DEAD BROKE

Why It's So Hard to Get Ahead

Josh rises early each morning. He starts each day with a nutritious breakfast—usually something high in protein, such as boiled eggs and yogurt, as well as a nice serving of fruit.

After breakfast, Josh relaxes and listens to a couple of his favorite talk radio programs. Sometimes he reads the morning paper. He uses this time to stay up-to-date on current events and engaged in world affairs.

After a morning of engaging the mind, Josh likes to get his blood pumping. He takes a deep breath of fresh air, stretches for a few minutes, and takes a leisurely stroll. If he feels like it, he might even join a local basketball game.

After he exercises, he rests and gets ready to eat lunch. Again, he tries to keep it small and nutritious—typically a mixed green salad and a hot sandwich. Once in a while, he cheats and will eat a cookie.

Friends are important to Josh, so he likes to spend the afternoons socializing—talking, playing games, or just watching TV with them. Josh is an avid reader and writer. He often spends his afternoons writing and poring over books.

After an early dinner, Josh hits the gym for an hour or so. He follows this with a high-protein snack and a shower. He spends the last few hours before bed watching a little TV, reading, and writing. Occasionally he'll chat with a friend or take in a little more talk radio before dozing off.

Eric also gets up early. He takes a quick shower and fills his coffee mug before racing out into the cold, dark morning. He navigates the streets as if he were on autopilot—he's been making the same forty-minute commute for over a decade.

A thirty-minute lunch break becomes an island of solitude in an otherwise stressful day. He slams down a quick sandwich and typically takes in more coffee—it's already been a long day and he's only halfway through it.

He mentally checks out as he clocks out at the end of the day. His drive home takes over an hour. Eric spends this time decompressing by listening to sports radio or music.

He greets his wife, who also just came home from her job. She laments about a particularly tough day, and they decide to splurge a little. They talk about doing dinner and a movie, but they decide to skip the movie and just go to McDonald's. Eric and his wife are struggling with debt. They owe more than $10,000, and the high interest rates are killing them. They've had to cancel their Internet service and one of their cars was recently repossessed.

They spend the last few hours of the night watching TV before they pass out.

Josh is learning, advancing, and growing. He takes care of his body by eating a balanced diet and by exercising five days a week. He keeps his mind sharp by staying abreast of current events in his community and around the world. He devours information in books and invests a great deal of time writing and being involved in his favorite causes. Even when things get a little chaotic, he still makes an effort to stay connected to friends and family—often seeing family once a week. He'll tell you he feels like there's nothing he can't do.

Eric has the same twenty-four hours in each day, but his life is very different. He spends much of it focused on work—getting ready for it, engaged in it, driving to and from it, and wishing he didn't have to do so much of it. His body suffers from his poor eating habits and lack of exercise. He feels and looks older than he is. He wants to escape his life and the mountain of debt and unpaid bills to a whole new life. He had dreams and goals, but they have been pushed aside and buried for years. He can tell you who won the big game last night, but he has no idea what's happening in his local community or in national politics. He'd like to hit the "undo" button on the last decade. He'll tell you that his days bleed together. He's not learning, advancing, or growing. He feels like a prisoner.

There are people like Josh and Eric in small towns and big cities across the country—regular people just living their lives. But what's remarkable about these two is that they are both prisoners. One bound by life and the other by chains. (Are you ready, M. Night Shyamalan?) Josh is an inmate at a California federal prison and Eric happens to be a prison guard. (By the way, Josh and Eric are real people. Josh is a journalist who wrote about prison life after refusing to turn over videos he took during a demonstration. And I read about Eric's story in the *New York Times*.)

You think you're free, but are you really? Eric has all the freedom in the world but no time to invest it or enjoy it. On the other hand, Josh has nothing but time to read, exercise, and develop. Maybe this isn't a fair comparison, but if things have gotten so crazy that the only way you can get time is to "do time," then something is definitely wrong.

You are faced with the same choice every single day. You can choose to just "do time" or you can choose instead to use and invest it. Unfortunately, most of us have chosen to turn on autopilot and cringe through another day. The good news is you don't have to commit a felony to get some time for yourself. As you'll learn in coming chapters, it only takes a little time, focus, and desire. But before you can get more time, get a life, and get more money, you need to snap yourself out of this coma you're stuck in . . .

THE LIVING DEAD

We have the freedom to do what we want, but life has beaten us down. We're faced with 5:00 AM commutes, long hours at work, stacks of bills, and growing debt. Our cumulative experiences in life have smothered our burning desires. Whether that burning desire was for more money, recognition, or connection, it is now long gone. A soulless body is all that is left—a physical vessel that can talk and walk but that is void of any purpose.

Think *Invasion of the Body Snatchers*. In it, seeds from outer space land on Earth and become pods. The alien pods create duplicates of humans as they sleep—killing the human in the process. The pods suck the life and soul from the humans, leaving only an empty shell. Sound familiar?

The Living Dead are those among us who are unfulfilled—those with forgotten dreams and ideals. They have given up on their passions, their dreams, their purpose, and are simply going through the motions of living. For them, life is an awful lot like an assembly line at a factory—wake up, go to work, eat lunch, work more, go home, make dinner, watch TV. It is mechanical and routine, and there is little change from day to day.

They're going through the paces and putting in their time. They're not taking chances. They are alive but not fully living. And then it happens. One day, they are hit with the bitter realization that they are not where they thought they'd be. The Living Dead are frustrated because they know that life could be better.

If you are one of the Living Dead, you know that, at one point, you had dreams and a bigger vision for your life, but you try not to think about it anymore. Thoughts of what could have been are depressing, and thoughts of what could be just anger you. The dream of any other kind of life seems impossible.

The Living Dead come from every corner of the world, from all backgrounds, and from every socioeconomic level—Asian, black, white, Latino, poor, rich, college educated, high-school dropout, etc. Being "successful" doesn't guarantee that you're not one of the Living Dead. A single mom working two jobs and struggling to make rent may have more "life" than an executive making six figures who lives in a gated community.

The Living Dead feel stuck. They feel like their future is predetermined. They feel like no matter what they do, they can't improve their lives.

In life, we all experience situations where we seem to lack control. It can be very easy for us to believe that we are powerless over certain aspects of our life. Worse yet, if we have this sense of defeat and powerlessness in certain areas of our lives, it can bleed over into other areas of our lives where control over events is possible—and infect our success and happiness like a virus. This is one of the reasons why the rich get richer and the poor get poorer. It's also one of the reasons why the happy get happier and the depressed get more depressed. The Living Dead feel that their life is already laid out in front of them and that, no matter what they do, they can't change its course.

Most of us feel a gap between where we are and where we want to be. This gap may initially inspire us, but if we are unable to make any progress toward closing the gap, it can cause us frustration, anger, and, ultimately, surrender and apathy.

But before we look at solutions, it's important to understand how you got here. Why is there such a large and growing gap in your life between your dreams and your reality? Are your expectations unrealistic? Do you shoot for the stars but get disappointed when you only reach the moon? Is it your fault? Should you simply want less?

The Buddhists teach that instead of constantly striving to get what we want, we should simply reduce our wants. They say unhappiness is caused by wanting what we do not have. A recent study of the people of Denmark may substantiate this concept. Danes consistently score higher on measure of life satisfaction than people in any other Western country because, at least in part, they have very low expectations. "It's a David and Goliath thing," says Kaare Christensen, the lead author of the study. "If you're a big guy, you expect to be on the top all the time and you're disappointed when things don't go well. But when you're down at the bottom like us, you hang on, you don't expect much, and once in a while, you win, and it's that much better."

So, does this mean you should settle for a life you know is less than ideal? Absolutely not. You should aggressively and continuously pursue your best life AND, at the same time, be completely grateful for what you already have. The key to lifelong happiness is feeling satisfaction with what you've done, gratitude for what you currently have, and continually pursuing personal greatness.

I don't think unrealistic expectations are to blame. In fact, I think you suffer from expectations that are too low. You're working so hard just to survive that you haven't had the opportunity to envision a better life. You've been beaten up and pushed around so much that the gap has become a way of life.

Here's a look at just how hard and demanding life has become for many of us:

- **Working more.** It's not just you. We're all working more than we used to. The federal Bureau of Labor Statistics reports that we worked five more hours a week in 2006 than we did in just 2003![1] Thinking

ANOTHER 8-HOUR SUCCESS

If you can see the future and you don't like what you see, what should you do? That was the question that plagued Ryan Kappel. Ryan was working a full-time job as a social worker and had two part-time jobs. His commute was over an hour and a half each day. When he got home from work, he felt drained and had no time or energy for hobbies or to enjoy life. "I looked around and saw what my life would look like if I wanted to make more money," he said. "As a social worker, I'd have to work sixty hours a week, be on call every weekend, work for thirty years, and then wait for a supervisor to retire or die before I could move up."

He knew he had to do something. "I felt trapped and wanted to escape. I wanted to put the control back in my hands." He knew the solution was to focus on his strengths and skills—his counseling. He couldn't stand the thought of commuting more, so he turned to the Internet. He looked up "online counseling" and discovered LivePerson.com—a Web site that lets experts set their own per-minute fee for e-mailing or speaking to clients. "I was skeptical at first, but I thought I'd try it," he says.

He spent what little free time he had on LivePerson.com getting clients and building his reputation. Soon he had a roster of regular clients and was attracting new ones from the glowing reviews his clients provided. For the first time, he saw the light. He was enjoying his work and making good money. Within a few months, he was able to quit both part-time jobs and his full-time job. "I'm making more now than when I was working three jobs," he said. "Plus, I don't have a commute and I have plenty of free time and energy to relax and pursue my hobbies."

about leaving the rat race and settling down in another country? Avoid Peru and Korea—two countries where half the people work more than forty-eight hours a week. If you're thinking the Peruvians and Koreans are slackers, you're probably one of the nearly half of American workers who put in more than fifty hours of work a week.[2]

- **Vacationing less.** It's hard to get away, and many people are giving up on it. While most other developed countries around the world require that their workers receive paid vacation time, the United States does not. Nearly a quarter of workers in this country don't receive any paid vacation time. You'd think that we'd carefully guard the few days we do get, but we do not. Almost a third of workers actually lose vacation days by not taking them within the year. For those lucky enough to get away, almost a quarter check work e-mail or voicemail while vacationing.

- **Commuting longer.** Extreme commuters are defined by the U.S. Census Bureau as those who travel more than ninety minutes to work each way. Sound crazy or impossible? The U.S. Census Bureau says the 3.4 million extreme commuters are the fastest growing group of commuters in the United States. That's twice as many as there were in 1990![3] Even the average commute is a full twenty-five minutes longer than it was two decades ago.[4]

- **More stress.** Take a deep breath. Most likely you need it. A recent report by the American Psychological Association says that one third of Americans are living with extreme stress, and nearly half of Americans believe their stress has increased over the last five years.[5] Another survey says that nearly 50 percent of all American workers experience "persistent and excessive stress or anxiety in their daily lives."[6] The phrase they use to describe our condition? A "national pressure cooker." That feels about right.

- **Increased fear.** The only thing we have to fear is—everything. Anxiety disorders are the most common mental illness in the United States—affecting forty million of us (nearly one in five adults).[7] The horror of 9/11 has only made things worse—35 percent worry they'll be victims of terrorism.[8] And according to a 2007 Gallup survey, 78 percent of us are worried about global warming.

OTHER 8 EXPERT

Michael Michalowicz is a serial entrepreneur and author of the fun and insightful book *The Toilet Paper Entrepreneur*. Here's how he answered the question, What one thing should readers do with their other 8 hours that will have the greatest positive impact on their lives?

The other 8 hours is all about recharging the emotional, mental, and physical batteries. Entrepreneurship requires tremendous, often exhaustive effort for full work days (and a full work day for an entrepreneur, by the way, is at least twelve hours). The only way you can sustain this—and you must to be successful—is to sleep deeply. You must release stress and reinvigorate your stamina. Do that every day, and you come out the winning entrepreneur.

- **Three billion-plus job applicants.** The world is flooded and it's not just because the icebergs are melting. There are about three billion people in developing countries who are desperate to improve their lives and hungry for work. They've entered the global workforce, résumé in hand. They are willing to work longer hours for less pay and no benefits. Corporations are all too happy to outsource anything and everything to cut costs. Suffice it to say that "job security" has become an oxymoron for many.

- **Fewer close friendships.** Psst. Let me share something with you. According to a recent survey, there's a good chance that you have fewer people sharing important matters with you. The study shows that we have significantly fewer friends than we had just twenty years ago. They found that the number of people who don't have anyone to discuss important matters with tripled from 1985 to 2004.[9] This increase is particularly curious in the face of all the new ways we have to be "connected" with each other—cell phones, e-mail, Twitter, instant messages, blogs, texting, Facebook, MySpace.

- **Having less sex.** Say it isn't so! Americans have sex less frequently than people in almost every other country in the world (Olga in Russia, Mobuto in Ghana, Helga in Germany, and Quang in Vietnam are all getting it more).[10] More and more couples are saying "I don't" after they say "I do."[11] Approximately forty million Americans have what experts call a sexless marriage—that is, they have sex less than ten times a year. Isn't that like going into a Baskin-Robbins and being told they ran out of ice cream?

- **Getting fatter.** We're getting bigger and we're doing it at breakneck speed. According to the Centers for Disease Control, in 1990, you could drive through each of our great states and you wouldn't encounter a state where 15 percent or more of the residents were obese. If you made that same drive today, you'd notice some big changes. Two states (Mississippi and West Virginia) have the dubious distinction of a 30 percent or greater obesity rate— that means that about one in every three people are obese. Not just overweight—obese. The rest of the states, while somewhat slimmer, still don't have anything to brag about. Of the remaining forty-eight states, twenty have obesity rates at 25 percent or greater and not a single state has an obesity rates less than 15 percent. It's no surprise that some researchers are predicting a whopping 75 percent of American adults will be overweight and 41 percent will be obese by 2015![12] It's amazing what a few years and a few million supersized meals can do.

- **Happiness plateaus.** Despite advancements in health care and technology, we are not any happier than we were twenty years ago. The Internet, e-mail, iPods, DVD players, BlackBerrys, reality TV, and our Britney Spears fascination haven't boosted our happiness at all.

The gap is real and it's getting wider. More and more of us are joining the Living Dead.

THE DEAD BROKE AND THE
AMERICAN SCREAM

This country was founded by people and on principles that proposed a better life. James Truslow Adams coined the term "American Dream" in his 1931 book *The Epic of America*. The American Dream is "that dream of a land in which life should be better and richer and fuller for everyone. . . . It is not a dream of motor cars and high wages merely, but a dream of social order in which each man and each woman shall be able to attain to the fullest stature of which they are innately capable."

Above baseball and apple pie, Americans are known for their unfettered optimism and hopeful pursuit of the American Dream. For centuries, this pursuit was justified, but there's less hope here now than in the Chicago Cubs dugout. It appears that more Americans are turning away from the optimism of this dream.

Over 50 percent of respondents to a 2008 Marlin Company survey said they didn't think the American Dream—the opportunity to have a nice home, financial security, and hope for the future—was attainable for the average American. To make matters worse, 75 percent said that achieving the American Dream is more difficult today than it was just eight years ago. Lastly, according to the 2008 Gallup-Healthways Well-Being Index, over half of the 100,000 respondents said they were struggling or suffering—mostly because they were worried about money.

I know what it's like to worry about money. From an early age I can remember my mother struggling to raise my four siblings and me. I'd often wonder how my friends' families could afford to take vacations and was always amazed at their full refrigerators. This gap between struggling to survive and financial security plagued me into adulthood.

Early in my career, I got a job at a stock brokerage firm in Beverly Hills, about two blocks from Rodeo Drive. I had to be at the office at 5:00 AM, so when I left my apartment at 4:45 each morning, I was nearly the only one on the road. This gave me the chance to drive leisurely through the residential streets of Beverly Hills and admire the huge multimillion-dollar houses in which everyone was still sleeping. The same questions haunted and inspired me each morning. What do these people do? How do they make their money? How can they afford this house? What decisions did they make long ago that helped them end up here? And the one I asked more than any other: What do I need to do to achieve financial success?

I'm no Leibniz, but I looked at my own situation and finances and quickly realized I would never experience this level of financial success unless something dramatic happened. I was living in a small apartment, waking up at 4:00 AM, working twelve hours a day, and making about $30,000 a year. Unless something changed, it was a mathematical impossibility that I'd ever claim 90210 as my zip code.

Although you may have no desire to live in Beverly Hills, you may want to live in a larger house, drive a better car, or be able to afford a vacation. Maybe you just want to get out of debt or pay for your kid's college education. Chances are you want more financial security and peace of mind, but it's tough just to pay the bills and survive, let alone get ahead. And you're not alone.

I'll also be the first to acknowledge that we're fortunate to live in the best country in the world, with the best form of government, and the best economic system. We have the freedom and opportunity to pursue what we want and to achieve the life we want, but there are several challenges that make achieving financial success and closing the gap more and more difficult:

- **Less financial security.** It is getting harder and harder to get by. A 2008 Gallup poll found that 50 percent of people surveyed were worried that they wouldn't be able to maintain their standard of living. Nine in ten Americans feel that they are working as hard as or harder than ever just to get by.[13]

- **Earning less.** Nearly half of all Americans make less than $27,000 a year. We earned less in 2007 than we did at the start of the century,[14] and men in their thirties make less money than their fathers did at the same age.[15]

- **Saving less.** More work + fewer vacations = less savings? Shouldn't we be financially rewarded for working more and forgoing our vacations? You'd think so, but that's not the trend. It wasn't always this way. In 1984, Americans were saving more than 10 percent of their income. Fast forward to today, and we have a negative savings rate.[16] It's as low today as it was during the Great Depression! Speaking of depressing, almost 10 percent of Americans don't even have a bank account.[17]

• **More debt.** Someone once said the only man who sticks closer to you in adversity than a friend is a creditor. If that's the case, there's a whole lot of sticking going on. Revolving consumer debt (that is, credit cards), car loans, and home mortgages are up dramatically, according to the Federal Reserve. That could be why about one in seven American families reported that their debt problems were serious enough at some point in their lives for them to file for bankruptcy or to use a credit counseling consolidator.[18]

• **Few investments.** It only makes sense that if we are earning less and saving less, we are unlikely to be investing for our future. Here are the numbers . . . nearly half of workers report a total savings of less than $50,000, and 22 percent say they have no savings of any kind.[19]

• **No money for retirement.** Retirement, once something to look forward to, is now something to fear. Only 18 percent of workers are very confident about having enough money for a comfortable retirement.[20] And more than half of thirty- to sixty-four-year-olds think they will outlive their money after they retire.[21] Can the numbers get worse? Here's one . . . 28 percent of retirees (those who are supposed to be living off their savings) say they have absolutely no savings[22]

• **Unable to retire.** The big payoff after working for forty-plus years? More work. According to the AARP, 68 percent of workers between the ages of fifty and seventy plan to work during retirement or do not plan to retire at all.[23] Almost half of these people say that they plan to work into their seventies because of money issues.[24]

- **Make it for 8, spend it for 24.** If you're trading your time for money, as most of us do, you make money for eight hours a day. When you "clock out," the income stops coming in. Our expenses work much longer hours. In fact, our expenses never take a break, call in sick, or take a vacation. Our rent, insurance, utilities, car payment, taxes, and phone bills extract their toll 24 hours a day. It's hard to get ahead when we make money for 8 hours a day but spend it for 24.

- **Taxes.** Taxes are the cost of living in a civilized country, but they don't make it any easier to get ahead. Each year the Tax Foundation calculates Tax Freedom Day. This is the day of the year when the nation has earned enough income to cover its annual tax burden. In 1900, that date was January 22. In 2009, it was April 13. It's hard to save for retirement and a better tomorrow when all the income we make during the first four months each year goes to taxes.

- **Inflation.** Inflation is the carbon monoxide of wealth—silent, invisible, flavorless, and odorless. Unlike the armed robber, inflation is the craftier cousin who comes in the back door, sneaks up the stairs, robs you of your goods, and, before he leaves, sits down at your kitchen table for a cup of tea. Inflation is unavoidable and perilous to your financial health.

- **Rising cost of education.** One of the prime drivers of financial advancement is higher education, except that it is becoming more and more expensive to get that degree. In the past several years, tuition has rocketed up 35 percent.[25] At the same time, federal aid has decreased. Tuition up + aid down = more debt for students. In addition to a degree, two-thirds of graduates leave college with student loan debt.[26] The average undergrad can expect to shoulder a debt burden of $20,000 (graduate students clock in at $45,000). The burden is too great for many low-income students, of whom 20 percent with good test scores never even apply to college.

PROBLEMS WITH TRADITIONAL
FINANCIAL PLANNING

These are real and serious hurdles to jump if we want a better financial life. What's the solution? Well, the solution has been traditional financial planning. The traditional approach to financial planning is pretty simple. Take away all of the jargon and fancy acronyms, and you're left with just three factors:

(1) Time—need a lot of it

(2) Savings—need a lot of it

(3) Investment Return—need a high rate

The traditional approach only works if you have Time + Savings + Return. If you lack any one of these pieces, and the Dead Broke usually lack more than one, you're going to have a problem.

The limitations inherent in traditional financial planning run deep and have created a dilemma. It's what I call Sophie's New Choice. Should I scrimp and save for the next forty years so I can then squeak by in retirement, or should I enjoy life a little now and pray I hit the lottery before I retire? These are our options? The choice is as subtle as Vinny asking, "Would you like it in the head or the chest?" But traditional financial planning has other limitations, too:

- **Age-related issues.** You don't have to be Dr. Mehmet Oz to know that the older we get, the more health issues we face. Aside from chickenpox and ear infections, I think every other health problem increases with age. This means that during our prime years, the years when we are the most vibrant and healthy, we are working; and when we retire, our health begins to deteriorate. Also, as we age, our energy decreases. We don't have the same bounce in our step. One retiree said, "Now that I've finally got the ability, I don't have the mobility."

- **Delayed gratification.** Would you rather have a cupcake now or tomorrow? If you're like most people, you want it now. Not just cupcakes, but everything—vacations, nice cars, security, time for hobbies, travel, etc. But our choice is not today or tomorrow. It is today or forty years from now. That's not delayed gratification, that's nearly-impossible-to-imagine gratification!

- **Late start.** One of the three key ingredients in the traditional approach is time, and to succeed, you need a lot of it. The traditional approach just doesn't work effectively if you start too late. If you're twenty-two and diligently contributing 10 percent of your income to a 401(k), time is on your side. But if retirement is nearing and you don't have anything saved, you're not going to make it with traditional financial advice. Don't take my word for it. Use any one of the retirement calculators online to see for yourself.

- **Live to work.** The preboomers had a job. The boomers had a career. The postboomers want a calling. Those born after the boomers want to live to work, not work to live. They want to find meaning and significance in the work they do. Trading time for money just to pay the bills isn't attractive to these generations.

- **Retirement focused.** Instead of looking at ways to improve life today, traditional financial planning focuses almost entirely on retirement, which could be twenty, thirty, or forty years in the future. If you're working overtime just to pay this month's bills, you need solutions and strategies to live a richer life now, not forty years from now.

- **Expense-only focus.** Traditional financial planning focuses exclusively on just one side of the cash flow equation—expenses. What can we reduce, eliminate, or postpone? How much can you sacrifice today for retirement forty years from now? Reducing excess and unnecessary spending is absolutely critical, but traditional financial planning neglects the other side of the cash flow equation—income! In addition to consuming less, we should also focus on boosting our income.

The traditional approach to improving finances and saving for retirement initially leaves most Americans confused and then, when they work through the numbers, frustrated. "How can I save for a distant future when I'm struggling to make ends meet right now?" Traditional financial planning is like measuring a mile with a ruler—it can be done, but it is very time-consuming and you're going to have one hell of a backache. This is why so many are saying forget it and instead are choosing to spend today and ignore tomorrow. This feels good in the moment, but it is obviously a horrible long-term financial plan.

It's easy to point fingers when someone is clearly living an extravagant lifestyle. Just tell them to cut back, right? Even though I've worked with a lot of people over the years, it is still frustrating to sit across from someone who earns a lot but spends lavishly and complains about debt and his or her poor financial situation. That answer is simple. But it's an entirely different situation when you're sitting across from a couple who are in debt and struggling but they've already sacrificed and cut their expenses to the bone. Where are all of the financial planners and solutions for that couple?

Let's be clear, I'm a big proponent of the traditional approach. I am a Certified Financial Planner.™ I have a master's degree in financial services. I am the president of a financial planning firm. I wrote a bestselling book based on the traditional approach. It can and does work. You should cover the basics and implement the traditional strategies to improve your finances, but you must temporarily forget about all of the traditional financial advice you've ever read or heard because it will prevent you from getting the life you want, and it will make you ineffective and frustrated.

Imagine you're driving a car. Traditional financial planning advises you to conserve gas regardless of how uncomfortable or how much longer it makes the ride. Of course, if that doesn't work, you'll be forced to choose a closer and less desirable destination, whether you like it or not.

The assumption is that you've got a limited supply of gas so you have to make it last as long as possible. It doesn't matter if it's 100 degrees out and that you're dying inside the car. If you can drive a little farther by having your windows rolled up and your AC off, then that is a sacrifice you must make. The focus is on stretching your existing resources as much as possible, regardless of the sacrifice involved.

Traditional financial advice focuses on depriving, reducing, cutting, and eliminating. All the financial experts are hell-bent on getting you to cut your expenses by shrinking your lifestyle. They want you to take your big goals and dreams and shrink them until they are shriveled and unrecognizable. Stretching your resources is a good idea, but when the entire focus is on conservation, getting by, and making do, you lose the capacity to identify opportunities. Think about it. If you're so focused on the dwindling gas gauge, you may not notice the six gas stations you just passed.

Fortunately, you have the other 8 hours. In the coming chapters, you will learn a completely different approach. Instead of focusing all of your attention on how to stretch the limited gas you have, the goal will be to find a gas station so you can fill up. Do you see the difference? You will learn to focus on your potential and what you can accomplish instead of only on what you have.

You want to grow, expand, achieve, and experience, but traditional rules tell you that you need to reduce, contract, and limit your life. I will show you how to jump out of the box you've been crammed into and to expand your means to fill your vision instead of shrinking your vision to fit your means.

The other 8 hours are the best resource you have to radically improve your life and finances. The other 8 hours is time. Time you can invest to produce a bigger and better future. Your first step to reclaiming your life and your finances is reclaiming your time—getting more of your 8 hours back and getting more out of them.

GET MORE TIME

If you feel like you don't have 8 minutes, let alone 8 hours, this section is for you! Before you can get a life and get rich, you have to get the one thing we all lack . . . time. Reclaiming as much of the other 8 hours as possible is our first goal because without it, we are stuck. We can't make more money, start a business, get in better shape, learn how to salsa, become more intimate with our spouse, or finally finish reading *Charlotte's Web* to our children. We need the other 8 hours to live and pursue our dreams and goals.

The goal of this section is NOT to free up more of your time only so you can put in more hours at the office or add unfulfilling commitments to your schedule. It is NOT about running around trying to do more. It is NOT about adding stress or anxiety to your already overscheduled and over-worked day.

The goal isn't to cram more *into* your day, it's to get more *out* of your day. The more of the other 8 hours you have, the more you can focus on those pursuits that make your life more fulfilled and get you closer to reaching your goals. You'll learn strategies to take back control of your time and your life, including:

- Reduce commitments that aren't important or rewarding.

- Partner with others and use their time.

- Eliminate activities that drain your time and energy.

- Become more efficient.

A rich life has nothing to do with having a full day and everything to do with having a day that is fulfilling. Take the first step of designing the life you want by getting more out of the other 8 hours.

CHAPTER THREE

GETTING THE OTHER 8

How You Can Get More Time and Get More Out of It

An American businessman was at the pier of a small coastal Mexican village when a fisherman on a small boat docked. Inside were several large yellowfin tuna. The American complimented the Mexican on the quality of his fish and asked how long it took to catch them. The Mexican replied, "Only a little while."

The American then asked why he didn't stay out longer and catch more fish. The Mexican said he had enough to support his family's immediate needs. The American then asked what he did with the rest of his time. The Mexican fisherman said, "I sleep late, play with my children, take a siesta with my wife, and stroll into the village each evening, where I sip wine and play guitar with my amigos."

The American scoffed, "I am a Harvard MBA, and I could help you. You should spend more time fishing and buy a bigger boat with the proceeds. With the proceeds from the bigger boat, you could buy several boats; eventually you would have a fleet of fishing boats. Instead of selling your catch to a middleman, you would sell directly to the processor and eventually open your own cannery. You would control the product, processing, and distribution. You would need to leave this small coastal fishing village and move to Mexico City and then LA, where you would run your expanding enterprise."

The Mexican fisherman asked, "But, señor, how long will this all take?"

To which the American replied, "Fifteen to twenty years."

"But what then, señor?"

The American laughed and said, "That's the best part! When the time is right you would announce an IPO and sell your company stock to the public and become very rich. You would make millions."

"Millions, señor? Then what?"

The American said, "Then you would retire. Move to a small coastal fishing village, where you would sleep late, fish a little, play with your children, take a siesta with your wife, and stroll to the village in the evenings, where you could sip wine and play your guitar with your amigos."

I first heard this fable at church a few years ago, and I've been in love with it ever since because of its powerful message. Are you, like the American in the story above, so focused on the end that you forget all about enjoying the journey?

TOO MANY BUNNIES IN THE MANSION

We feel overwhelmed and overstressed because we cram our schedules with too much work and too many responsibilities. We have more commitments than time. We keep adding more and more to our plates, thinking it will all pay off in the future. But all this blind effort doesn't guarantee future happiness; it only guarantees stress and frustration now.

To the bleary-eyed worker who doesn't have time to stop and catch his breath, the idea of having 8 hours may seem absurd. If that's you, this chapter is your wake-up call. You need to capture as much of the other 8 hours as possible so you can use this time to close the gap—to pursue your goals and your dreams. Without this time, you're stuck. This chapter will give you strategies and tricks to recapture your time and your life.

There are six strategies to help you get and maximize the other 8 hours:

1. Taking Control of Your Time
2. Learning to Say No
3. Getting 9 Hours Out of 8
4. Chunking

5. Plugging in Positivity

6. Using Technology

TAKING CONTROL OF YOUR TIME

We're going to dissect your average day and look for time wasters you can eliminate, noncritical tasks you can reduce, and pockets of opportunity you can seize. other8hours.com.

STEP 1—BIG PICTURE

Time is the great equalizer. The big-shot CEO who oozes money, power, and success doesn't have any more hours in the day than the single and overworked mother bartending at the club downtown. It's not how much time they have—they both have the same amount—it is how they invest their time that makes the difference.

The reality is that few of us actually have a full 8 hours available. It takes time to get ready in the morning, drive to work, eat, pee, and mow the lawn. Nobody is forcing us to mow the lawn, but we need to do it anyway.

So, what do you do during the other 8 hours? I'm sure some of this time is put to good use and some of it is wasted. The only way to know for sure is to take inventory of the way you spend your time. Complete the worksheet below, but keep in mind the following tips before you get started . . .

- **Guess.** This ain't NASA, folks. Put down the calculator. We're just trying to get a rough idea of where your typical day goes.

- **Include only workdays.** Don't include weekends. Unless you work on the weekends, those days are all yours!

- **Average it out.** If you work out three days a week for an hour, calculate the average per day by turning the hours into minutes (3 hours × 60 minutes = 180 minutes), and then divide by 5 days (180 minutes ÷ 5 days = 36 minutes) to get the average number of minutes per day. (Yes, I know I just told you to put away your calculator.)

- **Don't cheat.** This is a tool to help you determine how you actually spend your time, not how you'd like to spend your time (we'll get to that later). So, if your *goal* is to work out for an hour three days a week, but you never do it, time spent exercising would be zero.

- **Pick the primary task.** Most people do several things at once. For example, you might call a friend while driving to work or read a magazine while on the elliptical. How should you count this time? Only count the primary task. So, for our examples, you'd count your time as spent "driving" and "exercising."

You can create your own form or you can download one from other8hours.com.

Activity	Hours	Minutes
Sleeping/Napping—Time you spend sleeping or lying down with the intent to sleep. Time dozing off during meetings doesn't count.		
TOTAL SLEEPING		
Work—Time at work. Notice I didn't say time spent working, since this would be a very different number compared to time spent at work. Count lunch and breaks as "work."		
TOTAL WORKING		
Driving—Basically any time you are in your car going somewhere: commuting, dropping kids off at soccer, running errands, etc.		
Meals/Snacks—This includes not only eating food but also preparing it and cleaning up. Don't include shopping here; we'll get to that below.		
Personal—This is a big category. It includes things such as showering, using the bathroom, getting dressed, and having sex as well as the G-rated, boring things you do such as getting your hair cut, nails done, massage, etc.		
Exercise—Time at the gym, walking, biking, stretching, etc.		

Activity	Hours	Minutes
Watching TV—Obviously includes time spent watching TV and movies at home and in the theater.		
Personal growth—Time spent reading, learning, planning your future, taking courses, etc.		
Home maintenance—Includes grocery shopping, bill paying, phone calls to plumbers, etc.		
Family—Time with spouse/partner and/or kids when you are really engaged with them. Watching *Dora the Explorer* with your three-year-old would not be considered "family" time.		
Spirituality—Time spent at church/temple, in Bible study, in small spiritual groups, praying, meditating, etc.		
Helping—All the time you spend working and helping others without pay, such as volunteering, helping your neighbor, mowing your grandma's lawn, etc.		
Socializing—Time with friends, talking on the phone, texting, at parties, etc.		
Kids' School—Any time spent in PTA meetings, school conferences, working in the football concession stand, etc.		
Other leisure. This is a catch-all category for everything else, such as surfing the Internet, listening to music, blogging, etc.		
TOTAL OPEN TIME		
TOTAL TIME	24 Hours	

STEP 2—TASKS

Within each time category (for example, Socializing), write down all the things you do during this time. For example, talking on the phone, meeting friends for coffee, texting, e-mailing. Try to think about all of the tasks within each category. As another example, let's say you watch four hours of TV a night. List the shows you watch.

STEP 3 — TIME SPENT ON EACH TASK

Next, write down approximately how much time you spend on each task. Do you watch the local evening news for an hour each night? Do you blog for thirty minutes a day?

STEP 4 — PERK: POSTPONE, ELIMINATE, REDUCE, OR KEEP

This is where things get interesting. For every task you must select from one of the following: Postpone, Eliminate, Reduce, or Keep.

- **Postpone**—This is when you can shift the task into the future. For example, to create free time to complete a project, gain a new skill, or take a class, you might want to hit the "pause" button on another task. For me, I really want to become fluent in Spanish, but I also wanted to write this book. I could have done both, but it would have taken a lot longer to write the book and to learn Spanish. I made a conscious decision to postpone Spanish to focus more time on the book.

  Go through each of your tasks and see if you can postpone any of them. If you can, you will free up valuable time to focus on your more important goals.

- **Eliminate**—This means you can completely remove this task from your life. I want you to start cutting and slashing like a machete-wielding tribesman going through a jungle. Buh-bye. What can you eliminate? Better yet, what *can't* you eliminate? We do so much crap and make so many commitments that our natural reaction is to protest that we can't eliminate anything. But doing what you've always done will get you what you've always got. Don't be a big wuss. Start eliminating. Will you die if you cancel your Twitter account or if you stop watching *Lost*? For those things that you can't bring yourself to eliminate entirely, decide just to eliminate them for three weeks. If at the end of the three weeks you want to resurrect the task, go for it.

- **Reduce**—Maybe you just can't bring yourself to eliminate something completely, but can you reduce it? Absolutely. Go through your tasks and ask yourself if you really need to spend that much time on it. Can you cut it back a bit? You can reclaim so much of your life just by reducing unimportant and unsatisfying tasks. There's probably something in your life that sucks up your time that you could eliminate or reduce. Maybe it's fantasy football, celebrity gossip Web sites, YouTube, or MySpace?

- **Keep**—Undoubtedly there will be some tasks that you don't want to eliminate, reduce, or postpone. That's okay. For these, just check the "keep" column.

STEP 5—NIRVANA

Now sit back and ponder what you're going to do with all of this new free time you're going to have. An extra thirty minutes a day? An hour? Two or three?!?!

Our goal is to take back as many of the other 8 hours as possible. How close did you get? If you're not satisfied, review those tasks you haven't eliminated to see if you can reduce or postpone them further. If you are satisfied, you shouldn't be. We're just getting started . . .

LEARNING TO SAY NO

There was a popular book published a few years ago called *Getting to Yes*. It's a great title, but I want you to focus on the opposite—getting to no. You need to protect your time from yourself and others by digging a moat around it. Try the following two strategies:

ABSTAINING

Don't be a time slut. If you're the type of person who can't say no to favors and requests, others will take advantage of you. If you sacrifice your other 8 hours to benefit someone else, they will keep coming back for more and more until you've got nothing left to give.

So wise up! Make it your policy that your default answer is, "I'm sorry, I just can't help you with that." If that's too strong, follow it up with "because I'm working on a deadline, have a previous engagement, late for a meeting/appointment, taking care of my sick mother, getting checked for a rare and contagious disease." Whatever you say, you have to have a sense of urgency in your voice, and you need to extract yourself from the conversation as quickly as possible by saying, "Let's catch up soon, though."

BALANCING

Be more like the Governator. You may have heard that the federal budget deficit is over one trillion dollars. That means the federal government is spending a whole lot more than it receives in taxes. This is similar to someone who gets into credit card debt. Few know this, but state governments can only spend as much as they make. If the Governator wants to add a program, he has to subtract the money from somewhere else. This is called pay-go, as in you pay for things as you go.

Your job is to adopt a pay-go type of policy with your time. Before you agree to join a nonprofit board, train for a marathon, volunteer at a local soup kitchen, help a friend move, start Bible study, take a night class, or help your neighbor have a garage sale, you must eliminate that time from something else. Picture a balance that you need to keep level. If you add something to your schedule, you have to subtract something to keep it in balance. This will help protect your time by forcing you to limit your commitments.

GETTING 9 HOURS OUT OF 8

What could you accomplish with an extra hour a day? What about an extra three or four? Sound impossible? It's not. Buying and Boosting are two effective strategies you can implement tomorrow that will help you squeeze more out of the time you have.

BUYING

Generals don't win wars, the troops on the ground do. If you're over-whelmed with activities and responsibilities, you need to enlist some troops to fight more of your battles. Regardless of how wealthy or broke you are, you can "buy" time so you have more of the other 8.

NO MONEY OR TIME

Even if you don't have the money to hire others, you still have options to create hours a week of free time for yourself. Here are two strategies you can implement immediately that will help you reclaim the other 8 hours and that won't cost you a dime:

Frictionless Reciprocation. Sounds naughty, right? It's not. This is where you do someone a favor, and, at some future point, they return the favor. It's called frictionless because it takes little or no additional effort on your part. Don't confuse this with bartering, which is when you give up something of value in order to get something of value. There is friction in that transaction—you are giving up something of value. Frictionless Reciprocation is a simple strategy, but it must be done cor-rectly to generate free time.

The key to reciprocating is providing a frictionless service, which means doing something of value for somebody without its taking any of your time. For example, you pick up your neighbor's grocery items (because you're already going to the store for yourself). If your neigh-bor picks up your groceries next time, you didn't sacrifice any of your time helping your neighbor (remember, you were going to the store any-way), but you gained an hour because now you don't have to go to the store the next time you need groceries.

How do you create a frictionless favor? Whatever "service" you pro-vide must be something you were going to do anyway. You'll drive your neighbor to the store (because you are going to go anyway). You'll watch your friend's child tonight (because you are going to be at home with your kids all night). You'll drive your brother to work every day (because it is on the way to your office). You'll walk your landlord's dog every morning and evening (because you have to take out your own

AN**OTHER 8-HOUR SUCCESS**

Sometimes the first step isn't a step at all.

Five years ago, John Schulte was having trouble in his neighborhood with a gang of girls (yes, that's right, girls). They were harassing and assaulting neighbors, and their criminal activities were beginning to escalate. He wasn't a victim, but he had friends in the neighborhood who were mugged and assaulted by this gang of girls.

A few locals put together a community meeting with the police to discuss what was going on. The police suggested a neighborhood watch where everyone could take turns walking the streets in the evening. When they asked for volunteers, nobody offered . . . until John raised his hand.

Now, the volunteer group is referred to as the NECP (NorthEast Citizen Patrol), and they have a Web site where they list any problems in the neighborhood and they put out a weekly newsletter. What started with one volunteer has grown to over a hundred. This year, their area had the highest reduction in crime in all Minneapolis.

John says, "I see more families on the street now. Our neighborhood is safer. Open drug dealing and prostitution is gone. I've also met a lot of wonderful people and made some great new friends that I probably would not have."

John started the NECP while he was working a full-time job. He initially volunteered once a week at first, but now that the NECP has grown, the organization has become a main activity for him during his free time. John says, "To think, this all started with me raising my hand at a community meeting four years ago."

dog every morning and evening). You'll make your neighbor chili for dinner (because you're making it for your own dinner). You'll summarize the key points in that book for your colleague (because you were going to do it anyway). You'll take your friend's package to the post office (because you're going to the post office anyway).

The best uses of frictionless reciprocation are those favors that become part of your schedule and life. For example, you can watch your neighbor's kids every Friday night (because you do movie night and pizza with your kids every Friday), and in return, they can watch your kids every Saturday night. You've lost nothing but gained a romantic night out every week with your spouse.

To add a little extra juice to reciprocation, you could provide the same service to several partners. For example, every Monday, you make spaghetti for your family. You partner with your neighbor and make spaghetti for her family every Monday in exchange for her husband mowing your lawn. This might work so well that you partner with another neighbor and make his family spaghetti every Monday, too (there's very little extra time or effort in making dinner for nine as opposed to three) in exchange for getting your plants watered twice a week.

The best thing about frictionless reciprocation is that it is a win-win. You are providing a service that someone else highly values. As much as you appreciate and benefit from the partnership, your partners do as well.

Reciprocation can give you hours of freedom each week for free, but you need to make it happen. Here's how you can get started. First, jot down all of the frictionless (or near frictionless) services you could provide, and then jot down a list of potential partners. Then, match potential services with potential partners and run your ideas by them. You might need to tweak the service, the frequency, or the timing, but the important thing is to get started. Don't forget to increase your payoff by providing the same service to multiple partners.

Specialization. Like frictionless reciprocation, specialization also involves trading services . . . but the key here is using leverage. Provide a service that you love or excel at in exchange for a service that you dislike.

The goal is to gain time, enjoyment, or both. For example, I hate handyman-type jobs but enjoy going to the grocery store. My wife is quite handy with a hammer and a screwdriver but would rather stick toothpicks under her fingernails than go grocery shopping. Even though I don't save any time by trading this service with my wife, I'm much happier. I'm leveraging my enjoyment (we both are). This kind of thing occurs frequently in marriages, but you can also establish specializing partnerships with friends, family, and neighbors. For example, if you hate yard work but love working on Web sites, you could spend an hour a week teaching your friend HTML for an hour of his time working on your yard.

An even better use of specializing involves leveraging our enjoyment AND our time. That is, trading two hours for twenty hours. Instead of spending an hour a week teaching your friend how to build a Web site, you could build the Web site for him. Because of your specialized skills, it might take a couple of hours to build a basic site, but you could trade this for ten, fifteen, or even twenty hours of yard work.

If it appears you are taking advantage of a friend by doing this, you are not looking at the big picture. How much would you have to pay the neighbor's kid an hour to work on your yard? Maybe $10? So 20 hours at $10 an hour is $200. That's the value you are receiving. How much would it cost for your friend to hire someone to create a Web site? At least $200 and probably twice that. If anything, your friend is taking advantage of you!

The best partnerships are those in which you provide a high-value and unique service in exchange for a low-value and common service. Suggest running a Google ad campaign for a friend's company's Web site every month (high value/unique) if you can get his kids to mow your lawn and clean the pool every week (low value/common).

If you are short of time and money, frictionless reciprocation and specialization can provide you with hours a week that you can use to get a life and get rich.

SOME MONEY BUT NO TIME

If you have a little extra cash, you can hire yourself some troops to do your dirty work. Here are the steps:

1. **Create hit list.** Brainstorm all of the activities that take a ton of your time and/or you don't like doing. If you didn't have to do something, what would it be? Write down everything as it comes to you. You might need several pages for this exercise (I did!).

2. **Least wanted.** Once you have a healthy list of unwanted tasks, rank them. Which are the worst offenders?

3. **Get quotes.** Determine what it would cost to unload each of the tasks on your least-wanted list to someone else. Make guesses/approximations for now.

4. **Budget.** Figure out how much money you want to spend hiring someone to take over your least-wanted tasks. If you earn $20 an hour after taxes, don't pay someone $30 an hour to do your laundry. If you have a lot of small tasks, consider hiring someone for a few hours a week to take care of several different things.

5. **Pull the trigger.** There are several resources you can use to find help. TimeSvr (timesvr.com) has an excellent and cost-efficient outsourcing platform. For $69 a month, they will complete an unlimited number of basic tasks (those that can be done in less than fifteen minutes) and up to 8 hours of more time-intensive tasks such as extensive research, writing, or transcribing.

You'll find that most tasks can be done remotely, but if you need someone to come to your house to work, try Craigslist (craigslist.com). This is an excellent resource for finding talented local people. Also, check your community's newspaper online. You can probably search résumés and/or post a job. If you do post a job, just to be safe, never list your home phone number. Ideally, you should create a new e-mail address (you can create one for free in about two minutes at yahoo.com) and direct all initial communication to that address. Once you weed out 90-plus percent via e-mail, you can make contact using your cell phone. If you don't need in-person help, check out elance.com to find candidates.

The most common disliked tasks are also the easiest and most cost-effective to hire others to do. Here are several examples:

- Mowing lawn—Easy to find cheap and plentiful labor.

- Cleaning the pool—Usually inexpensive.

- Filing—Slightly more skilled, but you should be able to find someone cheap. Whenever you are going to have someone come to your house, and especially if they are going to see personal documents, it's important to call references or even run a background check.

- Housecleaning—Again, easy to find cheap and plentiful labor.

- Manual labor—Perfect for moving furniture, helping you clean the garage, etc.

- Exercising (just checking to see if you were paying attention).

- Cooking—You can pay for this, but it is also easy to reciprocate.

- Babysitting/Child care—You should have no problem finding a pool of qualified talent right in your neighborhood.

BOOSTING

Boosting is a great short-term way to boost income and time for those with very little money and/or a lot of debt. The strategy is to supplement your day job income with a part-time job at night. Doesn't sound very revolutionary, does it? Obviously your income will increase, but how can you boost your time if you are working more? It's because a boost job gives you the time and freedom to work on your own stuff.

A boost job is where you get paid to show up and do absolutely nothing. That's right. Unlike your day job, where you want to move up the ladder and increase your responsibility, your boost job needs to be just the opposite. The less you are responsible for, the better. In fact, the best boost jobs are those where you clock in, sit on your butt, talk to no one, do nothing, and then clock out.

If you're short on money and/or need to pay off debt, why not kill two birds with one stone? Make some extra money while working on your other projects. What could you do during your boost job? Learn a new language, do your homework, study for an exam, read Shakespeare, blog, work on an invention, write a book, start a consulting business, work on frictionless reciprocation tasks for your partners, etc.

The trick is finding a boost-friendly job. Here are the criteria:

- **Brainless & Actionless.** When you've found a job you could do successfully in a coma, you've found a perfect boost job.

- **Schedule.** The job has to mesh well with your schedule—don't try to cram it where it doesn't fit.

- **Flexible.** Ideally you'll find a job where you can work more hours when you need them and fewer hours when you don't.

- **Pay.** If you have a big ego, this is going to hurt. You'll want to look for something that pays between $8 and $15 an hour.

- **Proximity.** Because you aren't going to be making much, it's VERY important that the job be close to where you live—not more than a ten- or 15-minute drive.

- **Connected.** If possible, find a job where you have access to a computer, the Internet, and a phone.

Here's an example of boosting in action. Shelly works full-time during the day and goes to school two nights a week to complete her bachelor's degree. She has $3,200 of credit card debt that she hasn't been able to get rid of for years. She confesses that she spends too much time watching TV and that she doesn't get enough done. Shelly's goal is to become a Hollywood director, and she thinks that the best way to achieve this goal is to write a successful screenplay. She wants to get out of debt and decides she will try boosting.

Shelly gets a job at her college working in a computer lab two nights a week. She schedules her computer lab hours right after her school hours so she's already on campus. There are rarely any students in the lab, and when they are, they don't need any help. The first hour during her four-hour shift, she has a small study group with other students from her class. The next hour, she catches up on personal e-mail and phone calls. And the final two hours, she writes her screenplay. Shelly isn't giving up anything by working. In fact, she'd have to do all of these things even if she didn't have a job. And this way she is "forced" to schedule her activities because she might spend those four hours watching TV or chatting with friends all night if she wasn't on a schedule.

In less than a year, Shelly is getting As in her classes, feels connected to her friends and family, and is halfway through her screenplay. Oh, and one more thing. Shelly just paid off her credit card debt with the extra income from her boost job.

BOOST-FRIENDLY JOBS

Here are a handful of boost-friendly jobs you can consider.

- **Babysitting/Child care.** This only qualifies if the kids are already asleep and they don't often wake up during the night.

- **Nursing home caretaker.** Same as above. It only makes sense if everyone is already asleep and they don't require much help.

- **Security guard.** Don't get a job where you need a gun or in an area where you'll see any action. Consider a position where you need to watch monitors or a gate with few visitors.

- **Dispatch operator.** You must find one that gets very few calls a shift, not one where the phone rings off the hook.

- **Computer lab attendant.** Great for students.

- **Driver.** Find a job where you transport stuff, not people—preferably over longer distances where you will have time to make calls and listen to audiobooks.

- **Toll-booth attendant.** Because of electronic "fast passes," fewer drivers need to stop and pay.

- **Gym front-desk clerk.** This can be a great boost job if you find the right gym. You'll want the late shift at a gym that isn't too busy and where you don't have to check in people your whole shift.

- **Kiosk attendant.** Have you noticed the Rosetta Stone kiosks at the mall? I asked one of the employees sitting at a computer what he was doing and he said, "Learning Chinese." Boost, baby, boost!

- **Hotel front-office clerk.** The later the shift and the more remote the hotel, the better. You might see two or three people a shift, which will leave you plenty of time to work on your own projects.

Before you jump into a part-time gig, make sure it meets the requirements. It's a waste of time for you and your employer if you quit after a week. During your evaluation, do the following: ask to watch a shift, ask what other facilities they have and notice which are busier/slower, talk to other employees about their experience, ask about workload, if you can make phone calls, and if you can use the computer during down time. Tell the prospective employer you are a student and would like to find a job where you can study and do homework. Even though you're barely getting paid minimum wage, it's important to be honest with your prospective employer about what you're looking for.

CHUNKING

In psychology, chunking is a strategy for making more efficient use of memory. For example, trying to remember "**IMAT TRA CTE DTOF UR RYSH EEP**" would take forever and you'd forget it tomorrow. But you could instantly remember "I'm attracted to furry sheep." Why? Even though the order of letters hasn't changed, grouping them differently produces a different result. Psych people call this chunking (the grouping part, not the attraction to sheep).

For our purposes, chunking is a strategy for making more efficient use of your time and schedule. Chunking allows you to get more done by grouping multiple tasks together.

"You can't pull the wool over our eyes! You're trying to ram a cool new word for 'multitasking' down our throats, but we all know multitasking has been proven to be unproductive," I hear you protesting. You are right: multitasking has been proven in study after study to decrease productivity, but chunking is *not* multitasking.

Multitasking doesn't work because it involves two or more activities competing for the same resources. (Think nine kittens and eight nipples.) A typical multitasker may try to listen to voicemail while reading a report, talk to a friend while writing an e-mail, read the morning newspaper

ANOTHER 8-HOUR SUCCESS

Art is Samantha Hahn's life. She teaches art to children and is an illustrator. A couple of years ago, she started a Web site (samanthahahn.com) to showcase her work. She didn't have lofty goals for the Web site. She just wanted a venue to share her work with others. Today she freelances on surface patterns and illustrations. Her work has been featured in *Glamour* magazine, on Hallmark cards, and in Barnes & Noble.

She pours her energy and time into her projects during the other 8 hours. She's been able to juggle a job and freelancing because she's "highly scheduled" and because she's become more efficient with her time. "It puts a fire under you when there's not enough time," she says.

More importantly, she told me her freelancing "doesn't feel like work." She gets paid to work on projects she loves and that give her creative fulfillment. She loves teaching art, but her work during the other 8 hours gives her pleasure and meaning that teaching alone never could.

while talking to her spouse, or play a board game with the kids while watching the evening news. The problem with all of these is that these tasks are competing for the same limited resources.

So, how does chunking avoid the pitfalls of multitasking? The trick is to choose two tasks that don't compete for the same resources by combining a mental task with a physical task. Here's how you can become a chunking fool in no time . . .

1. **List dead time activities.** Dead time is not time when you have nothing planned; it is time spent doing a brainless activity that feels like a waste of time. No matter who you are or how productive you think you might be, we all have some dead time throughout our

day. Examples include brushing your teeth, taking a shower, getting dressed, standing in line, sweeping the floor, watching commercials, taking out the garbage, driving, sitting in waiting rooms, working out, washing your car, cooking, attending meetings, picking weeds, doing the laundry, jogging, vacuuming, flying, riding bus/subway/train, mowing the lawn, doing the dishes, etc.

Think about an average day and list all of the areas of dead time you find. Look for pockets of dead time that are predictable and recurring. Write them down as you think of them.

2. **Brainstorm the positive activities you want to do more often.** Step 1 had you list dead time activities, but improving your life is all about doing the things you're not doing but want to do. If time weren't an issue, what activities would you do? Maybe you'd read every John Grisham novel or more articles in your industry's journals. Maybe you'd handwrite letters to your top clients or to family or call each of your friends once a week. If you're having trouble coming up with a good list, think of those things you enjoy and/or that will get you closer to reaching your goals. For example, if your goal is to get in better shape, some of the activities that would help you reach that goal might include stretching, jogging three days a week, lifting weights two times a week, and walking every day for thirty minutes. Each of these would be activities you would list.

3. **Determine if the activities require your head or your body.** Mark the activities in step 1 and step 2 as either "head" or "body." In other words, does the activity require you to think (head) or be physical (body)? Head examples include attending church, watching TV, memorizing new vocabulary, reading, listening to an audio program, etc. Body examples include lifting weights, washing a car, cooking, driving, doing laundry, jogging, showering, flying, commuting (subway, bus), working on the lawn, walking, doing dishes, etc.

4. **Make the connection.** Look for opportunities to combine a head activity with a body activity. For example, you could listen to the

Portuguese audio program while you stretch, memorize ten new words by posting them in the shower and near the kitchen sink, walk while calling your friends, listen to *The Grapes of Wrath* while driving into work, etc.

Unless your father is your mother's cousin, most people have only one head and one body. For chunking to work, you need to combine just one head activity with just one body activity. For example, at my church, you can take a hike on a trail with a preacher while he gives a Bible study. A friend makes all of her calls while on a StairMaster. What about you? Could you chunk these . . .

- wash your car (body) with your children while you talk and play with them (head)

- jog (body) with your spouse and talk to him (head)

- drive to work (body) and listen to an audio book (head)

- cook (body) while talking to your friends (head)

I'm a big fan of having a "to read" folder. Anytime I come across something I want to read, such as a magazine article, blog post, or report, and I don't have time to finish it, I tear it out or print it and throw it in my "to read" folder. I take this folder almost everywhere (dentist, Jiffy Lube, bathroom). Whenever I have a few minutes of dead time, I always have plenty of good stuff to read and don't have to rely on the lame magazines at my doctor's office.

PLUGGING IN POSITIVITY

Really big positive change doesn't require a lot of effort or time. Sometimes the small things can produce massive effects—like a small spark in a dry forest. A fun way to get more out of your day is through sparking. Sparks are positive reminders to think or do something, and they can create dramatic changes and results in your life. Here's how you can add a little positivity to your day:

1. **Choose one spark.** Some sparks are a reminder to think, such as repeating an affirmation, thanking God for all you've been given, saying a prayer, imagining your perfect future, or going over your top three goals. Sparks can also be reminders to do something, such as taking five deep breaths, stretching, sitting up straight, relaxing your muscles, closing your eyes, standing up, etc. Whether your spark is thinking or doing, choose one that is easy and powerful for you. For example, I get so wrapped up in what I'm working on for the future that I forget about what I've accomplished and what I have. So, a powerful spark for me is to think of three things I'm grateful for. This takes me away from future-based thinking and brings me back to today. On the other hand, you might be stuck in the problems of the present. A powerful spark for you might be imagining your perfect future.

   Whatever your spark, make sure it takes less than a minute.

2. **Choose a dead time moment.** The key to sparking is connecting the spark to a brief but recurring activity. It's easy to go a little nutty and try to find a hundred different dead time moments, but take it slowly at first. I only want you to identify one for now. Examples include turning off your alarm, waiting for the shower water to heat up, opening the refrigerator, pouring a cup of coffee, going to the bathroom, stopping at a red light, listening to hold music, dialing your voicemail, waiting for your computer to boot up, waiting for an elevator, taking off your shoes, opening your front door, checking the mail. When choosing your dead time moment, look for one that occurs at least once every day, and try to match the spark to the moment. For example, a spark reminding you to spend more time with your kids when Monday Night Football starts . . . not so good. Likewise, a spark reminding you to stand up and stretch at a red light . . . also not so good.

3. **Make the connection.** Once you have the spark and one recurring dead time moment, you need to connect them. Whenever the dead time moment occurs, you need to light your spark. For

example, I have the bad habit of taking shallow breaths. So now, I take several deep breaths every time I call someone and wait for them to pick up. It doesn't cost me any more time, and it's good for me.

At first, you might forget to spark and/or it might feel clumsy, but keep doing it. After a few days, it will become automatic, just like brushing your teeth in the morning. It's important to introduce one spark at a time. Once it becomes a habit, then introduce another. Also, only one spark per moment. Don't try to cram several sparks together. The power of sparks comes from one concentrated thought or action.

You can have some fun with sparking by creating props. Here are a few ideas. Hang a sign inside your garage with a motivational quote about making the most of each day that you can read before you go to work. If you find yourself thinking about work after you get home, tape a message on your front door (who cares who sees it!?!?) about making each moment with family count. After a tough day at work, a little note can shift your attention back to your family. Post a note in your mailbox with a Bible passage that resonates with you. Along with the daily Pottery Barn catalog, you'll also get a little inspiration when you get the mail.

How about a digital spark? What if you could instantly connect to your most powerful goal or get a blast of inspiration several times a day? If you don't mind getting a little attention, this one may be for you. Instead of being the annoying guy with the "Louie Louie" cell phone ringtone, you can create a personalized ringtone. Record your favorite Bible passage, you yelling "Carpe diem!" in a French accent, your kids or spouse saying they love you, your top three goals, etc. Record anything that will give you a shot of hope and encouragement and that you won't mind broadcasting to everyone around you. Check out other8.com for instructions and links on how to create your own ringtone.

Don't try to do too much, too soon. Start slowly. Introduce just one action at a time. Let it sink in and become a habit before you begin another one. Also, leave yourself some dead time. Don't snuff out every last second of every day.

USING TECHNOLOGY

Technology is a spy movie nun who blesses you and then throws a ninja star into your back as you walk away. It tricks you into thinking it will be your salvation, but you end up confused, frustrated, and paralyzed. Still, if you use the right technology correctly, it can help you get more of the other 8 hours.

I'm not a techie, but there are a few tools I use that have helped me:

- **Xobni** (xobni.com)—This application does what Outlook should do but doesn't. It's free and makes it easy to find e-mail and attachments. Don't be a ymmud, use this program.

- **MindManager** (mindjet.com)—This is software based on mind mapping. It's a visual technique for taking notes, jotting down ideas, and seeing the big picture. The cheaper version works great and is probably all you need.

- **Evernote** (evernote.com)—Supercool (and free!) program to help you organize your thoughts and notes. It provides a single place for you to keep a running tab of everything you'd normally put in a journal or on a Post-It note.

- **RSS reader/feeds** (various)—Instead of visiting the same ten individual Web sites each morning, you can create your own page with all of the best information from each. It's a real time saver and is easy to use.

- **RescueTime** (rescuetime.com) or **JournalLive** (journalLive. com)—Slick Web applications that effortlessly track how you spend your time on your computer. They are free and easy to use.

- **Mint** (mint.com)—Have you tried to organize your finances using Quicken but found it time consuming or difficult? Check out Mint.com. It's a free Web-based program that pulls together all of your financial accounts (bank, credit card, loan, investment, etc.) on a single page and updates them automatically.

- **MP3 player** (various)—I use an iPod, but any MP3 player will do. If you are going to use your travel and commute time to its fullest, you need an MP3 player. Clunky CDs are so 1990s.

- **YouTube to iPod** (dvdvideosoft.com)—Not all YouTube videos feature stupid pet tricks or Asian inmates dancing to "Thriller." There is some great educational and inspirational content as well. The problem is finding the time to watch all of it. I'm a big believer in highest and best use of time. When I'm in front of my computer, the best use of my time is getting work done or research, not watching videos. Solution? Use a free program to extract the audio in the video to MP3 so you can download it to your MP3 player and listen to it in the car or while working out.

- **Mozy** (mozy.com)—The best online backup software you can find, and for less than two gigs it's free. If you need more memory, their plans are supercheap. You can easily set it to backup in the middle of the night or when your computer is idle.

- **GoToMyPC** (gotomypc.com)—Probably the single greatest invention since a hotdog on a stick. All you need is an Internet connection to access your computer from any Web browser in the world.

- **Dropbox** (getdropbox.com)—A free program that syncs files between computers. For example, you can have several computers (work, home, laptop, mistress's home) and have the latest versions of all your files at all locations.

- **Google toolbar** (toolbar.google.com)—Don't waste your time going to Google to search. Install a free toolbar into Explorer or Firefox to make searching fast and easy.

- **Digital voice recorder** (various)—Don't leave home without it. These are perfect for taking notes while driving or to record brainstorming sessions. Many cell phones now give you the ability to record memos, too.

- **Jott** (jott.com)—You call a phone number and leave a message. A few minutes later you get an e-mail with your message converted to text. Awesome for notetaking on the go.

- **Two monitors**—Once you go stacked, you'll never go back! You will save yourself a whole lot of time by using two monitors (I use three!). Instead of constantly flipping back and forth, two monitors will allow you to have more windows open and viewable at once. Studies have shown it can increase productivity by 20 percent to 30 percent![1]

- **Audiobook playback** (iPod)—Most of us speak about 110 to 150 words per minute, yet we often read at speeds between 200 and 300 words per minute. I'm a huge fan of killing dead time by listening to audio books, but I often find that the narrator speaks too slowly—so slowly, in fact, that my mind wanders. To increase comprehension and efficiency, increase the playback speed on your iPod or iPhone.

- **Audible.com** (audible.com)—I love, love, love this service. It's a subscription-based audiobook download service. You select the book (they've got them all), and then it effortlessly downloads into iTunes and on your iPod. Within a few minutes you could be learning a new language, studying the latest marketing strategies for small businesses, or listening to *Walden*.

If you really think about it, *The Other 8 Hours* is all about investing your time in activities that pay the highest returns—whether the returns are financial, physical, or spiritual. How you invest your other 8 hours determines your happiness and financial success. You must free up as many of the other 8 hours as possible and protect them like your life depended on it (because it does).

That's easier said than done when, throughout the day, you are bombarded with requests, activities, and responsibilities that overwhelm and distract you. If you are to succeed, you must stop doing those things that suck your time and our energy. You must stop the bleeding . . .

CHAPTER FOUR

LIFELEECHES

Reclaim Your Life by Avoiding These
24 Time and Life Suckers

You decide you are going to skip the gym's pool and get some exercise outside in the warm summer air. You're standing on a dock at a local lake. The occasional chirping of a family of birds in a nearby tree breaks the silence. All is peaceful and still. As you gaze at the still lake, you wonder why nobody else has discovered this beautiful setting.

Just inches below the surface of the water, things couldn't be more different. The lake is teeming with activity. There are thousands of hungry leeches peering through the murky water in a frenzy, waiting for you to dive in. They can smell your blood, and they can hardly control their undulating bodies.

You take a couple of deep breaths, raise your arms into the air, and plunge into the depths of the water. You're wriggling and kicking and rising toward the surface to catch your breath. Most of the leeches don't have a chance to attach when you plunge, but then one digs in, and then another. You're taking long deep strokes and feeling great. Then another leech sinks its jaws into your flesh and begins to suck the life from your veins. You start to lose the snap in your kick, and your arms begin to feel like they have weights on them. As you slow, another leech grabs hold of you. Then another and another and another. You're about twenty yards from land, and you start to worry that you're not going to make it.

After what feels like an eternity, you make it to dry land, but you're in a daze. Your head is spinning and your body is numb. You're covered in what looks like mud or oil. You try to rub off the black slime that covers your body, but it doesn't come off. As you strain to get a better look, you realize that what looks like mud is actually hundreds of pulsating leeches intent on sucking every last drop of blood from your body.

Like the lake swimmer, leeches are sucking the life out of your body. Do you collapse to the ground and let them have their way with you? Or do you decide that you're going to remove them one by one and recapture your life? This is a life-or-death decision for our swimmer, and it is a life-or-death decision for you, too.

In chapter 2, I discussed the Living Dead and the idea that you can be alive but not fully living. If living feels like doing time, you're not filling the other 8 hours with things that inspire or energize you. Trust me. I've talked to a lot of people who sleep for 8, work at a good job for 8, and feel completely wasted and dead. So what's the problem? LifeLeeches.

LifeLeeches suck time and energy from us. Yes, energy in the let's-use-the-stairs-instead-of-the-elevator physical energy, but also our life energy. Life energy is what gives us that mental spring in our step. When our life energy is high, it provides us with hope, optimism, and drive. It's the feeling of being "in the zone" and on top of the world. When our life energy tank is low, we feel negative, pessimistic, and down on ourselves.

LifeLeeches are activities and situations that drain you of time and energy, and ultimately, suck the life from you. It's our job to shield ourselves from as many LifeLeeches as possible, but you don't have to go crazy with it, either. The blood loss from just one or two real leeches isn't dangerous. Likewise, if you read through the list of LifeLeeches and find that you've just got a couple of small ones attached to you, you're probably fine. But if several LifeLeeches have clung onto you, you've got to get them off as quickly as you can before they drain you.

1. **TV.** Quick , what's the average life expectancy for someone in the United States? According to the Centers for Disease Control, it is 77.8 years, but the guys in white lab coats at the CDC got it wrong. Sleep and work take 313,176 hours of our life. This leaves us 368,352 hours—42 years. That's our real life expectancy.

    Think about it . . . watching a couple of hours of TV might not seem like a big deal (most people watch 4 hours and 35 minutes

per day!), but if you have only 8 real hours a day, those two hours
suddenly represent 25 percent of your day! Next time you start
flipping mindlessly through the channels, ask yourself if you really
want to invest 25 percent or 50-plus percent of your day on TV.
When you consider your real life expectancy, an hour here and an
hour there during the other 8 hours isn't trivial anymore. This is
the granddaddy of all LifeLeeches. It sucks away more time from
more people than anything else. Enough said?

The Solution: I'm not recommending you chuck your TV. There
are worthwhile programs, and TV provides many people a great
way to decompress. There are shows I look forward to watching
and would not want to eliminate completely from my life. What
I want to eliminate is uncontrolled and excessive television watching. As soon as the tube fires up, our minds cool down. Research
shows that watching TV induces a comalike state of mind.

The single best way to limit TV is the DVR . . . but beware. It
can be used to control time spent watching TV or it can be a very
easy way to watch even more TV. Here are the rules. First, you are
not allowed to watch live TV. Second, record only a handful of
shows that you really want to watch. Third, deselect the option for
the DVR to record shows it thinks you might like.

Another great way to limit TV but not miss the best shows is
to rent full seasons of the shows you want to see. I've done this
with several shows, including *Entourage, Lost,* and *Arrested Development.* The upside is you don't have any commercials to fast forward through and you can burn through an entire season without
having to wait each week. You can watch them on your own time.

2. **News addiction.** My wife had the nasty habit of watching late-
   night local news in bed right before going to sleep. This was a
   habit that lasted one night before I put my foot down and said
   enough. Actually, I pleaded my case, pointing out the many reasons it was harmful—fortunately, she said she'd go without for a
   few nights to see how it went, and she's never wanted to watch local news again. It's not just news before bed, but it's local news of
   any kind in any form. It's one of the most egregious LifeLeeches

you'll experience. It's a complete waste of time and it is harmful to your sense of well-being.

The Solution: Give it up. You're not missing anything. Trust me. If you want to be informed, bookmark a news Web site such as CNN. Go to it once a day to get a snapshot of what's happened and be done with it. If something newsworthy happens in your area, it will end up in the national media. If it isn't big enough for them, it shouldn't be big enough for you.

3. **Internet and social media.** Where do I start? I confess that I use the Internet every day throughout the day, and occasionally, I discover that it has used me. The Internet is sneaky because you can use it for good, but you can also get sidetracked by it very quickly. How many times have you said, "I'm just going to check one thing," and an hour later, you find yourself knee-deep in a Britney article on some Argentinean's blog (maybe I just shared too much information)? Whatever your poison, the Internet has it on draft. Maybe you're a YouTube junkie. What about MySpace, Facebook, or SecondLife? Is your home page the Huffington Post or ESPN?

   The Solution: You need to slow down and think about the reason you are online before you pull up your first site. Write your Internet goal or goals on a Post-it note and attach it to your monitor. Before you click on any link or visit any of your favorites, look at your goals. If the link will help you reach your goal, click away. If the link won't get you closer to reaching your stated goals, resist the urge to surf.

   You also need to set limits on the sites that suck your time. The easiest way to do this is to set a timer for the number of minutes you're willing to be online. If you determine you will allow yourself thirty minutes online, set the timer for twenty-five minutes so you will have five minutes to wrap up whatever you're doing when the timer beeps.

   If a particular Web site is THE LifeLeech, you've got to break out the big guns. In this case, block the site from your Web browser. (I know, I know. If you're desperate, you can always unblock it, but at least it will force you to think about what you're doing first.) If you really want to get clever, get one of your techie buddies to change the settings on your firewall to block the site, but tell him you don't want to know how he did it. Or you could always use the aptly named Firefox Web browser add-on Leech-Block (search for "leechblock" in Tools/Add-ons in Firefox). You can use it to block those "time-wasting sites that can suck the life out of your working day."

In addition to using a timer, you can quarantine this Life-Leech. An effective way to insulate your Internet use time from spreading and taking over your productive day is to schedule online time between or immediately before other commitments you know you won't break. For example, schedule thirty minutes of Internet time before lunch, a meeting, or your son's baseball practice. If you've got to eat, meet a client, or drive your son to practice; chances are you'll tear yourself away from the computer (no matter how irresistible it might be to watch "Funny or Die: The Landlord" one more time on YouTube).

4. Perfectionism. I'm not sure what the psychology of a perfectionist is, but I know it's dark and twisted. The need to do and have everything "just right" is a terrible disease—something the perfectionist admits to while claiming that he can't help it. Perfectionism not only drains you of time and life energy, but it can drain those around you. If you're a perfectionist, live with one, or work for one, you know what I'm talking about.

If you're a hardcore "everything has to be perfect" person, a paragraph isn't going to help. If it's bad—almost obsessive—I'd really recommend you see a therapist. There's something going on somewhere that you may be able to address to help free you from the anxiety and overwhelming pressure you feel.

The Solution: Sometimes good enough is good enough. Instead of wasting time and life energy trying to achieve 100 percent with everything, just focus on those few things where 100 percent really matters. I'd say 95 percent of what I do is far from perfect, but it is good enough. The time and energy I save doing just what's necessary, I invest in the other 5 percent—those projects that really do matter. For me, the things that really matter are working with my clients, writing, and being the best father and husband. Figure out what is important to you and where it makes sense to achieve perfection. Everything else? Think pass/fail instead of killing yourself to get an A.

5. **Maximizing.** Almost a decade ago I read an article about Maximizing versus Satisficing—a concept made popular in Barry Schwartz's book *The Paradox of Choice*. To Maximize, you analyze and compare every option you can find with the goal of finding the very best choice. To Satisfice, you limit the options and accept the first one that will satisfy you. Maximizing is correlated with depression, perfectionism, and regret, as well as generally feeling less satisfied with consumer decisions.[1]

   The Solution: Schwartz suggested that we first identify what is important and what we really want. Once we know this, we can start the search process. As soon as something fulfills your criteria, stop searching and comparing! Once you've made your decision, focus on the positives of your choice and avoid the temptation to continue searching and comparing. You've made your choice. Move on.

6. **Being disorganized.** How many hours have you wasted just this week looking for your keys, a folder, an e-mail, or an electronic document? One of the side effects of information overload is trying to develop a system for storing things for easy retrieval.

   The Solution: I work with a four-step process to help me stay organized. The more there is, the more there is to organize. The first thing I do is limit what comes my way. I religiously remove myself from e-mail lists and e-mail forwards as well as from physical subscriptions and mailing lists. Second, I operate under the policy that everything is chuckable unless proven otherwise. I must convince myself *not* to throw something away. Third, anything I must keep, I scan into a PDF and organize with a document management program (I use FileCenter, by lucion.com). Once I scan it, I throw away or shred the original. The advantage to scanning everything you'd normally file is it takes up no space, you can find documents immediately, and you can back up these files. If you receive faxes, save yourself some time by using eFax. Faxes are converted to PDF and e-mailed to you. This allows you to skip the scanning process altogether. If you have trouble managing and/or locating e-mails, you must use xobni.com. It's free and it has saved my sanity. Fourth, if I must keep an original, I give it to my wife to file. While I'm really good at managing electronic documents, I'm horrible at filing physical documents.

7. Health. Nothing ruins a perfectly planned and efficient schedule like getting sick. To be efficient and productive and enjoy your life, you must feel good and have the physical energy to tackle your day.

The Solution: Live longer and live fuller by taking care of yourself. Exercise, eat right, wash your hands often, don't pick your nose (seriously, this is how most people get sick), take a multivitamin, drink lots of water, and get regular checkups. If you can extend your life by a decade and/or boost your vitality by exercising just a couple of hours a week and eating better, that's one hell of a return on your investment. Get more time by extending your life and the quality of your life.

8. Gossip. Water cooler gossip and behind-the-back "did you hear about" is not only a waste of your time, but it can also jeopardize your reputation, be hurtful to those being discussed, and drain your life energy. Nothing, and I mean *nothing*, good comes from gossip.

The Solution: Decide right now that you will not take part in gossip. If someone tries to drag you into a gossip session, cut him off immediately. An effective strategy is to say, "Well, you can't believe everything you hear." Do this once or twice and people will know you're not into playing the gossip game.

9. Celebrititus. A serious condition of spending more time and energy obsessing over the lives of famous people than your own. The breaking point for me was when news coverage of Paris Hilton eclipsed reports on the war in Iraq and Afghanistan. But it's not just the occasional Britney or Lindsay story that can divert our time and attention, there are television shows, magazines, and Web sites that dedicate themselves to reporting on all things celebrity. I know people who can spew forth fact after fact about the latest celebrity gossip and then complain that they don't make enough money or that they don't get to spend enough time with their family.

The Solution: Where we spend our time is an indication of what is important to us. If your life is so boring that you need to know what everyone else is doing with their lives, the solution is to create a more interesting life. I want you to be so fulfilled and engrossed in pursuing your goals and dreams that you don't have the time or the desire to know who just broke up with whom. I want your life to be so exciting that the paparazzi are climbing *your* trees!

10. **Video games.** My name is Robert, and I am *not* a video game junkie, but I know someone who is. Actually, I know a lot of people who spend a lot of their other 8 hours playing games. That sucking sound isn't coming from the game you're playing, it's your life being drained away. A lot has changed since Missile Command and Kaboom!. The graphics are amazing and the choices are endless. Now you can play with people around the world over the Internet as if they were sitting next to you.

    The Solution: Okay, maybe I'm being a little dramatic here. Like the alcohol ads say, drink in moderation. But if you're like most people, you'll find that it's just not that much fun to drink in moderation. If games are taking over your life and you can't seem to control it, rip the cord out of the wall as fast as you would if it were a ticking time bomb that happened to be conveniently plugged into a wall.

11. **Porn.** I'm sorry, did I break your concentration, guys? There are two camps of people when it comes to porn: those who can't stand

it, and those who can't get enough of it. If you're in the first camp, skip ahead. However, if you spend a good deal of time watching porn, you've got to break this addiction. That's right, Internet porn is allegedly as addictive as crack. Porn is about as bad for you as the dialogue in those films.

The Solution: Cold-turkey. This is one of the LifeLeeches that you've got to eliminate. It will rob you of time and life energy without providing any positive benefits. Google "porn addiction" to find many online resources to help you break the compulsion. Use the Web site blocking tips discussed earlier or use software that blocks porn sites such as NetNanny or CYBERsitter.

12. **Being reactive.** Do you feel like a slot machine ball? Just when you start getting some momentum going, something comes from out of nowhere to bounce you in a completely different direction, and then another and another? Whether it's from our Black-Berrys, text messages, e-mail notifications, voicemails, etc., we are inundated with requests. We've become adept at responding to every blip as if it were life or death. We aren't able to filter the good from the bad or the truly important from the meaningless. We award everything we receive equal importance and respond to it all immediately. The problem with this automatic reaction is that most things don't need our immediate attention, but when we feel the compulsion to react immediately, we take time, energy, and focus away from the things that really are important and meaningful.

The Solution: We'll never get back to the simplicity and serenity of the idyllic 1950s. You can't stop, or even effectively slow down, the stuff that comes at you, but you can control your response (or, in this case, your lack of response). Here are some tips. Turn off the notification when your PDA receives an e-mail. If this is too severe, turn off all notifications unless an incoming e-mail is marked "Urgent" or "High Importance." Disable all of the alerts on your computer e-mail program (for example; Outlook). With all of the bells and beeps and flashing notices, you'd think getting an e-mail was the second coming. Turn them all off. They are completely unnecessary; you should check your e-mail only at a few scheduled times during the day. Create tech-free zones. Include both times during the day that you are going to unplug and also locations that are free from technology (bedroom, children's rooms, parks, playgrounds). Some people protest that it's better to be at the park with their kids—even if they are on their cell phone—than not to be at the park at all. On the surface this makes sense, but it's completely wrong. Kids don't think this way. If you're at work, they don't fault you for not playing with them. But if you're at the park working, they see that you are ignoring them. That's much worse, in their eyes. You'd be better off staying at work until you can devote your full attention to them.

13. **Answering the phone.** This could have been in the "reactive" section above, but it is so important I wanted it to be its own Life-Leech. There are few things that can distract you from your work,

---

OTHER 8 EXPERT

Merlin Mann is, well, the man. He writes one of the most popular blogs around at 43folders.com, which is aimed at "finding the time and attention to do your best creative work." Amen! Here's how he answered the question, What one thing should readers do with their other 8 hours that will have the greatest positive impact on their lives?

At some point in "the other 8 hours" of a given day, make time to read a book that's: a) unrelated to your job and b) about a topic you know little about. Could be a novel or a history book or biography. But it has to be a real book; not a magazine or Web site. The idea is to set aside as little as thirty minutes every day to unhook and learn something new. In my experience, regularly absorbing new and unfamiliar material is black coffee for your brain.

conversation, or train of thought like answering a phone call. You're going about your day and someone thinks that you'll drop whatever you're doing just to talk to them? Why? I know this is not a popular idea, but phone calls are avoidable intrusions.

The Solution: Easy. Stop answering the phone. Voicemail was created for a reason. Call them back when it's convenient for you. You can either screen your calls (still distracting, but at least you don't have to engage in a conversation) or simply let everything go directly to voicemail. Like e-mail, you can schedule a few times during the day to check messages and return calls.

14. **Complaining.** Doing it or being around it is hazardous to your happiness and success. Complaining and general negativity is a huge LifeLeech. If you are in the habit of complaining, you are not only infecting others, you are undermining your own happiness and success. Secondhand smoke kills. Even if you're not a complainer yourself, just being around those who complain will damage you.

The Solution: There is help. If you're a complainer, you probably don't even realize it. The first step is awareness. A friend of mine wears a bright purple rubber wristband on his left hand. If he complains or is negative, he has to move the bracelet to his right hand. The goal is to keep the bracelet on his left hand for thirty days. In order to get the whole family involved, or at least to get some accountability, you can turn this into a game. If my wife or I hear the other complain or be negative, we say "five minutes." This means we get a five-minute massage at the end of the night. It's possible to rack up twenty or thirty minutes throughout the day very easily. I consider myself a very positive person, but the first day we started playing this game, I spent a good part of the night giving her a massage. I discovered just how much complaining was part of my life. More importantly, I learned to break the habit. Now my wife complains that she doesn't get as many massages as she used to ("five minutes" for that complaint!).

If you're around others who complain, you've got to take immediate preventative action. Here are two tips. First, the more someone complains, the more positive you need to become. It will either get them to become more positive (not very likely) or it will annoy them and they'll stop talking to you (more likely). Second, if the first tip doesn't work or you don't have the patience for it, stop hanging around them. If someone starts to complain, excuse yourself, or if you have the guts, tell them about the bracelet idea. They just might get the hint. Try to surround yourself with positive people. Their optimism and bright outlook will help undo the damage and protect you from future negativity.

15. **Reading.** Yes, I recognize the irony. Reading for pleasure is not a waste of time. Reading because you feel compelled to or without a purpose, is a total waste of time. There are countless articles, trade publications, blogs, Web sites, and newsletters for nearly every industry. You can waste a lot of time and energy (and many people do) trying to read all of them and worrying that you are missing something.

The Solution: Unless you're reading for pleasure, the goal is to learn something. Learning isn't passive; you can't sit back and read like you would sit back and watch TV. To get the most from the time you invest reading, start with these tips. First, don't waste time reading the wrong stuff. Before you commit several hours to reading a book, invest twenty minutes making sure you should read it. Think of this as the book's "movie" trailer. You want to get a feel for the book and the content. Read the table of contents and index. If something catches your eye, flip to that page and skim it. Did you learn anything? Did you want to read more? Skim the introduction and conclusion. If the trailer doesn't inspire you, don't waste your time reading the whole book.

Assuming you've found a book that passes the trailer test, it's time to become an active reader. Never read without a highlighter and/or pen and paper handy. Before you start each chapter, ask yourself what you think you might learn. As you read, take notes, highlight sections, write in the margins, and constantly ask how you can use this in your life. I love to underline (highlighting fades over time) and then give the book to my assistant to type up the notes. This system gives me a short synopsis I can refer to later. I also send these summaries to friends and colleagues. It saves them a ton of time and they reciprocate with books they're reading.

16. Meetings. When in doubt, schedule a meeting! Unfortunately, that's the philosophy of most people. No matter where we go, we can't escape meetings. While most meetings occur at work, there are many others that rob you of your other 8 hours: PTA, homeowner associations, church meetings, etc. I'm not down on the PTA or church; I'm down on their usually unorganized and inefficient meetings and lack of leadership.

Meetings and the organizers behind them usually have the best intentions, but most lack structure and control. An effective meeting is determined before it even starts by having a very clear purpose and tight agenda. This is not to say there can't be pockets of spontaneity, but to foster creativity, there must be structure.

The Solution: If you're involved in an organization that has ineffective meetings, you have two choices. Get more involved so you can make them more productive, or get out. You do not have the option of staying as is. You will waste too much time, and the frustration you feel will kill your life energy.

Here's what you can do. First, sit near the back and leave early, if possible. I know this may sound childish, but we're talking about your life here. The other 8 hours are yours to grow and to live, not to waste at a lame meeting.

If you can't leave early, how many meetings can you skip and not get into "trouble"? For the meetings where your attendance is required, prepare a list of things to work on while you're there. Nearly every meeting, and especially those by ineffective leaders, is full of handouts. If important (rare), read them during the meeting. If not important, come prepared with your own reading material. Avoid books and magazines; they are too noticeable. Instead, bring Web site printouts or articles (printed on loose-leaf standard paper) so they can blend in with any handout.

17. Attending conferences. Is it me, or do most conferences suck? Almost all of them are a complete waste of time and money.

The Solution: If you feel compelled to go, do your research first. Who's presenting? What are they talking about? How long is the conference? Can you download the PowerPoint presentations in advance? If possible, skip the conference and get it on CD or MP3. This way you can listen to it on your own time and skip the worst presentations altogether.

18. Driving. More and more of us are spending more of our precious time behind the wheel, and much of the time spent is typically considered dead time. This dead time can be brought back to life.

The Solution: Talking on your cell phone via a hands-free set (if it's legal), listening to audiobooks, and thinking are the best uses of drive time. If you have a longer commute, write down a list of people you need to contact before you start your trek. Start at the top and go down the list. Lastly, you can sit in silence and think. But to get the most from your drive, it must be *active* thinking. Think with a purpose. Try to solve a problem, come up with a marketing strategy, invent a new product. Think of solutions as opposed to engaging in passive thinking, where you reflect on random thoughts and events.

Also consider the time of your drive—make business calls on the way in to work when you're fresh and your mind is sharpest; listen to audiobooks and talk to friends and family on your way home when you need some time to relax. Carry a handheld digital voice recorder so you can "take notes" without having to take your eye off the road.

19. Car pooling. This practice saves gas, but most people do it incorrectly. Here's how it usually goes down. Joe mentions he commutes an hour to work. Bob laments that his drive is a good forty-five minutes. They talk a bit more and discover they take the same freeway. Synapses flash and someone gets the brilliant idea that it would save money if they carpooled. The wheels are set in motion, and Joe and Bob carpool to the office. They're in the car, together, for an hour and a half each day. They develop a rapport. They gossip about their fellow co-workers. They complain that management doesn't get it. They talk about the game the night before. In essence, they chitchat for almost eight hours a week. I call this car spooning. Let's cuddle and make nice. It's fine to make a friend and to have conversations, but don't waste a huge opportunity to use *some* of that time more productively.

The Solution: Carpool the right way. Before you commit, make it known you like to get the most out of your time in the car. You want to be free to talk on your cell phone, e-mail, listen to audiobooks on your iPod, read, and sleep. Schedule alternating weeks where you trade off who drives. If you are direct about your needs during that drive, your carpool partner may welcome the opportunity to use that time more effectively, too.

20. **Doing more than is necessary.** A friend of mine complains that his wife cooks gourmet dinners. Poor him, right? He says she spends at least an hour and a half preparing the meal every night and then he spends a good forty-five minutes after dinner cleaning up. The problem is he doesn't want a gourmet dinner every night. He says this becomes such a huge undertaking that it takes precious time away from them doing other things together. She thinks she's doing something terrific but he doesn't appreciate it. It's actually become a pretty serious issue.

The Solution: Don't break your back doing something that nobody values. But how do you know what they value? Ask them! Most people probably don't even notice half of the hard stuff you do. Why not save yourself some time and sweat and use this time to do the things they actually value?

21. **Trying to change others.** There are few things in life as special as someone who wants to improve his life and overcome challenges. Unfortunately, there are few people in life who are willing to change. Too often we see the potential in others that they do not

see in themselves. We then spend years trying to get them to recognize their own potential. We spend more time and energy trying to get them to change than we do trying to improve our own lives. Of course, it usually ends in frustration and defeat. It reminds me of a saying a friend of mine who has battled alcoholism her whole life told me once. AA is for people who want it, not for those who need it.

The Solution: Unless you are a shrink who gets paid to change people or are helping someone who truly wants to change, don't waste your energy. Instead, focus on making the most of yourself.

22. **Upgrading.** This LifeLeech is about upgrading "stuff"—getting everything from the latest iPhone, TiVo, 3 Series, PlayStation software. When the newest iPhone makes the national news and people camp out overnight to get one, we've taken consumerism to a whole new level. Regardless of who's to blame, we feel compelled to buy the latest technology, upgrade to the newest software, and have the most recent model of everything. We're partly to blame, but we're no match against the companies armed with billion-dollar marketing budgets that bombard us with ads that make us feel like what we have is inadequate and would have us believe that the new version will solve all our problems. It's not just the waste of money that makes this a LifeLeech, it's the waste of time. Every new upgrade, phone, and tech gizmo requires a tremendous amount of time to learn.

Even downloading seemingly innocuous free upgrades can waste valuable time and distract you. For example, whenever I write, I listen to music on iTunes. Nearly every week I get prompted to download a new version. I used to diligently download each new version as it came out. Sometimes it would take ten minutes to download and then another ten minutes to install. If it required a reboot, I'd be out nearly a half hour. For what? I never noticed any difference whatsoever in ANY of the upgrades. And it's not just Apple; I'm constantly getting messages I need to upgrade every time I start my computer.

The Solution: Don't fix what ain't broke. I don't download any upgrades unless they are critical updates to my operating system or upgrades to my antivirus software. Once every six months, I'll update a few of the programs I use often, but I do this when it is convenient for me, not just because a box pops up telling me to do it. As far as getting the latest phone or gizmo, determine if all the new bells and whistles are really important to you. Most of the time, the changes are insignificant. You're better off saving your money and your time by keeping what you already have and know. If you do need to upgrade, wait a few months so they work out the bugs first.

23. **Working for a workaholic.** Want a great way to cut the other 8 hours in half? Put in fifty or sixty hours a week working for a company or a boss that doesn't respect your time. If you are just starting out in your career, it's important to put in your time. Sometimes it takes working fifty or sixty hours a week to get noticed, get projects completed, or gain more responsibility. That's just the nature of learning a new career and being at the bottom on the totem pole.

On the other hand, if you are not pursuing your dream career or have been putting in your time for no recognition or reward, it may be time for a change.

The Solution: Here's a nasty little fact. You're going to spend more time with your boss at work than you will with your loved ones. Even though it may have taken dozens of dates and months before you were ready to commit to your girlfriend, you will jump in the sack with the first job offer.

The job search is no different from dating, so you've got to spend some time getting to know your potential partner. And just as you instinctively do during the dating process, you have to stay alert for the warning signs. Things to look out for:

It's best to ask a few of these questions at the beginning of the interview as a "getting to know you" chitchat before the real interview begins. If you are waiting in the reception area, start chatting with the receptionist and getting a feel for the place. You'll learn about the culture, and you'll make a good impression (receptionists have a tremendous amount of pull in an office). Also, at the end of the interview, you can ask your potential boss a few more questions. Again, these are getting-acquainted questions. It's a great way to end the interview. If you come across as Perry Mason cross-examining a witness, it will be a huge turnoff and you'll never get the job. If you approach these questions casually and with the intention of trying to get to know him better, you'll come across as sincere and interested.

- Ask about his commute and what time he gets in and leaves the office. If he gets in at 6:00 AM and leaves at 7:00 PM to beat the traffic, guess where's he's going to be all day? Guess where he'll want you?

- Try to talk to other workers. Ask them about their typical day and travel plans. They'll often be your best source of unfiltered information because they're not trying to sell you on how great the company or boss is.

- Look around the interviewer's office. Any family photos? Kids? If you see kids, ask about how he is able to work and raise a family. If you hear about how supportive the spouse is at taking care of the kids, this is short for he's never at home and always at work.

- Schedule a follow-up interview thirty minutes after the office has "closed." If he says it's too late to meet, that's a good sign. If he agrees, check out who else is working at that time. Is the office empty or is everyone still there? When you leave the interview, is everyone still there?

24. **Sleeping.** A third of our life is spent sleeping. That's about twenty-five years we're unconscious. Most of us don't get enough sleep and spend our days loading up on stimulants so we don't doze off driving home. But there are a few of you out there who actually get too much sleep and are wasting your other 8 hours in the process.

The Solution: How do you know if you are getting enough sleep? Test it. Try 8 hours a night and see how you feel. Jot down how tired you feel when you wake up and throughout the day. Then keep testing by cutting your sleep by fifteen minutes. Try each new time for a week. You'll know when you've found your sweet spot when you feel pretty good about fifteen minutes after you wake up (don't count on springing out of bed feeling fully refreshed) and when you aren't yawning all day.

If you crash in the afternoons (usually between 3:00 and 5:00), you might try sleeping an hour less at night but taking an hour nap during your crash time (some flexibile employers will let you do this). This way you are not giving up any more of your 8 hours, but you are writing off the time when you'd be dragging and unproductive anyway.

We covered a bunch of LifeLeeches just waiting to drain your time and energy, but there are a whole lot more. Check out other8.com to share your tips and to read more LifeLeech solutions.

I hope you've learned some strategies in the last two chapters to help you reclaim more of the other 8 hours. The rest of the book addresses what specifically you should do with this time in order to get rich and get a life.

GET MORE MONEY

Now that you have a little more free time, this section will show you how to use the other 8 hours to make more money (the last section of the book will show you how to "get a life"). We're living in an amazing time where it's possible to catapult our finances to a new level with a little creativity and free time. As you read this, there are people just like you who are taking advantage of today's resources and technology not just to supplement their income but to radically improve their finances.

The old rules say you need to work harder and longer. That you need to cut your expenses and sacrifice today for an uncertain and distant future. But what if you've followed the old rules and are still struggling to survive? What if there's a gap between where you are and where you'd like to be? And what if there's no way of closing that gap with the old rules? Should you give up on your dreams and settle for a life that is less than ideal?

Fortunately, there's a better approach. You can become a Cre8tor™—someone who uses the other 8 hours to create. This section will show you the opportunities to create and provide you with tips, strategies, and resources to thrive using the Cre8tor approach.

In this section you will learn:

• What a Cre8tor is and how you can become one.

• How to profit from the consumer mentality.

- How to minimize risk and maximize success.

- Answers to the most frequently asked Cre8tor questions.

- Ten Cre8tor Channels to start making money.

CHAPTER FIVE

SHIFT FROM CONSUMER TO CRE8TOR

The New Strategy for Creating Wealth

The roar of the crowd reverberates off the columns and down the dusty corridors leading to your cell. The rhythmic thumping and stomping offers a slower and deeper contrast to your fast and sharp heartbeat. That internal beat is interrupted when the door flies open. "That one," two men command, as they point at you. Moments later, they drag you down a narrow underground passage and throw you onto the stadium's dirt floor.

You stand near the middle of a massive open-air stadium. There are thousands of people standing, stomping, and chanting. A beast of a man strides out onto the stadium floor. Bare hands and bare feet. He's at least 6'5" and 250 pounds.

The beast circles your paralyzed body. He toys with you and slaps you around. How did you end up here? You quickly tell yourself that question is less important than how you are going to get out of here alive. How can you beat him? He's bigger and stronger, and he's a much better fighter. You could throw a few punches and fight him like you've seen done in the movies. This optimistic pep talk ends when you notice you're standing in a pool of someone else's blood. You need a new strategy.

You quickly rush in, fake a punch, and rush out. He covers up and then takes a swing—missing by a mile. You're gauging his distance and his reaction time. You fake another punch and then kick him in the groin. A loud gasp echoes through stadium, followed by cheers.

You reach down and grab a handful of dirt and fake another kick.

He drops his hands to protect his groin, and you fling the dirt in his eyes. You jump on his back and lock him in a neck choke. He struggles violently to shake you, but you hold on for life. After what seems like minutes, he drops to the ground unconscious.

The crowd is silent. The guards aren't sure what to do. Apparently this has never happened before. Nobody anticipated this. Nobody except you. Then the gates to the stadium slowly open. The crowd is on its feet chanting as you walk toward freedom . . .

Maybe I watched too many Jean-Claude Van Damme movies in my youth, but there's an important lesson here. Sometimes playing by the old rules can be dangerous. Sometimes you need to do something new and different in order to succeed.

JUMPING THE GAP

Your financial life has a certain trajectory—similar to a train on a track. There will be twists and turns, but you can easily determine where you will end up if you stay on the financial track you're on. What if the traditional methods of working hard, cutting expenses, and saving don't work for you? Brown bagging it every day won't cause you to jump tracks and end up somewhere completely different. The guy living in the mansion overlooking the ocean didn't buy that house by clipping coupons, and the chick passing you in a $400,000 Maybach didn't buy it by eliminating her morning latte. For most of us, the gap between where we are and where we want to be is so wide that we'll never be able to close it by following traditional financial advice.

What's the solution? If you're tired of scraping by, you've got to create. If you want to move out of your apartment or make more than minimum wage, you've got to create. If you want a big house overlooking the ocean, to travel first class, to quit your job, or to drive your dream car, guess what? The answer is in the other 8 hours. The answer is to shift from being a full-time consumer to being a part-time Cre8tor.

A what? A Cre8tor is a creative entrepreneur who has a day job but wants more. He isn't content with the status quo, and is less than thrilled with the thought of working another forty-plus years. He knows that the only way to "jump the tracks" to get to a new financial level is to do something different during the other 8 hours. A Cre8tor utilizes his strengths, passions, and/or expertise to create something unique and valuable—maybe he'll start a blog, work on an invention, write a screenplay, or start a business. If you settle for a paycheck, you'll only be worth what your employer pays you. But if you create something valuable, there's virtually no limit to your worth.

A long commute, brainless boss, and an empty bank account can wreak havoc on your outlook, hope, and purpose, but a side project or venture can bring inspiration to your life. When you're passionate about what you're creating during the other 8 hours, you can endure even the worst day. It will change your whole morning routine. Think about the excitement and anticipation you felt on Christmas Eve as a kid. You probably couldn't sleep all night and were the first one up on Christmas morning. This is the kind of excitement you can feel when you are creating something you are passionate about. Creating provides purpose, and for the living dead, it provides a reason to get out of bed in the morning. It provides the hope that life can improve. When you create, it engages your mind and your soul.

You need to start looking at the world a little differently. You need to create instead of consume and build instead of buy. You have to turn everything you've learned on its head. Instead of always thinking about what you can buy, you need to shift your thinking to focus on what you can create. Instead of being brainwashed by billion-dollar ad budgets to think that consumption leads to happiness and success, I want you to reject that premise. I want you to be the guy or gal taking the money—instead of handing it over.

Don't get me wrong. I love to consume as much as the next guy. I am not encouraging anyone to sell his possessions and meditate in the mountains of Tibet for the rest of his life. I happen to like stuff, and I've got plenty of it . . . cars, house, an iPod, a cell phone, computers, a big-screen TV, DVD players, DVRs. I love buying new toys, and I'm sure you do, too, but excessive consumption has gotten us in quite a mess.

OTHER 8 EXPERT

Bet you can't guess what one book has changed my life the most in the last five years . . . *Skinny Bitch*. Thanks to the authors' hilarious approach, I've been a vegetarian for over a year. Coauthor Kim Barnouin answers the question, What one thing should readers do with their other 8 hours that will have the greatest positive impact on their lives?

One of the most important things that can bring about the greatest impact in a person's life is mindful manifesting. Think of what it is you want to create. It can be anything: a new career, a new relationship, to lose weight, or to buy your dream house. Have a clear mental picture of what you want. Then ask yourself how it would feel to have it. If you are truly passionate about what it is you want to create, that feeling will bring you such joy that the vibration of the feeling together with the thought of what you want will spark the energy to make it happen.

Consuming has morphed from being a luxury to being a hobby. We've become a consumer culture; almost everything sells us something. The goal is to find a balance between consuming and creating.

Shifting from consumer to Cre8tor is the solution to the financial fear and frustration you may be feeling. Creating can bridge the gap between where you are and where you want to be, but you may still be wondering if it is worth the time and energy.

SPEED FOR YOUR WALLET AND SOUL

Should we really spend some of our precious other 8 hours creating, or would we be better off having fun and enjoying ourselves? Studies show that most of us are not fulfilled mentally or emotionally in our day jobs. We work, not because we are passionate about what we're doing, but for a paycheck. Even though you might be stuck at your day job doing something that doesn't fully capture your mind and heart, that doesn't mean that what you create during the other 8 hours has to feel like work. In fact, it shouldn't feel like work at all. I want you to be excited and passionate about what you create and about the potential results you can achieve.

There is a full spectrum of possibilities that you can achieve by becoming a Cre8tor:

- **Mansion money.** Make no mistake about it. If you create something special that takes off, you could generate an obscene amount of money that could instantly catapult you to a whole new level. Mansion money is an amount of money so large that it allows you to do whatever you want, including quitting your job and buying a mansion. This is the big kahuna. This is what people dream about. It's a game changer, and it happens all the time.

- **Mo' money.** Maybe you're not interested in an IPO, but could you find a use for a few extra thousand a month or an extra hundred thousand dollars a year? Some ventures will never make the cover of *Fortune*, but they can still produce a great deal of income you can use to pay off debt and/or take your lifestyle to the next level.

- **Be your own boss.** If you're tired of getting up before the sun rises, commuting longer than you'd like, working at a job you don't love, working for people you don't respect, and working more hours and for more years than you want, becoming a Cre8tor can help you design a new life where you call the shots. Millions of entrepreneurs have been able to quit their unfulfilling day jobs and create more passion and excitement in their lives by starting their own business.

- **Movin' on up.** Even if you don't have a desire to strike it rich or work for yourself, what you create during the other 8 hours can help you secure a better job or move up the ladder at your current job. By writing a book or an article, by speaking at an engagement, by blogging, or by using any number of other strategies I'll

discuss later, you can attract new clients, gain credibility and recognition, and take your career to a new level.

R U A CRE8TOR?

It's not easy and it's not instantaneous to transition from full-time consumer to part-time Cre8tor. We're facing an uphill battle. Research
shows that we are bombarded with over a million ads a year brainwash-
ing us with the messages of buying and consuming. Creating might
not feel natural. When is the last time you saw a message suggesting
you start your own side business, turn your passion into a product, take
that idea you've had for years and invent something, or write that book
or record that song or shoot that documentary?

And even if you did hear a message encouraging you to use the
other 8 hours to follow your passions and create (you're reading this
book, after all), chances are you might resist. You might still be reading
and nodding, but for many that inner voice may have reared its ugly
head. You know which inner voice I'm talking about. It's the one that
is saying, "You can't do this. You can't create anything. You're not
smart enough. You're not creative. You don't have any special or unique
talents. You'll never make more money than you're making right now."

Every successful person has had doubts. They have had an inner
voice too, but what set them apart is that they plunged ahead despite
any reservations they had. They took the leap.

You may think that it's too late to create anything valuable or unique
because "everything has already been done," but that would have been
like watching *The Ed Sullivan Show* for the first time and thinking all
the good ideas for TV shows had been done.

It doesn't matter where you came from, where you work, how little
you make, or where you live. Everyone sees the world a little differently,
and because of that, anyone can create something special and unique.
Sometimes the best ideas and solutions come after defeat. Your struggles and failures are powerful. You can tap into your strengths and
uniqueness and create something that nobody else has.

AN**OTHER 8-HOUR SUCCESS**

From idea to *Dr. Phil* in about a month.

It is March 2009 and I get a call from a friend. He says he is worried about getting laid off and wants my advice on what he should do. He's got a few bucks set aside, but he also has several thousand in credit card debt. He wants to pay off his credit cards with his savings so he'll feel better.

"That's a terrible idea!" I tell him. He thinks I'm joking. "No, really. I think that is the worst thing you can do right now," I add. He still thinks I'm joking. Once he realizes I am not joking (this takes several minutes), he politely tells me that's what all the "experts" say to do.

I tell him that most traditional financial advice is dangerous during a recession. I tell him, "Cash is king! Pay just the minimum on credit cards, stop contributing to your 401(k), get a loan," and on and on and on.

That's when I get the idea of writing a no-nonsense, down-and-dirty eBook with nothing but how-to tips and strategies to survive the recession. I call it *Plan Z: How to Survive the 2009 Financial Crisis (and even live a little better)*—www.planzbook.com. I write it during the other 8 hours. I want to spread the message far and wide, so I decide to give it away for free.

I then enlist six separate partners to help me. I get the cover design, book layout, Web hosting, Web design, editing, and audio recording/ production for free. About a month after having the idea, I have a seventy-five-page eBook, Web site, and audiobook finished and it didn't cost anything but a little time.

Oh, and one more thing. Dr. Phil invited me on his show to discuss my "counterintuitive" strategies and to be part of his Recession Survival Squad.

From idea to *Dr. Phil* in about a month. I love being a Cre8tor!

With very few exceptions, anybody who has attained any level of financial success has created something. It might be a book, a CD, an invention, or a Web site. Look around you. Everything you see was originally just an idea in someone's head. Look around again. The computer, the desk, the bench, the coffee cup, the couch, the pool, and even this book you're holding were just ideas at one point. It took vision, determination, and action to turn those ideas into what you see today.

We are living in the most exciting and mind-blowing time we have ever experienced. It is rich with opportunities that didn't exist just a few years ago. Unless your last name was Rockefeller or Carnegie, it used to be difficult to become rich. Becoming a millionaire wasn't even a dream or an ambition. It was such an impossibility that it wasn't worth a moment's thought.

Because of technology, efficiencies, and a global economy, it's much easier to become rich with much less effort than at any other point in history. But before we get into the various ways you can spend the other 8 hours making money, let's address a few of the most frequently asked questions in the next chapter.

CHAPTER SIX

THE BIG LIST OF FAQs

What You Need to Know Before You Get Started

"Crack!" The sharp sound of gunshot pierces the evening air. You hesitate for a fraction of a second and then you push off the blocks. You've cleared everything from your mind so that not even your thoughts will weigh you down. You feel only the blood pumping through your heart and your feet pounding on the track. You hold your head up and keep your back straight. Your legs are rocking up and down and your arms are pumping back and forth in a sweet rhythm. You've trained for years. You've sacrificed time with family and friends. And it all comes down to this race. You cannot lose. You become faster and faster with each step—your strides get longer and quicker. You crash through the finish line at full speed. All of the time in the gym and on the track has paid off. This was what you worked so hard and trained so long to achieve, and it was worth it.

Then you notice that the cheers are loud, but they're not for you. You look up at the board and see a "2" next to your name. You wipe the stinging sweat from your eyes, hoping it has clouded your vision. You squint, but the "2" is still stuck, like an ugly appendage, to your name. Your eyes dart to the times. Your time, 10.83. The winning time, 10.82. You lost by .01 of a second. The outcome of the last six years of your life was decided by a hundredth of a second?!?!

You didn't lose at the finish line or even halfway through the race. You lost the race at the starting blocks. The millisecond hesitation determined your fate.

Becoming a Cre8tor is tough work, and you need as many advantages as possible. But before you shoot out of the blocks, you need to get a good start. Read through these FAQs to help you start out on the right foot, because how you start can determine how well you finish.

GETTING STARTED

1. What are a few things I can start doing tomorrow that will help me become more creative?

2. What should I do if I'm *really* not creative?

3. What's a Cre8tor Club?

4. I don't think I'm old enough to start my own business. Should I wait until after I graduate from college or find a career?

5. I want to use the other 8 hours to improve my life and to make more money, but I can barely pay the rent every month. I'm so focused on just surviving that I can't do anything else. What should I do?

6. What are the chances my venture is going to catapult me to a new level?

AVOIDING LANDMINES

7. I've got a day job; is there anything I need to know before I start something on the side?

8. Why are my friends and family so critical of my idea and desire to better my life?

9. Why is my spouse so unsupportive?

10. How should I deal with the potential for failure?

11. How can I protect my idea?

12. How can I avoid being ripped off?

13. My venture has stalled, but I've put a lot of money into it. What should I do?

14. Should I ever use a credit card or home equity loan to start a venture?

FINDING "FREE" HELP

15. How should I approach graphic designers, Web programmers, PR pros, marketing gurus, consultants, and other service providers to get them to help me for free?

16. Where can I find service partners willing to reduce or eliminate their fee?

17. I've got a service provider interested in my idea, but how should I structure the partnership?

18. How much revenue should I give to a service partner?

19. If I have to pay some money, why not just pay someone cheaper in full so I don't have to give away any profits later?

20. Which service partners should I try to partner with?

ATTRACTING INVESTORS

21. Should I try to get investors for my venture?

22. How do I raise money?

23. How do I find investors?

GETTING STARTED

Q—*What are a few things I can start doing tomorrow that will help me become more creative?*

A—Here are several things you can try that will get your juices flowing:

- **Capture ideas.** Coming up with a good idea is hard enough, so don't lose a good one because you aren't prepared to capture it. Ideas (good and bad) don't work nine to five. They'll come to you in dreams, while driving seventy mph on the freeway, in meetings, during dinner, and in the shower. You must have a system to

ANOTHER 8-HOUR SUCCESS

Miriam Hughes is proof that inspiration can come from anywhere.

She was employed in the pharmaceutical business but felt unfulfilled. She came home after a tough day and vented her frustration to her boyfriend, saying she was so tired of her job and the "crap" involved. Without missing a beat, her boyfriend joked, "Why don't you pick it up, then?" Her neurons fired and that was when she had the idea of a dog-poop scooping business. She loved dogs and liked being outside, and when she did a little research, she discovered there was little competition.

While she was working her full-time job, she was able to get a few clients right away. She would scoop the poop during her lunch hour, after work, and on weekends. Friends, co-workers, and family thought she was crazy for doing this and were actually concerned about her new career choice, but she said she found that the work brought a sense of humor and humility to her.

After some initial success, she decided to expand her services. She was interested in dog training but wasn't sure how to go about it. One day she was in PetSmart and noticed that they were looking to hire a trainer, so she applied for the job and they hired her with no experience. As she perfected her dog training skills on the job and went to school to study canine behavior, she decided to break out on her own. She now owns the poop-scoop company as well as a dog training company (missbehave.com).

Miriam proudly says, "If I hadn't left my corporate job when I did, I don't know where I would be. I truly believe I'm healthier, happier, satisfied, and in control of my life. I always say, 'Do what you love, some of what you don't, and the money will follow!'"

capture the essence of the idea quickly and easily. There is no best method. I've found it takes multiple systems to effectively capture ideas in different settings. For example, if I think of something at church (maybe a new volunteer project or a Bible passage I want to look up), I'll type a two- or three-word note in my cell phone. If I'm in front of my computer, I'll type the idea in Evernote. If I'm driving down the freeway, there's no way I want to try to type anything on my phone, so I use a small digital voice recorder. And what happens if I get a brilliant idea in the shower? I jot it down on a scuba diving slate board I keep in there. Find a system that works for you. If you're not tech savvy, break out your parchment paper, ink bottle, and feather quill.

- **The $1 million question.** This is a fun question to ask yourself or a game to play with others; the best answer gets a prize. Ask yourself, If my life depended on it, how could I make $1 million in 365 days? What would you have to do? What could you do? This question forces you to think bigger than you're used to thinking, and it forces you to focus on just one simple (but not easy) goal. It's something you can ask yourself often because the answer may change. Of course, if after a month of repeatedly asking yourself this question you still have the same answer, you should seriously consider pursuing it!

- **Hang out with your kids.** Nothing can increase your creativity more than hanging around children. Everything is a possibility to them, and make-believe is better than reality. Learn from their sense of wonder and unstructured thinking. Hanging out with older kids is also a great way to pick up ideas. Pay attention to what they wear, what they're talking about, how they are relating to one another, and any trends you notice. Your observations may spark ideas later. Recruit your own kids to do reconnaissance. It gets them involved and it teaches them how to spot trends and look for opportunities.

- **How can this be improved?** I love this exercise. Like so many other things, it's fun to play alone, but it is even better to play with others. Pick any product or service that comes to mind, and then come up with as many ways to improve it as you can in one minute. Again, the goal is not to come up with an improvement you are actually going to implement (but you may), but to get you to start looking at things as a Cre8tor.

Q—*What should I do if I'm* really *not creative?*

A—Use other people's ideas! No, this does not mean I want you to steal someone else's idea. It means that you should partner with that person. Let them come up with the concept and the ideas while you provide a service or do the legwork. A successful venture requires a full human body. You have the head that is responsible for coming up with the idea and then you have the body that takes the idea and translates it into action. The head thinks. The body does.

Society is so enamored with the head people—those who come up with the ideas—but nothing is created until someone takes action. It may start in the head, but it ends with the body. Are you a thinker or a doer? Maybe you're both? What is your dominant strength? Do you

OTHER 8 EXPERT

Twyla Tharp is an Emmy and Tony Award-winning choreographer and the author of *The Creative Habit*. If you don't think you're creative, get her book. Here's how she answered the question, What one thing should readers do with their other 8 hours that will have the greatest positive impact on their lives?

In order to function well, even to sleep our best, exercise is a given. Must be done—stretching, aerobics, strengthening. A minimum of forty-five minutes, six days a week. And then there is reading; I like to pick one author to live with for a while.

come up with a lot of ideas but never do anything with them? If so, you're a head. Are you a go-to person at work? Are you good at managing projects and implementing? If so, you're a body.

Whether you're a head or a body, the point is that it takes a whole body to successfully pull off a venture. If you're a head person with a lot of good ideas, that's great. Just know that being a head person doesn't mean you have a pass on Easy Street. You may need to find yourself a body to get stuff done. On the flip side, if you're a body, you may have to find a head.

If you discover that you are an extreme thinker or doer, it may make sense to partner with someone with the opposite strengths. One way to do this is to start a Cre8tor Club.

Q—*What's a Cre8tor Club?*

A—A Cre8tor Club is a group of friends or colleagues who come together to brainstorm and bounce ideas off each other. There are two types of clubs: support and equity.

Support Clubs: As the name suggests, these clubs are a forum that allows members to provide support and encouragement as well as share ideas. Participants may bounce ideas off each other and provide tips to others. For example, a member may ask the group if anyone has a referral to a good .NET programmer, while another member may ask the group the best way to secure a marketing partnership with a Fortune 500. Still another member may have legal questions about a licensing deal he is trying to close, while another member may want to get feedback on a couple of different logo variations.

Often these clubs are nothing more than a group of colleagues and friends who share an entrepreneurial mindset. Informal or formal. It doesn't matter, as long as everyone feels comfortable and there is a good exchange of ideas and dialog.

It's helpful to have members from different backgrounds and with different skill sets. Ideally you'd have a lawyer, a tax expert, marketing folks, technology geeks, etc., so the members can share the collective experience of the group.

Support clubs should not allow visitors during meetings because often the discussions are quite personal and confidential. There needs to be a great deal of trust; otherwise, the club won't function at its highest level. If anybody can visit, few will want to discuss their ideas or open up.

Equity Clubs: This is similar to a support club in that it's a group of like-minded people who share an entrepreneurial spirit, but the difference is that any ideas discovered and ventures created are done collectively—each member participates in the venture and is a financial partner. These can operate as mini-incubators, with several ventures going at once, or the group may work on just one venture at a time. Think of the equity club as a miniorganization, where the members work and contribute their expertise to a shared goal.

It's important to have diversity of skills and experience in the support club, but it is even more critical for an equity club. If you have twelve "heads," you'll walk away from each meeting with a ton of great ideas, but nothing will ever get done.

Q—*I don't think I'm old enough to start my own business. Should I wait until after I graduate from college or find a career?*

A—The wonderful thing about capitalism is that it doesn't matter if you're gay, Muslim, gorgeous, college educated, or ten years old. Justice tries to be blind, but capitalism really is. Don't look at your age as a liability. It's a huge advantage. Anytime is the right time to build the life you want and to use the other 8 hours to get rich, but there is absolutely no better time than when you're young. Many of today's great companies, such as Microsoft, Dell, Google, and Facebook, were started by young people who had very little to lose and much to gain. You can take crazy risks with few repercussions. Live at home as long as you can. Free rent, free food, free utilities. Use your money to invest in yourself and in your ventures. When you're young, you also have more free time than you'll ever have. No spouse, no kids, no homeowner association meetings, no demanding boss. Use your free time and money to build companies. Use your network to find partners and to collaborate. Lead, create, build. It will be the best education you'll ever get.

Q— *I want to use the other 8 hours to improve my life and to make more money, but I can barely pay the rent every month. I'm so focused on just surviving that I can't do anything else. What should I do?*

A—Don't beat yourself up. I've known many people (some close friends) who have gotten themselves into some really bad situations. It's surprisingly easy to do, and scary how fast things can take a bad turn. There are a million reasons you can get into trouble—high medical bills, loss of a job, illness, bad investment. Whatever your situation, focus less on the why and more on how you're going to survive and overcome it.

You need a short-term strategy to survive and a longer-term strategy to get out of your hole. The short-term strategy is triage. Stop the bleeding and get off life support. The longer-term strategy is about developing a financial base so you can then pursue the Cre8tor Channels in chapter 8 (see also Cre8tor rule #1 in the next chapter).

SHORT-TERM STRATEGY

PERK—This is a quick and effective way to cut your expenses.

STEP 1—List all of your expenses and add them together. Include recurring monthly expenses (for example, rent) as well as those that occur less frequently (for example, auto insurance).

STEP 2—Now the fun part! Next to each expense, write either P for Postpone, E for Eliminate, R for Reduce, or K for Keep:

- **Postpone**—These are expenses that you can put off for a while. For example, new tires, clothes, etc.

- **Eliminate**—These are expenses you can completely eliminate, such as a gym membership you never use, premium cable channels you never watch, or newspapers you subscribe to but never read.

- **Reduce**—Any expense that you are willing to cut back on qualifies for Reduce. For example, if you go out to lunch every day at work but are open to bringing a lunch twice a week. In this case, you are reducing the frequency of the expense, but not eliminating it entirely. Likewise, you could continue to go out to lunch every day, but at less expensive restaurants. Both situations reduce your expense.

- **Keep**—Many fixed expenses, such as rent, insurance, and food, are necessary and cannot be eliminated, postponed, or reduced.

STEP 3—Now recalculate your revised expenses. Voilà! It should be less than when you started. So, that's it! If you've followed along, you're thinking one of two things: This is amazing. In the time it takes to watch a rerun of *Seinfeld* I've slashed my expenses. Or, you're thinking: This was a waste of time, because I wasn't able to cut my expenses at all.

If you're in the first camp, congrats! Implement the other short-term strategies discussed below as well as the longer-term strategies. If you're in the second camp, it means you wimped out and didn't Postpone, Eliminate, or Reduce. Usually this means you weren't aggressive enough. Your Netflix account, umpteenth shoe purchase, eating out habit, and trip to Vegas are not Ks. If you are serious about cutting your expenses, go back through your list and start replacing the Ks with Ps, Es, and Rs.

Of course, sometimes all those Ks really are Ks. If you're completely tapped out and all of your income goes to necessities, such as rent, insurance, food, and transportation, there may not be much you can do with your expenses; but there may be plenty you can do if you focus on your income . . .

- **Boost job.** Boost jobs were discussed in chapter 3. As a reminder, they are part-time jobs that provide a little extra income, and because they don't require any thought or effort, you have time to work on your own projects. Nobody wants to work two jobs, but if you're having trouble paying the electric bill or getting out from under a mountain of debt, you need to increase your income. The advantage with a regular part-time gig and a boost job is that you are going to use this time to develop your longer-term strategy.

LONGER-TERM STRATEGY

- **New skills.** If you're on a dead-end career track and don't see things getting any better for you, use the other 8 hours to get some new skills. But not just any skills. French for beginners and water-color painting don't count. I'm talking about very specific and marketable skills you know companies are seeking. Something you can learn and immediately use to get several better-paying job offers. Maybe it's data entry, customer service skills, medical billing, or paralegal training. Don't bother with a degree—these are too general, and you won't learn a specific skill you can use on Monday morning. Instead, get a certificate or designation. These are much more specialized and are what some companies want to see on a resume.

- **Bouncing.** If you don't have any skills and are stuck in a real dead-end job (one where moving up to fry guy is a promotion), you need to get creative. Stay employed at Dead End, Inc., but use the other 8 hours to learn a specific and marketable skill (see above). This one skill won't get you your dream job, but it should pay better than your current job and give you new experience. Once you have this new job, use the other 8 hours to learn a new skill. This new skill might help you move up the corporate ladder where you are employed, or (more likely) it might help get you into a completely different industry. Again, this new skill needs to be in demand, and the job you get should pay better than the job you have. Guess what? You keep doing this—learning a new skill and getting a better-paying job—until you are making enough to pay the bills and build a financial foundation.

- **New career.** Whether you've bounced your way up or you are just not satisfied with your current career choice, you can use the other 8 hours to get a new career. First you need to figure out what you want to do. Focus on your strengths and identify a career that you'd not only be good at doing but happy doing. Learn what it takes to get that job. Do an informational interview. What education is required? What skills are needed? Get a book from the library and research the career. Nearly every industry has its own trade magazines. Get old copies. Start reading what the people in those industries read. Attend a trade show or conference. Immerse yourself in the career you want. This takes time, but that's what the other 8 hours are for.

Q—*What are the chances my venture is going to catapult me to a new level?*

A—There is virtually a 100 percent chance you will stay stuck where you are if you don't do something different. The only way you are going to jump to that next level is if you become a Cre8tor. If you don't like where you're going, you've got to do something. So will your venture catapult you to the next level? Maybe. Every day, people start ventures. Some become huge successes. Others provide a little extra boost of income for their owners. And some wither and die. You probably won't make it on your first or even your second, third, or fourth attempt. It may take several misses before you find your rhythm. But it's worth it. That's just part of being a Cre8tor.

AVOIDING LANDMINES

Q—*I've got a day job; is there anything I need to know before I start something on the side?*

A—Yes. There are several potential landmines you must navigate.

- **Employment agreement?** Some companies require their employees to sign an employment agreement, and these agreements often contain language that limits what an employee can do while she is employed by the company. If you've signed an employment agreement, dust it off and read it carefully. Look for language about outside employment and noncompete clauses. If you see this kind of language, talk to your HR department and let them know you are thinking of doing something on the side. Their first concern will be whether it competes with their company. If it doesn't, let them know this up front. That will alleviate many of their concerns. Come to a mutual understanding and get the agreement modified to allow you to pursue your side venture. One way to defuse the situation and to take the focus off you is to tell them you are simply helping your spouse with his venture but that you wanted to go by the book and consult with them first. Most companies will appreciate your candor and won't have an issue with you doing something after-hours as long as it doesn't compete or interfere with your day job.

- **Disclosure.** If you don't have an employment agreement, you may still have to disclose your side project. Some industries (securities brokerage, for one) require full disclosure of any businesses you are involved in. If you're not sure about the law in your industry/company, talk to your HR department.

- **State law.** Most inventors and business owners who have day jobs overlook state laws when starting a new venture, and that can be a big mistake Some states (California, for example) have laws that make it possible for your employer to own what you create even if you work on it at home. That invention you've been working on till 1:00 AM for the last eighteen months? It's not yours. The book you've been writing for two years? Not yours. So what's a Cre8tor to do? Protect yourself. Get the okay from HR that you can work after-hours on your own project and then have them sign away their rights to your work product. As long as you can show the company you are not using their trade secrets, equipment, or time, it shouldn't be a problem. My advice is to keep the language broad and all-encompassing so that anything you create is yours.

Lastly, don't take advantage of your employer. They are counting on you AND paying you to get a job done. Unless you have a boost job, don't make calls, send e-mails, or do other work on the job. In addition to putting your job at risk, it just isn't cool.

Q—*Why are my friends and family so critical of my idea and desire to better my life?*

A—You will likely face negativity and pessimism from those who are closest to you—your friends and family. Why would those who care about you the most also be the most critical? There are only two reasons. They either don't want to see you fail or they don't want to see you succeed. It's that simple. They're either trying to "protect" you from defeat, or they're worried that your venture might actually take off. I've seen this time and time again. Misery loves company and despises success. If you catapult your life to a new level, your friends may feel threatened.

You must be prepared for negativity. You must be prepared to hear your family and friends be critical of your desire to better your life and of your enthusiasm for your idea. That criticism might arrive in obvious forms ("That's a stupid idea") or it might be the less blatant but equally deflating kind ("That's interesting. Good luck with that"). It's going to hurt. It might throw you so much that you decide to give up before you even get started. I don't want this to happen to you. So let's go through some of the more common criticisms you'll hear and try to understand why those who mean the most to you can also be the meanest to you.

- "Don't you know most businesses fail in their first year?"
  Businesses fail all the time. You need to know that going in and not be surprised if your first or fifth or fifteenth venture doesn't work out as well as you'd hoped. But if you follow the Strike 4! strategy discussed in chapter 7, a swing and a miss doesn't have to be the end of the ball game.

Keep your eye on the prize. Focus on your dream and on what you can control. Look around. Not every business fails. There are millions that are flourishing, and there's no reason why yours won't flourish too.

- "You've never started a business before."

   Not starting a business because you've never started a business is not a good reason. Start small if you want. Learn the ropes. Take classes. But just start. The first time might feel awkward, but you'll learn what works and what doesn't. Sometimes you've just got to take the plunge.

- "I just don't think people will buy it."

   Who died and made this person Donny Deutsch? This is probably the most common response you'll hear, and it can instantly take all of your hope and excitement and flush them down the toilet. This is why I encourage you not to tell your family/ friends about your specific idea until you've done some of your own research. Test your ideas online very cheaply using Google Adwords by running a text ad for your idea and seeing the response rate. Get some outside feedback. Maybe your idea really is stupid, but no one person can know this. Do a little research and find out for sure.

   History is littered with people who were rejected but who persevered. For example, there was once a writer who had an idea for a book about a boy wizard. She took this idea to twelve publishers and they all told her, "No way and no thanks." Finally, a London publisher took a chance and published *Harry Potter and the Sorcerer's Stone*.

Q—*Why is my spouse so unsupportive?*

A—There are three reasons why you might have an unsupportive spouse.

1. Maybe your spouse just doesn't like you anymore and doesn't care what you do. Solution? Therapy first and then your venture.

2. Maybe you're the best thing since sliced bread but you have a spouse with issues. Solution? Therapy first and then your venture.

3. The most common reason is that your spouse is afraid. Afraid you'll take too much risk and lose the kids' college savings. Afraid you'll spend all of your time working and that you'll neglect the family. Afraid that you will try and fail and be disappointed. These are legitimate concerns that you need to address on day one. Otherwise it could become very difficult for you to spend time on your new venture.

Here's what you have to do to get your spouse to become more supportive.

- First, don't get defensive. Spouses put up resistance for a number of reasons. They are giving you resistance because they are worried about losing something—money, time with you, or both. Don't make it worse by sulking or yelling. Don't turn your Cre8tor venture into a fight.

- Second, try to alleviate the fear. What are they most afraid of losing? Money? Focus on the Strike 4! concept discussed in chapter 7 and explain how you are not going to spend any retirement savings on this venture. Time? Make it clear that you will still be involved and that, if you must, you will give up Monday Night Football or a hobby to have time for this.

- Third, get them involved. Don't make it a "me" thing. Make it an "us" thing. Starting a venture can be exciting and it can be a great way to get closer to your spouse. Instead of spending less time together, you might get to spend more time with each other.

- Fourth, ask for their help and ideas. Get them involved as early as you can so they can help shape the idea and feel like they're part of the process. Listen, starting a venture is tough and it takes a lot of work. You hope that it will be fun and inspiring work, but you'll need all the help and support you can get.

- Fifth, talk about the benefits. Ask them what their dreams are and what they would want if money or time wasn't an issue. Work together to create a photo collage of your goals and dreams to get the juices flowing and put it up where you can both gaze at it and get connected to your bigger life.

Q—*How should I deal with the potential for failure?*

A—It's this "f" word that is more obscene and crude than the other, more well-known "f" word. What is our obsession with failure? People see a business failure as a colossal mistake. It's not. But if you have a fear of failure, a few feel-good platitudes aren't going to be enough to give you courage. Over the years, I've gained some insight into the fear of failure.

If you give 100 percent and still fail, doesn't that mean that you weren't good enough? So what do you do? You stop taking chances, or, when you do, you only give 50 percent. This way, when a venture fails, you will have a reason to explain why it failed—lack of time, lack of effort, etc. The reason is not YOU.

This type of thinking will damage your efforts. When I start a new venture, I feel like I have nothing to lose and everything to gain. What would happen if I started a venture and it failed? Guess what? I've started ventures and they have failed (gasp!). Big freakin' deal. You get up to the plate, swing for the fences, and sometimes you miss. Babe Ruth is famous for his home run record, but you might not know he also held the record for strikeouts for decades. "Every strike brings me closer to the next home run," Babe said.

And that is the beauty of being a Cre8tor. You get to keep swinging and swinging. Don't get me wrong. I hate to lose and I hate to fail. I'm guessing Babe wasn't jumping for joy every time he whiffed, but he understood that he'd be up to bat again. We have the opportunity to start as many ventures as we want. One failure doesn't end the game.

Regardless of the overall success of your venture, you can guarantee some level of success if you follow these tips:

- **Learn.** As a Cre8tor, you have to approach each venture as a learning experience. One of my favorite mottos is: "Sometimes you win and sometimes you learn." Starting a new business is like getting a crash course MBA. People pay hundreds of thousands of dollars and spend years in college to get this education, but you have the opportunity to learn those lessons in the real world. You have to approach the world and your venture as a learning experience. You must be open to learning and growing. Regardless of what happens with this venture, you can take what you've learned and apply it to new ventures for the rest of your life.

- **Network.** Bestselling author Tim Sanders says, "Your network is your net worth." Every venture you start will lead you to new people. Don't be casual about the relationships you form—be proactive. Everyone you meet has the opportunity to teach you something. Learn from each person's successes and failures. Everyone you meet has the opportunity to introduce you to someone else who can help you—maybe not today and maybe not with this venture, but maybe a year from now in a completely unrelated venture. Be aware of those connections and nourish them.

- **Don't burn bridges.** Whatever you do, treat others with respect. Don't lie or take advantage of them or of a situation. Deals go bad all the time, but relationships shouldn't. Protect your reputation. It's a small world and it's getting smaller. Bad relationships are likely to come back to haunt you. Be honorable and professional.

Q—*How can I protect my idea?*

A—The only way to guarantee nobody takes your idea is to never tell anyone about it or do anything with it. Of course, that won't get you far, because you need to share your idea at some point. Follow the tips below to protect your idea:

- **Don't blabber.** When you have a hot idea, you want to toss it around and share it with others. You should get feedback and ideas from others, but at this very early stage, you need to be careful about whom you choose to tell. Discuss it only with close friends. There will be a time to open it up and discuss it with others, but your idea is just too vulnerable at this early stage. Someone could easily beat you to it.

- **NDA.** This is a nondisclosure agreement. If you want to share your idea, process, invention, product, etc., with others, you can have them sign an NDA. It's a crucial document that limits what they can do with the information you provide them. Use it with vendors, potential partners, prospective investors, wholesale buyers, and others. Don't worry, it's a common agreement that they are often asked to sign. Search "NDA template" online for free samples you can customize.

- **Provisional patent.** A patent gives you exclusive rights to an invention and is issued by the United States Patent and Trademark Office. It can take years and $10,000+ to obtain. A patent on the right invention can be worth billions, but not too many folks tooling around on an invention in their garage have an extra $10,000 to invest in a patent. The solution? A provisional patent. This filing costs a couple of hundred dollars, protects your idea/invention, and let's you use "patent pending" for your work. Once you file a provisional patent, you have twelve months to then file a full patent. During those twelve months, you can test the commercial appeal of your product, raise capital, get partners, and invest time in your project while knowing you're covered. It's a low-cost way to buy protection.

- **Trademark.** Also issued by the U.S. Patent and Trademark Office, this only protects the company or product name. It's good to have a trademark, but unless you have a few hundred extra dollars, I'd focus first on the other areas before I'd worry about getting one.

- **Document everything.** Keep e-mail discussions and make copies of letters. Use registered mail. Build a case to prove this was your idea and provide as much support documentation as you can.

If you approach someone with just an idea, it is very easy for a better-capitalized company with a team of people to take your idea and run with it. If you go to them, however, after you've created a prototype and logo and have filed a provisional patent, they will be much less likely to take your idea.

Q—*How can I avoid being ripped off?*

A—Some people are just bad. Not only will they try to take your ideas, but they'll also try to take your money. I've been ripped off. Learn from my stupid mistakes by following these tips:

- **Go to people you know first.** Ask your friends for references. Writing a check to a friend's friend is usually safer than writing a check to some guy in Cleveland you've never met.

- **Know who you are working with.** Before you transfer any funds, find out as much as you can about an individual or company. Have the person send you a copy of his driver's license. Ask how long he's been in business. Learn his story and get to know him personally before you commit to using him professionally. If you're dealing with a lot of money, it can make sense to run a background check on him first.

- **Have a clear written agreement.** This is very important. Without a clear agreement, it's your word against theirs. Be specific about what you want the other party to provide and include an arbitration clause naming your county in the agreement.

- **Use an escrow account.** Whenever possible, use an escrow account to pay service providers. Money is held by a third party and released only when you authorize it. Some sites, such as elance.com, make it easy to use an escrow account.

- **Pay with a credit card.** If you can't use an escrow account, pay with a credit card so that, if there's a problem, you can contest the charge through your credit card company.

- **Get references.** If they're so great, surely they must have some references you can check. Get at least three and talk to them. Find out what they liked and what they didn't about the individual or company. If they're giving you names of people to call, chances are the people you're calling are going to say nice things. So another thing you can do is reach out to the companies in their portfolio. For example, if you're looking to hire a Web designer, check out their portfolio of clients online and then try to contact several of them.

Q—*My venture has stalled, but I've put a lot of money into it. What should I do?*

A—Putting more time and money into a venture hoping something will change is courageous, but it's also stupid. If the venture isn't moving forward and doesn't show any hope of moving forward, let it go. The money and time you've put into it are "sunk costs." They're gone. Dumping more into it won't get it back. Move on to the next venture.

Q—*Should I ever use a credit card or home equity loan to start a venture?*

A—Yes. If you're halfway up the mountain and things are looking good but you've run out of cash, you may need to use your credit card or take out a home equity loan to go to the next level. Use extreme caution, though. It's better to raise capital or bring in partners, but as a last resort, it can make sense. There have been many successful companies that were founded by a credit card and/or a home equity line. Just do it carefully, if you must do it.

FINDING "FREE" HELP

Q—*How should I approach graphic designers, Web programmers, PR pros, marketing gurus, consultants, and other service providers to get them to help me for free?*

A—Free is such a wonderful word. Unfortunately, nobody in his right mind is going to do anything for free. People want something in return. But that's where there is an opportunity for you. You don't have much cash but need various services to start your venture. They have skills and expertise but not a great idea for a company. It's a win for you and a win for them. Sounds simple, but there are a lot of steps and hurdles you have to overcome in order to make a partnership like this a success.

1. **Think partnership.** You have to think in terms of a partnership. It can't be, "Let's see how much free stuff I can take from others." That'll never work. It must be win-win. You want your partners to pray that you become a multigazillionaire, because if you are making money, it means they are making money. You want them to feel like they are partners in the venture—that they have a vested interest in the success of the project. If you pay someone by the hour, you'll get an hour of his time. If you pay someone based on a venture's potential future success, you'll get his time, ideas, life, sweat, blood, and tears. Go into it looking for a partner instead of someone to give you free stuff. See the next several questions for how to find partners and how to structure a successful win-win partnership.

2. **Great idea.** Nobody worth working with will partner on a half-baked idea. Don't even think about recruiting service partners unless you have a really good idea. How do you know it's a good idea? Talk to your inner circle. If you're part of a Cre8tor Club, get the members' input. If most people think it's a winner, then you can feel good about finding partners.

3. **Communicate the potential.** You can have the next "big idea," but if you can't communicate it well, you won't be able to attract service partners, investors, or even customers. Most Cre8tors talk too much or too little. To fix this, memorize an elevator pitch that hits on the top points. An elevator pitch is a concise, carefully planned, and well-practiced description of your idea or company

that your mother could understand in the time it would take to ride up an elevator. One of the things potential service partners will be listening for is what you bring to the table above and beyond the idea. Do you have connections? Prior successes? A marketing plan? Make your credentials known.

4. **Build buzz.** Ever been skinny-dipping? The first person to jump in risks the chance that nobody will follow. But by the time four or five people jump in, all the risk is gone. Your mission? When talking to potential partners, sell them on the fact that you have several other interested partners. Nobody wants to be first and nobody wants to be last.

5. **Establish credibility and trust.** The biggest hurdle you must overcome is trust. You are asking someone who may never have met you to give away his service and his time. You must establish trust and credibility immediately. If you've had prior successes, talk about them. If you haven't, discuss your other professional achievements. You want partners to see that you are a successful person who is taking a chance on a new venture and that "we're all in this together."

6. **Make a compelling offer.** Let's break this down. You are asking someone you may have just met via e-mail to give you something with the hope that you have the skills and connections to make it a success. Make the person a killer offer she simply cannot refuse. Make the offer so compelling she'd be insane not to help. When she reads your offer, you want her to be as giddy as a schoolgirl. Remember, these are your partners. If you do well, you want them to do well too. Don't be stingy. If you hoard the goods, nobody will lend services or expertise to help you. See the following questions for tips on how to structure a partnership deal.

ANOTHER 8-HOUR SUCCESS

We look for inspiration in all kinds of places, but few of us find it at the bottom of a bottle. On a warm summer evening in New York City, brothers Eric and Will Stephens went online to search for a bar that carried their favorite beer, but came up empty. When these two young guys (twenty-six and twenty-three, respectively) were faced with such a dilemma, they had two options: choke down a Coors Light or start a business. Fortunately for all the beer drinkers out there, they chose to start BeerMenus.com, a site that allows you to search for bars that carry your favorite beers.

When they started working on the Web site, they were both working full time, but they realized they needed some help. In true Cre8tor form, they partnered with a Web developer who was willing to use his other 8 hours to help build the site—paying him in equity instead of cash.

Another thing they've done right, they started small. Before they built a massive Web site, they first talked to bar owners about the idea to get their feedback. "Because we were using our other 8 hours, we needed to start small and to test the model," Eric said.

Eric still works full time and does BeerMenus.com on the side, but his brother has been able to quit his job and work on the company full time. Eric is hopeful that within the next year, he'll also be able to call it his day job. And if things continue the way they have, that shouldn't be a problem. They have a tremendous following and have been featured in the *New York Times*, the *New York Post*, *Wired*, and many other publications. Salud!

Q—*Where can I find service partners willing to reduce or eliminate their fee?*

A—They're everywhere. They're online and they're down the street. Do you have a huge print project? Talk to your local print shops and see if they're game. Maybe they'll charge you for the material but not for their time. I've found that most people are looking for that something that will take their finances to the next level. They may not have the ideas, time, or even the drive to start their own venture, but if they can get a piece of a promising company with very little risk, many jump at the chance.

And it's not just small-fry that are using other people's time. TD Ameritrade partnered with an Argentine software firm to create a stock trading application for the iPhone. Nothing new there, but in this case, TD Ameritrade paid the firm nothing up front. Instead, the developer gets part of the commissions from trades on the application. If a small company in South America can partner with one of the largest U.S. investment firms, there's no reason you can't find willing partners for your project.

Q—*I've got a service provider interested in my idea, but how should I structure the partnership?*

A—If it's a service partner and not, say, an investor, don't give away equity (ownership of the company). There are too many legal requirements, people don't understand it well, and it's a pain in the butt. Keep it supersimple. I like to structure my deals based on the income the venture produces. It's easy to calculate, it's easy to understand, and it's easy to structure. If it's an ad-based Web site, give away a percentage of net ad revenue. If you're selling widgets, give away a percentage of sales or profits.

Q—*How much revenue should I give to a service partner?*

A—The short answer is, as much as necessary. Here's how you should structure your deals:

1. Determine how much the service you are receiving would cost if you paid in cash. For example, if you need a logo created, how much would you have to pay in cash to get it?

2. Determine how much you are willing to pay in cash (if anything) and how much the service partners would need to "invest" in the venture. For example, if they charge $800 for a logo and you are willing to pay them $200 in cash, they would need to defer $600. This $600 is their "investment" in your venture. I call this amount the Invested Capital (IC).

3. Structure the deal so it's clear what their potential return could be, how much they could earn from their IC, and when they get paid. I like to structure my deals with the following parameters:

   a. I think it's only fair that the service partners get their IC back as quickly as possible. If I am working with four service partners, I'll give them each 20 percent of the initial revenue (I keep 20 percent as well) up to each partner's IC.

   b. I also use a sliding revenue scale. They get a bigger percentage on a smaller amount of revenue (25 percent on the first $5,000 of revenue) and a smaller percentage on a larger amount of revenue (5 percent on revenue between $75,000 and $100,000).

   c. I make sure that there is a big potential payoff for each service partner. I want them to be excited about the company and its potential.

   d. I also always put a cap on the maximum payoff any service partner can receive. But again, this is usually a big number. A service partner should have an incentive to work with you on your project.

Let's use an example so you can see how this works in the real world. You have got a great idea for a Web site. You talk to your friends and colleagues and they think it's great. You find an awesome Web design firm and they quote you $5,000 to create the site. You want to work with them, but you can't afford $5,000 (the most you are willing to pay is $500 in cash through an escrow account). After you dazzle them with your elevator pitch, you tell them you are interested in paying them some cash up front and giving them a share of the potential ad revenue. Here are the terms of the deal:

Project Cost	$5,000		
Cash up front	$500		
IC in Dollars	$4,500		
% Net Ad Revenue to Service Partner	Net Ad Revenue	IC Multiplier	$ to Service Partner
25%	$18,000	1	$4,500
15%	$168,000	5	$22,500
10%	$618,000	10	$45,000
5%	$2,418,000	20	$90,000
1%	$15,918,000	30	$135,000
TOTAL AD REVENUE PAYOUT			$297,000

First, they get a whopping 25 percent of ad revenue up until they get their full IC returned to them. This reduces their risk considerably and increases the chance they will agree to forgo (at least in this example) 90 percent of their payment.

Second, notice the decreasing sliding scale? As revenue increases, the service partner gets a smaller and smaller piece.

Third, did you notice the $297,000 figure? Chances are that your potential service partners will too. For a small investment of their time, they could make nearly $300,000!

Fourth, there's a cap. The service partners should make a killing if you make a killing, but there should be a limit on how much they can make.

So, here's what the service partner is thinking: "Here's a guy with a pretty cool Web idea. He's willing to pay me a few hundred bucks now with the hope that, if the company does well, we'll all do well. It will take some time to do the site, but it's not like I've got a line of customers around the block. I could probably work on this part-time and after hours to get it done. If the site does anything at all, I'll quickly get my investment back and then it's all upside from there. Here's a chance to turn a little bit of my time into a boatload of money." And that, my friend, is exactly what you want your potential service partner to think.

Of course not every venture you start will be the next Google. It's important to talk openly with your partners and to set expectations. They need to know that going in. If a project doesn't work, move on to the next one.

Q—*If you have to pay some money, why not just pay someone cheaper in full so you don't have to give away any profits later?*

A—Not everyone will do a 100 percent IC (that is, not need to accept any cash up front). For those who won't, you may have to pay them a small amount of cash to work with them. So why not just find someone cheaper and not even bother with a partnership? Simple. Leverage. If a company charges $500 for a logo and you pay them $500, you're not using any leverage. You're giving them 100 percent of their fee. If you partner with a firm that would normally charge $2,500 for a logo but you worked out a deal so that you only have to pay them $500 (with the remaining $2,000 as IC), you're using leverage. You're using your $500 to purchase a $2,500 logo. You're using a small amount of money to buy a much better logo. Who cares if you have to give up some of the profits later on? If you have a sucky logo (or Web site or whatever), you probably won't earn anything anyway. But if you have a great idea and a great team of service partners who deliver a great product/service, there's a much better chance the venture will be a success.

Q—*Which service partners should I try to partner with?*

A—High cost and specialized services are usually best. Technology, marketing, PR, design, etc. Sometimes professional service providers such as CPAs and attorneys will do it, too. Think about all of the services you'll need for your venture . . . logo, Web site, marketing, advertising, public relations, designer, legal, accounting, manufacturing, sales, etc. Chances are you can find a partner for each of these areas.

ATTRACTING INVESTORS

Q—*Should I try to get investors for my venture?*

A—Many of the successful companies and products you see today were funded with money from other people—venture capitalists, angel investors, friends, and family. The best thing you can do—at least initially—is to forget about raising money. Instead, spend more time on the product, researching competitors, marketing strategies, focus groups, and creating a competitive advantage. I've seen too many smart people come up with a great idea and then spend all of their time trying to get funding instead of developing their company.

Q—*How do I raise money?*

A—If you've already done all the legwork to make your venture as good as it can be and still need to use other people's money, start by writing a brief business plan. It should include the following:

1. **Problem.** What is the problem your product/service hopes to solve?

2. **Product/service overview.** What is the product/service the company sells and how does it solve the problem? Describe it in detail.

3. **Competitive advantage.** Who are your competitors? What makes your product/business better than what's already out there? In other words, why will people want to buy from you?

4. **Team.** Who is on board? What have they done? Why are they right for this venture?

5. **Marketing plan.** The best ideas and products will die a slow and painful death if they are not marketed properly. What will you do to attract customers? Advertising? PR? Partnerships?

6. **Revenue model.** How will you make money? You need to run the numbers. What are your costs? How much will you make? How quickly can you pay back your investors?

7. **Use of funds.** Why do you need the money? How long will it last?

8. **Milestones.** What are your milestones or goals? When do you expect to have a working prototype? When will the site launch? Which companies do you want to partner with? When do you expect to start making sales?

Q—*How do I find investors?*

A—Share your idea with friends and family. Ask your CPA or attorney for referrals to private investors (angel investors) or venture capitalists. Be prepared if you get a meeting. Develop a twenty-minute PowerPoint presentation highlighting the areas in your business plan.

Use these resources:

- Angel Capital Association (angelcapitalassociation.org)—Lists a ton of angel clubs across the United States.

- ActiveCapital (activecapital.org)—A government site run by the Small Business Administration.

- National Venture Capital Association (nvca.org)—A 35-plus-year-old trade organization for the venture capital industry.

- FundingUniverse (fundinguniverse.com)—Provides the entrepreneur with tools such as business plans and financial templates and connects them with angel investors.

Those are the top frequently asked questions, but before you can learn the specific strategies for how to use the other 8 hours to make more money, you first need to know the rules.

CHAPTER SEVEN

THE CRE8TOR RULES

The 8 Rules to Minimize Risk and Maximize Success

Even though this happened many years ago, it is still embarrassing to admit. I must have been eight or nine years old. It was a fall night and the air was cold and the ground wet. I could see my breath as I ran out onto the field. My helmet was twisting and turning, and I had to use one hand to hold it down so it didn't pop off.

Whistles blew and everybody ran to their positions. I asked one of the guys where I was supposed to be. With a look of disgust, he pointed his finger to a spot and grunted, "There!" I looked around, trying to see what everyone else was doing. I was hunched over with one hand on the grass, staring down another kid who hovered inches from my face. The quarterback on the other team yelled, "Hike!" That's when the fun began.

I grew up in an "e" house—no, not an electronic or Web-enabled house, but an estrogen house. Aside from an occasional appearance from my much older brother, it was just my mother, three older sisters, and me. I think I was the only fifth grader who knew that an emergency mask wasn't really for an emergency. Manicures around the kitchen table were common. Sports? Not so much.

Even though I lacked exposure to structured sports, I was naturally athletic. I was the king of recess football, so someone suggested I join a team. I didn't know the coach or any of the kids, but somehow there I was on the field that night.

"Hike!" Everyone jumped up and began grunting and pushing. I noticed a lot of the other kids fall, but my guy and I did pretty well. We pushed each other a little, but were still quite cordial. I remember thinking that football was pretty easy. We did a few more plays, and each time, we pushed each other around a bit. The coach benched me shortly afterward, and I never understood why until years later when I learned the rules. I wasn't supposed to just stand there . . . I was supposed to try to get past my guy to tackle the kid with the ball!

As a Cre8tor, it's easy to jump into a project, but if you don't know the rules of the game, you can waste a tremendous amount of time and money. You can trick yourself into thinking that all of your activity is getting you somewhere when it might not be. Just because you are working hard and working a lot doesn't mean you are getting closer to your goal. You must make sure that every action gets you one step closer to where you want to be.

Follow these eight Cre8tor rules before you get out on the field:

Rule #1—Keep Your Day Job

Rule #2—Go Nuclear

Rule #3—Know Your HABU

Rule #4—Limit Risk

Rule #5—Swing Often

Rule #6—Market

Rule #7—Monetize

Rule #8—Own

RULE #1—KEEP YOUR DAY JOB

The first rule is that you still need to follow the traditional financial planning rules—at least until you achieve success with a new venture. You need to keep working hard and saving. You're going to need the stable income from your job, and you may need some extra money to get started. This will provide you with a safety net while you transform yourself into a Cre8tor. As much fun as creating is—and it really is fun—and as much potential as there is when you create, this game doesn't provide a surefire way to overnight riches (I'll leave that promise to the get-rich-quick con-men on late night TV).

OTHER 8 EXPERT

Tim Sanders changed my life and he can change yours, too. He is the author of three books, including *Love Is the Killer App* and *Saving the World at Work*. Always inspirational and educational, here's how he answered the question, What one thing should readers do with their other 8 hours that will have the greatest positive impact on their lives?

When you aren't working, you should be feeding yourself with love, knowledge, and reflection. That's the three ways I use the other 8 hours. I gather love by promoting the growth and happiness of other people: family, friends, strangers. I feed my knowledge by acquiring and consuming content that solves problems in my life as well as those of others. I'm drawn to futuristic work that I can connect to. Most importantly, at least one of the "other 8 hours" is devoted to thinking deeply about what I've done, will do, and have learned along the way.

My mother-in-law recently moved from the suburbs of Chicago to southern California, and she expressed some concern about driving in an unfamiliar city. About a week after she moved, she took a drive. Several hours passed, and we began to get worried. We knew she'd be fine, but we were concerned that she was lost and getting anxious. Finally, well after sunset, she bounced into the house and said she had had a wonderful time finding new shops to visit. When we told her we were worried that she was lost, she just laughed and said, "I discovered the 'home' button." Her car's navigation system allows her to program her address, so no matter where she is or how lost she gets, she can just hit this button and it provides her with turn-by-turn directions all the way home.

The traditional rules are your "home" button. When you use them, you can take a turn down that dark street and explore new areas because you'll always have a way home from there.

RULE #2—GO NUCLEAR

Since we've got our "home" button with traditional financial planning, whatever we create in the other 8 hours needs to be something that is quick and, ideally, provides us with disproportionate results. The time, energy, and investment we put into it should be disproportionate to the results we can achieve. Put simply, we need a lot of bang for our buck.

Before you jump into a new business or venture, it's critically important to ask yourself these two questions:

(1) What will I need to put into it (time, money, and energy)?

(2) What can I get out of it (money, contacts, credibility)?

Once you answer these questions, you can determine if the project is worthwhile.

	Maximum Effort / Minimum Results	Maximum Effort / Maximum Results
E F F O R T	Terrible	Okay
	Minimum Effort / Minimum Results	Minimum Effort / Maximum Results
	Pretty Good	Awesome
	RETURN	

MAXIMUM EFFORT/MINIMUM RESULTS

Any venture that requires a great deal of time but that doesn't have the potential to produce a high return falls into this black hole category. If you're running at full speed but barely going anywhere, you've found a maximum effort/minimum results venture.

For example, spending your weekends scouring garage sales looking for knickknacks to resell on eBay is a good example of a bad venture. Why? You're spending a ton of time driving around, haggling, and

ANOTHER 8-HOUR SUCCESS

Michael Brooke changed his life with $5 and some of his other 8 hours.

Michael's passions are skateboarding and writing. While he was working a full-time job selling copy machines to publishers (which he claims he wasn't very good at), he started a Web site dedicated to all things skateboarding. His initial investment was $5 a month to keep the Web site going at that time. He wrote articles and responded to e-mails during his free time.

During a sales call, he mentioned to one of his publishing customers that he had a Web site about skateboarding. That person said, "Really? We're looking to do a book on the history of skateboarding. We'd love to talk to you more about it." Next thing he knew, he had a contract. While working his full-time day job, he spent his nights and weekends researching and writing a book. The skateboarding book sold 40,000 copies and he became coproducer of a 52-part television series based on the book.

After the book was published, the publishing company offered him a job in their magazine division. It was there he decided to broaden his skateboarding Web site to print. During the day, he worked selling advertising space on a wine magazine, and in the evenings, he developed *Concrete Wave* magazine.

Michael said his success has just snowballed ever since that chance meeting during a sales call about copiers. "Today," he says, "What I do for a living doesn't even feel like work. It's great, I get to work from home and dream about skateboarding all day."

listing stuff that you might make a few bucks on. Can you make money? Yes, but you'll be working for less than minimum wage.

It's amazing how easy it is to get sucked into this black hole where maximum effort can, at best, produce very little reward. Avoid these projects like the plague because they'll rob you of time, energy, and money.

MAXIMUM EFFORT/MAXIMUM RESULTS

Here you're swinging for the fences. You're going to hit a home run or strike out hard. It's all or nothing. When it works, it's great. The feeling of satisfaction from giving it everything and from its taking off is incredible. The problem is that there is no leverage, and if you do strike out, the repercussions can be devastating. It's common for people to lose their life savings and to spend years of their life breaking their back on a venture that ultimately fails.

If you need to invest a lot of your own money in a project or need to quit your day job to get it started, you've probably got yourself a maximum effort/maximum results business. A friend of mine spent almost two years planning and developing a med spa. She and her husband did everything on their own. They formed the company, looked for retail office space, negotiated leases, purchased products, bought insurance, and marketed it. They personally guaranteed loans and leases and sacrificed time with their four kids. They've got an amazing company, but it's been a struggle. If it is successful, they know they can make hundreds of thousands of dollars of profit every year, but they said that if they knew how much work was going to be involved or how many sleepless nights they'd have worrying about their finances, they probably never would have done it.

MINIMUM EFFORT/MINIMUM RESULTS

I'm not a huge fan of this approach, but it can be a safe way to get your feet wet. When I was in college, I became a distributor (I think that's what they called them back then) for Amway. I can't even begin to describe the excitement I felt and the transformation that took place in my outlook and perspective. I had never taken a business or economics class, but suddenly I had my own business. I was responsible for marketing and sales. I became an entrepreneur, and it felt amazing. Although I didn't make any money from my new business, I learned a great deal.

The same thing can happen to you. You might start something small with very little potential, but it will teach you skills that you will use down the road. You might catch the Cre8tor fever and ultimately work your way toward a minimum effort/maximum results venture. If not, at least you didn't put a whole lot of time and money into the project.

MINIMUM EFFORT/MAXIMUM RESULTS

Now we're talking. These are high-leverage activities where there is a disproportionate impact from the effort you invest. What is a disproportionate impact? How far will a gallon of gas take you? If you drive a Prius, maybe forty miles or so. That's pretty good leverage, but we could do better. Instead of a gallon of gas, let's say you had a gallon of uranium. How far could this take you?

1. From Los Angeles to New York and back 34,670 times?
2. Around Earth 41,016 times?
3. To the moon and back 2,619 times?
4. To the sun and back 19 times?

Actually, you could do ALL of these things combined with the energy from just one gallon of uranium![1] I call this going nuclear. It's about extracting the greatest results from the least effort. It's all about using leverage and creating efficiencies. Don't confuse me with the infomercial guys. "Least effort" doesn't mean no effort. Unless you're playing the Lotto, any worthwhile endeavor will take work and effort. Going nuclear is simply about engaging in those projects that offer the greatest potential for the least effort. Some of the ventures discussed in chapter 8 are nuclear-type, minimum effort/maximum results ventures such as inventions, licensing products for resale, and working for stock.

RULE #3—KNOW YOUR HABU

In real estate, there's a concept called highest and best use (HABU). Properties are valued based on the best use of the land that will produce the highest value. For example, appraisers may value a two-bedroom house on a busy street next to retail shops as if a strip mall occupied the land, because the best use of the property that produces the highest value is a strip mall and not a house. In other words, other two-bedroom houses in the town might be worth $200,000, but an investor may pay $600,000 just for the land in order to build a strip-mall.

When you use the other 8 hours to create, you must focus on your HABU—your unique talents, skills, and experience that produce the most value. The dead weight that so many people drag around with them is that they do not feel fulfilled at work. Part of the reason for this lethargy is that most people feel underutilized and don't have the flexibility to do what they do best. We get boxed into positions and job descriptions that we can do adequately, but that usually don't tap into our core strengths. "If only my boss would let me . . ." is a common complaint among those who feel underutilized and stuck in positions that don't capitalize on their unique strengths.

This is why creating during the other 8 hours is so much fun. You create your own job description. You are your own boss and you can focus on what it is you enjoy the most and do the best. It also explains why you find some people who never want to retire and who work sixty hours a week for fifty years but claim they've never worked a day in their life. If you love what you do, it doesn't feel like work.

You might not be performing at HABU during your working hours, but in order to maximize your chance for success and for you to enjoy the other 8 hours, you need to focus on projects that use your best and most unique talents. Duh, right? I wish it were so obvious.

Over and over and over again, I see people starting businesses and getting engaged in projects that are so completely outside of their best use. They focus exclusively on what will provide them the "highest" value—that is, those projects that look like they'll make them the most money—but they don't first consider what their personal "best use" is. I've seen guys who can't set the time on their VCR (I guess I'm dating myself) try to start technology companies. I've seen others who can't balance their checkbook try to start finance companies. I've seen somebody try to launch a video game application who had no gaming experience (and, in fact, didn't even like games).

And guess what? All those ventures failed. Why? You need to be passionate about what you're doing or you'll give up after the first setback. The more you love what you do, the more you will persevere. Also, when you capitalize on your unique qualities and gifts, you're making it easier on yourself. If you start something you're halfway into or that doesn't capture your talents, you're making it much harder to succeed.

Brain surgery is one of the highest-paid professions—with practitioners averaging about $500,000 per year. Take Patrick Dempsey (and my wife really would like to take him)—the "McDreamy" doctor on the TV show *Grey's Anatomy*. His HABU isn't being a real brain surgeon. No, he makes more money in two episodes pretending to be a doctor than what a real brain surgeon makes in a year!

So what's your best use? A lot of books and quizzes aim to help you answer this question. One of the better ones is Marcus Buckingham's *The Truth About You*. It's a toolkit with an interactive book and DVD. He says your strengths are those activities that make you feel stronger and that weaknesses are activities that leave you feeling weaker. You might be great at something and make a ton of money doing it, but if it leaves you feeling weak and drained, it is not your strength, it is a weakness. Marcus's program requires you to jot down activities for a week that give you strength and a feeling of power and then analyze them. The following week, Marcus asks you to keep track of the activities that weaken you. Once you've done this, you may, for the first time, understand your strengths and weaknesses. This is simple stuff, but it can be oh so powerful.

As you read through the various Cre8tor ventures in chapter 8, I want you to focus on those that feel right for you—those that mesh well with your experience and interests. Don't go for the "sexy" ones just because you think they'll be the most exciting or because you think they have the most potential. Make your decision based on who you are and after an honest assessment of your abilities.

RULE #4—LIMIT RISK

Unless you're sports-challenged, you know if you get three strikes you're out. But what if that weren't the case? What if you could swing and swing and swing without ever striking out? This is a concept I call Strike 4!

I have a metal paperweight on my desk with the inscription "What would you do if you could not fail?" It's a nice ornament with a positive message, but over the past several years I've realized that it's the wrong message. Anybody can fail at anything. It's important to know this going in. A much better and more useful message would be, "What would you do if it didn't matter if you failed?" To me, that's much more realistic and powerful, and that's what the Strike 4! strategy is all about—limiting risk.

If you start a new venture without first thinking about and limiting risks, you can put your finances—and, worse yet, your relationships—in jeopardy. Here's a scenario that gets played out all the time. Someone gets an idea and talks his spouse into starting a business. They both put their heart and soul into it. They quit their jobs and deplete their savings, investments, home equity, and retirement accounts. But for whatever reason, it fails. Now with no job, income, or savings, it becomes harder and harder to pay the bills. They use credit cards to buy groceries and pay the mortgage. Tensions rise and stress builds, leading to arguments and divorce.

What starts as a way to build a dream life, become your own boss, or make a fortune can turn into a nightmare if you don't limit your risk. Instead of taking a lot of risk and jeopardizing a cataclysmic strikeout, the Cre8tor's goal is to limit the risk of financial catastrophe. This means containing projects so a swing and a miss doesn't have the potential to ruin your life.

ANOTHER 8-HOUR SUCCESS

Mothers make excellent inventors because they must often adapt quickly to changing situations. They disregard theories and focus on practical solutions. They're also on the front lines, where they can see problems and opportunities well before the folks running the big product development companies.

And that's exactly what Mindee Doney did. "I was struggling to treat my daughter's bad cold by putting saline drops up her nose," she recounts. "I stood there thinking there's got to be a better way. So I grabbed a wipe and soaked it in saline solution to finish the cleanup." It worked so well, she went looking for saline wipes. Guess what? They didn't exist. "And that's when the light bulb went off," she says.

She was excited about the potential, but also nervous. After analyzing her HABU, she found holes. "I'm creative and good at marketing, but I lacked the financial and sales skills I knew the company would need," she says. So, she presented the idea to a friend who had the skills she lacked. "It was a perfect partnership," she said.

The next hurdle was time. Both Mindee and her partner were full-time mothers. "We got up a little earlier and went to bed a little later," she said. "We had to carve out time during the other 8 hours to focus on the business. We'd often have conference calls after the kids went to bed till after midnight, and I'd be able to work when the kids did their homework or on the weekends." They also included their family as much as they could. "I created a workshop in my kitchen," she says, "and we put together a 'scent party' focus group with family and friends to help us choose which fragrance we should use for our wipes."

In just a little over a year, they've had phenomenal success. Their product, called Boogie Wipes (boogiewipes.com), is now sold in over 25,000 stores, and they expect over $6 million in sales this year. They've been on the *Today* show and *The Big Idea* with Donny Deutsch.

Here's how you can limit your risk:

- **Follow Cre8tor Rule #1.** Keep your day job (at least for now). It's important to have that steady and predictable income during the day while you swing for the fences at night.

- **Other people's talents.** As a Cre8tor, you should enlist the support of others. Find service partners willing to invest their time for a piece of the venture's future income instead of up-front cash. The same person who would laugh you out of his office if you asked him for a $2,500 investment may gladly trade $2,500 of his services for a small piece of ownership in a promising new venture. Why? Like you, most people are looking for an opportunity to get ahead without risking too much. If someone can invest a little of his time with the hopes of making a huge return, he may jump at the chance.

  See chapter 6 for detailed recommendations on how to minimize your costs by getting others to work on your venture for free.

- **Other people's money.** Read the FAQ chapter for detailed recommendations on how to raise money for your venture from angels and VCs.

- **Negotiate fiercely.** As a Cre8tor, you must be relentless about getting what you need. You don't have the luxury of a six-figure budget. You need to get your ventures up and running as cheaply as you can. One way to minimize risk is to negotiate everything.

Don't accept anything as is. Negotiate discounts, concessions, bonuses, terms, etc. It will feel awkward at first, but keep practicing. You'll discover two things very quickly. Almost everything is negotiable, and most people can't negotiate to save their life. Learning to negotiate effectively is one of the best skills you can ever learn.

- **Piece together the team.** If you have a limited budget, one of the best ways to reduce costs is to piece together a team of service providers instead of working with just one or two firms, especially if you can bring on service provider partners. One freelancer can work on the logo; another does the database design for the Web site; and yet another firm designs the Web site. You may sacrifice more of your time to manage the team, but you should be able to reduce your financial risk with this approach.

- **Limit liability.** If you are producing a product or providing a service that could lead you to get sued, you must protect yourself against lawsuits by incorporating or creating a limited liability company and by having the proper liability insurance. Don't risk financial disaster by going naked (without shielding your personal assets from your business assets). See the resources section at the end of the book for discounts on a few popular incorporation services.

- **Make small bets.** In the investing world, everyone talks about risk tolerance—a measure that determines how psychologically comfortable you are with the possibility of losing money. This is good to know, but risk *capacity* is just as important. Risk capacity determines how much risk you are financially able to take. A Navy SEAL who races NASCAR as a hobby may feel totally at ease taking huge financial risks, but that doesn't mean he has the financial capacity to take those risks. In other words, he may feel comfortable (high risk tolerance) risking $100,000 on a long shot, but if he has only $100,000 to his name, he won't be able to survive if that long shot fails.

    It all comes down to risk capacity—that is, how much money can you afford to lose without it destroying your finances and your ability to pay your rent? Start small and start slowly. Immediately committing thousands of dollars to an idea is as ridiculous as walking up to a woman you've never met and asking her to marry you. You need to put a little out there and get a little back. Then you can put a little more out there and get a little more back.

Here are a few guidelines to determine how much you can risk. If you're in the start-up exploration stage, don't commit more than about 2 percent of your income or savings to any one project. For example, if you make $30,000 a year, limit your initial exposure to around $600. Let's say you have a great design in mind for a new T-shirt line. You could conservatively spend $600 to hire a graphic artist or designer to create digital artwork of your new line. You could then take these digital T-shirts and post them on your Facebook or MySpace page to get feedback. Maybe enter a contest and see how you do. You could inexpensively put up a Web site and run a Google Adword campaign to see how many clickthroughs you get, or, for products not closely tied to search terms, you could run a remnant ad and track hits to your Web site or phone calls.

If you pass this initial stage, then you can commit a little more to the project—maybe up to 5 percent of your income/savings. So if you get a good response to your digital T-shirts, then, and only then, should you consider printing actual shirts. There is no point in printing actual shirts before receiving feedback on the design. And when you do the first run, start slowly. Instead of printing 1,000, do a test run. Maybe 25 or 50 shirts. Once you have the shirts, go to local boutiques and try to get an order for them. If you get an order for 100 shirts, then you can commit some more dough.

Bottom line: You do not want to get into the situation where you could suffer serious financial hardship if your venture doesn't succeed. Start slowly. Get others to contribute their skills and services. Test. Then, and only then, risk a little more.

- **Cut your losses.** Live to fight another day by pulling out of dead-end projects. If you find that you are putting more time and/or money into a venture that looks less and less promising, you might be in a dead-end project.

RULE #5—SWING OFTEN

Cre8tors are painfully aware that strikes are inevitable. You will swing and you will miss. It doesn't matter how gifted you are or how many self-improvement programs you listen to. But, and this is key, a swing and a miss is not a failure when you live by the Strike 4! approach. A swing is simply one swing closer to a hit.

If you're content earning a little extra money, a single side project might be all it takes, but if you're trying to hit a home run and catapult your finances to a whole new level, it pays to swing often. When you see someone who has had phenomenal financial success, you don't see all of the swings and misses it took to hit the home run. You see the confident supermodel perfectly styled and coiffed strut down the runway, but you don't see the utter chaos and confusion backstage.

The most ambitious Cre8tors will have two or three or more projects in the works at any given time. The assumption is that just one will make it. Even though you may swing and miss with the others, I guarantee you will learn from each one. You will pick things up, meet new people, and look at the world differently. That combined experience will eventually help you swing and hit one. Think of the misses as batting practice.

Even if you direct all your energy to one venture, you must be flexible and willing to adapt and change. I've seen too many people get locked into a project and become unwilling to change paths—even slightly—because they invested so much time, money, and energy that a change would feel like failure or giving up. Some of the greatest successes have come from changing direction. For example, back in 1999 a company called Pyra Labs developed a project management Web application. While still in development, they changed gears to create what is now the technology behind blogging. A few years later, they sold it to Google.

RULE #6—MARKET

Creating—whether it's recording the CD for the musician, writing the novel for the author, building the Web site for the programmer, or developing the prototype for the inventor—is the easy part. The hard part is getting people to know the product exists and then convincing them they need to buy it.

Daphne always had an artistic flair. She works as an administrative assistant during the day and takes care of her five-year-old son at night. In her spare time, she creates jewelry to give to her friends and family for birthdays and Christmas. For years, her friends have told her she should try to sell some of her work. The thought of being able to quit her job and work part time making money pursuing her passion overwhelms her with excitement and possibility. After a particularly nasty encounter with her overly critical boss, she decides to take the plunge.

She buys a few hundred dollars' worth of inventory and makes several dozen pieces. Her friends love the new designs and buy a few pieces. They tell her she's going to be huge, and Daphne starts believing. She puts a few hundred dollars more into building a simple Web site so she can receive orders online. A few weeks pass without a single order. She decides she needs more designs, so she buys more supplies and spends the next few weeks designing and making more jewelry. She adds these to the Web site. A week passes. Still no orders. A month passes. Still no orders. After several months without receiving a single order, her self-worth and bank account are deflated. She pulls the site down and dumps all of the jewelry in a box and shoves it to the back of her closet.

Daphne had so much going for her. She had the expertise and passion. She was utilizing her strengths and unique talents. She found and dedicated time during the other 8 hours to create something. Her work was magnificent. So what went wrong? Daphne created, but creating isn't enough. And this is where so many entrepreneurs like Daphne fail. They fall into the trap of thinking that once they create "it," whatever it is, customers will beat a path to their door (or Web site) to buy it.

The Cre8tor knows that even the best products won't sell unless people know about them. Creating a product that you don't market has about as much of a chance for success as Daphne has selling the box of jewelry stuffed in the back of her closet. There are resources that will help stop you from putting your creation in the back of the closet and help get more of your stuff in your customers' hands. Go to other8hours.com for the latest information.

RULE #7—MONETIZE

The Cre8tor has two objectives . . . have fun and make money. If you want to use at least some of the other 8 hours to make more money, you need to monetize, which is just a fancy word for converting a product or service into money.

One of the biggest mistakes I see is well-intentioned people spending a lot of time and money creating things they aren't able to monetize. Watch a few of the videos on YouTube. Many of them are fairly sophisticated productions, with clean editing, a good soundtrack, and decent lighting. This takes time and energy to pull off, and many videos are part of a series that require an ongoing commitment. In other cases, people will spend hours upon hours writing reviews of books, movies, products, and services, and they'll research and answer questions on Web sites such as Yahoo! Answers and on discussion boards for a little recognition.

It's not uncommon to see videos that have been viewed 100,000 or even a 1,000,000-plus times or blogs with hundreds of thousands of loyal and active readers. But fame alone doesn't buy a new car. Views, members, readers, follower, or friends won't pay for a new house. Too many people think the recognition is the objective, but it is only a tool for the Cre8tor—just one piece of the puzzle. Recognition may have become the new currency, but it can't pay the bills. Listen, I get it. It feels good to be part of a community and to receive recognition from peers. Every thumbs-up may increase your self-worth account, but the Cre8tor also wants to increase his bank account.

The people who spend their time and energy on these projects are the same ones who complain they don't have enough time or money and that they aren't moving up in their company as quickly as they'd like. They're investing a great deal of their other 8 hours in a hobby that isn't making them a dime or helping them advance their career.

It's not enough for a Cre8tor to be a "Top 100 Reviewer" or to get accolades. It's got to bring in the money!

Before you turn on the video camera or dust off the keyboard, think about how you can monetize your contribution. Creating a YouTube video that gets watched two million times is cool, but how can you capitalize on this? Include your Web site address at the beginning or end of the video and encourage them to sign up to be alerted when you have new content?

You could even promote your content so it becomes a sensation and gets the interest from those you want to see it. For example, a teenager from Holland failed an audition for *Dutch Pop Idol*, but instead of sinking into a hole, she decided to promote herself. Esmee Denters created a video of herself singing a Justin Timberlake song and it became a YouTube hit. It became so popular Justin watched it himself. He was so impressed he met with her and signed her to his record label. What's the lesson? Was she just lucky?

Absolutely not! Luck is buying a winning lottery ticket. What Esmee did was not luck. She practiced and practiced and practiced. She perfected her talent. She then tried out for *Dutch Pop Idol*. Suffering a setback, she persevered and decided she'd take her future into her own hands. She produced a video and promoted it—not because she was bored and had nothing better to do but because she wanted to get noticed.

A Cre8tor may love what she does and it may feel like a hobby, but make no mistake that she is focused on converting her creation into dollars.

RULE #8—OWN

You work for someone else, you get a paycheck. You work for somebody else, you get a bonus. You work for somebody else, you get medical insurance. You work for somebody else, you get an expense account. You work for somebody else, you get them rich. Unless you're a star athlete or A-list entertainer, you won't get megarich working for someone else. True wealth is from ownership.

For example, 50 Cent didn't need to go to business school to understand the importance of ownership. In a *Fortune* article promoting his book, *The 50ᵗʰ Law*, he and coauthor Robert Greene explain that he "doesn't concern himself with the upfront money; he's thinking three years down the line—how he can own the material or own the company or get equity."

If you work for the "man" during your work hours and want to use the other 8 hours to explode into a new lifestyle, you need to focus on ownership. Remember, you have your safety net. Take the plunge. Roll the dice. You have no excuses.

If becoming a Cre8tor sounds like fun, the next chapter will show you the top 10 ways you can use the other 8 hours to make more money.

CHAPTER EIGHT

THE TOP 10 CRE8TOR CHANNELS

Your "How To" Guide to Make More Money

Man enters bookstore.

There's a yearning in his eye. He's searching for answers and solutions. He picks up two books.

Clerk: *"May I help you?"*

Man: *"What's this one about?"*

Clerk: *"It tells you how to get rich in under an hour."*

Man: *"That's just what I need."*

Clerk: *"I read it on my lunch break, and it's going to change my life."*

Man: *"What's this other one about?"*

Clerk: *"It says that the only way to improve your life or finances is to do something during the other eight hours of your day. You know, when you are not working or sleeping."*

Man: *"But that's when I watch* American Idol*?"*

Clerk: *"I know. I love AI!"*

Man: *"I'll take this other one."*

Clerk: *"We can't seem to keep it on the shelf!"*

Our lives have become so overscheduled and complex that we gravitate to anything that looks easy and promises to lift our burden. The rougher the road gets, the more we search for quick relief. As a result, we're hooked on the promise of magic pills and quick fixes.

I call these faux fixes McSolutions. They promise riches but provide little substance. Just when you swear off them, they tempt you with another hard-to-resist quick fix.

These types of solutions may work momentarily, but you can't fool yourself for too long. Once the euphoria wears off, reality rears its head again. Repeat after me, "McSolutions have betrayed me. They have seduced me with their empty promises and slick packaging. I will not succumb to their deception anymore."

If you're ready to get your hands a little dirty, there are limitless ways you can use the other 8 hours as a Cre8tor to make money. This chapter will give you an overview of ten different types, or Channels, as I call them. These summaries will get you to first base but won't take you all the way. Entire books have been written about each of these, so use this chapter to narrow the list to one or two that might be right for you.

Some of these Channels can catapult your finances to a new level and others can help you pay off debt or pay for a nice vacation. None of them are McSolutions and all of them require varying amounts of time and effort. Which one you choose should depend on your financial goals, available time, and ambition.

As a Cre8tor, you can use your other 8 hours to sell thoughts, things, or time:

THOUGHTS

1. Blogging
2. Inventing
3. Writing Books, Screenplays, and Music

THINGS

4. Starting a Company
5. Reselling, Affiliating, and Licensing
6. Taking Advantage of Fads/Stunts

TIME

7. Working for Stock in a Company
8. Advancing or Jumping Careers
9. Freelancing
10. Turning Hobbies into Income

BLOGGING

Blogging Channel Toolbar					
Start-up Time	🕐	🕐	🕐	🕐	🕐
Ongoing Time	🕐	🕐	🕐	🕐	🕐
Start-up Costs	$	$	$	$	$
Income Potential	$	$	$	$	$
Help Needed	👤	👤	👤	👤	👤

Are you passionate about something? Do you enjoy writing? A blog is an online journal and bloggers are authors of those online journals. Would you like to spend a few hours a week writing about topics that excite you? If so, blogging may be for you.

If you have something to say, you can quickly and easily create a blog and start writing about it. Seriously, in about three minutes, you could have your very own blog. Time to break out the champagne bottles? Not so fast. Because any Tom, Dick, or Sally can author a blog, earning money from blogging is a challenge (but it is not impossible). In fact, there are almost as many people making a living as bloggers as there are lawyers, and there are more Americans making their primary income from blogging than Americans working as computer programmers, firefighters, or even bartenders.[1] There are successful blogs on everything from new gadgets to gardening and feng shui, but if you want to make money blogging, you need to follow some rules.

OTHER 8 EXPERT

Seth Godin has written countless bestselling books, including *Tribes, Purple Cow,* and *Permission Marketing.* He also writes a must-read blog (sethgodin.typepad.com). Here's how he answered the question, What one thing should readers do with their other 8 hours that will have the greatest positive impact on their lives?

The one thing you can do to change what you do has to be a different thing because you've already tried the things you've tried and those haven't worked so well, right?

So my one thing is to start a blog. Give up thirty minutes of TV a day and write.

RULES

1. **Create valuable content.** This is rule numero uno. You must have something to say about a topic you are interested in and know something about. For your site to attract and keep visitors, you must provide those visitors with something worthwhile. If there were only two blogs on the Internet, you could probably get by with mediocre content. But there are millions of blogs just a click away. Your content must be worth reading.

2. **Focus on a niche.** To increase your chances of success, you need to blog about something you are passionate about and something that 10 million other bloggers aren't already feverishly penning. Maybe you're interested in celebrity gossip, but unless you have an inside source to Britney or a unique perspective on the subject, chances are you won't be able to offer anything to set you apart from the other million celebrity gossip bloggers. You need to find something to write about that will help you stand out from the crowd. For example, after watching the Golden Globes, Danielle Friedland was inspired to start a blog about pregnant celebrities. Her niche blog attracted advertisers such as McDonald's and Eastman Kodak. Now her blog is under the *People* magazine umbrella.

3. **Identify popular markets.** You need a niche, but you also need a topic that is popular enough to get visitors and earn money. Blogging about adopting autistic kids from Indonesia is certainly a unique niche, and it may be something you are interested in, but even if you captured 100 percent of this market, your blog wouldn't even make enough money to pay your monthly Web site hosting fee.

4. **Be opinionated.** Whether you're blogging, giving a speech, or on national TV, you have to take a stand and provide an opinion. Nobody is interested in "on one hand . . . but on the other hand . . ." CYA double-talk. This doesn't mean you need to be as

obnoxious as Limbaugh, but it does mean that you must clearly and unapologetically share and stand by your opinion, because, at the end of the day, your personality and opinions are what will make or break your blog.

5. **Get personal.** A good blogger needs to open up. A blog needs to be more like a conversation between friends and less like a news report. Your readers want to know you. Help them discover who you are by sharing personal stories, challenges, defeats, and victories. I've found that too many people want to project a perfect image of themselves, but this isn't effective when you're blogging. Readers connect much better with "real" people—those who admit to mistakes and struggle with challenges—than they do with Mr. or Ms. Perfect.

6. **Create a brand.** A brand is the emotional reaction someone feels when they hear your name. What do you feel when you think about Oprah, Bill O'Reilly, Paris Hilton? You don't have to be famous to have a brand. You've got a brand right now. In fact, you probably have dozens of brands, and that's the problem. You need to craft your own brand and communicate that brand to others. Before you write your first blog, consciously determine what your brand will be and make sure you are reinforcing that brand with each blog post.

7. **Market the hell out of your blog.** You have to get the word out to build traffic and a loyal following. Check out the tips section below for advice on how to do this.

8. **Build multiple streams of income.** Ads are a great way to earn income, but don't get boxed into thinking that they are the *only* way to make a buck blogging. The most successful bloggers don't rely on just one source of income. They have carefully crafted their blogs so that they provide several sources of income.

MONETIZE YOUR BLOG

- **Ad revenue.** There are four ways you can make money displaying ads on your Web site:

  1. **Pay Per Impression (CPM).** You get paid based on the number of times you display an ad on your site. It's pretty easy to earn money this way, since you make money anytime anyone comes to your Web site. More visitors=more ads=more money. Simple stuff.

  2. **Pay Per Click (PPC).** Some advertisers will only pay you if a visitor to your Web site clicks on the ad (called a "click-through"). A PPC ad pays you a certain amount (usually between $.05 and $.50) each time a visitor clicks on an ad displayed on your site. The money is typically better with PPC than CPM, but there is a risk. If nobody clicks on the ads you display, you won't earn anything. PPC only works if the ads you display match your visitors' interests. If you blog about vegetarianism but run ads for Morton's Steakhouse, chances are you won't get many clickthroughs.

  3. **Pay Per Action (PPA).** There are other advertisers that won't pay you for impressions or clicks but will be happy to pay you if a visitor from your site completes an action—buys a product, registers, takes a survey, etc. There's a great deal of risk with this approach. If your visitors aren't the action type, you might end up displaying a lot of ads but not making any money.

  4. **Sponsorships.** Instead of using an ad campaign service that randomly displays ads, you could instead sell ad space to one company for a set amount of time.

- **Donations.** People may send you money because they enjoy your blog. It's like a telethon but without Jerry Lewis. Think I'm kidding? Steve Pavlina is a popular self-improvement blogger. He says that his second biggest source of income is donations. But if you don't ask, you won't receive, so be sure to place a "Make a Donation" link on your blog that makes it easy for your hard-core fans to mail you a check or donate through a PayPal account.

- **Products.** If you love a product and want to tell the world about it, a blog is the perfect platform. If you want to take your income to the next level and have found a product that is a good fit for your blog, you can license it, buy it at wholesale and sell it at retail, or even create a product yourself. Brainstorm which products you love that you could sell on your blog. They should be products you think your visitors will love and that are also a good fit with your blog. Then make it easy for your visitors to buy them from your site.

- **Affiliate programs.** If you don't want to create your own product or deal with buying and shipping a product, a supersimple solution is to join an affiliate program. With an affiliate program, you link to products on other Web sites and are paid each time a visitor buys something—typically, you get a percentage of the sale price. The more they spend, the more you make. For example, if you mention a book on your blog and link to it at Amazon.com, you would earn a commission anytime one of your visitors clicks the link and buys the book. See the Resources section for several affiliate programs you can plug into.

- **e-books.** If you blog, there's a good chance you like to write and have something to say. While you won't be successful charging a membership fee for your blog, you can make money directly from your writing by creating an e-book related to your blog. For example, if you write about health and fitness, you could write an e-book about how to lose fifteen pounds in two months with a new fitness and nutritional plan. A good e-book is between twenty and fifty pages and looks to solve a problem your visitors are facing. Keep it simple and keep it short. Also, keep it cheap. Test various response rates to different price points until you find the optimum sales price.

- **Books.** If you're really feeling ambitious, you can write a book. Many popular bloggers have done this, including Gina Trapani

(*Upgrade Your Life*), Leo Babauta (*The Power of Less*), John Jantsch (*Duct Tape Marketing*), Mike Michalowicz (*The Toilet Paper Entrepreneur*), Christian Lander (*What White People Like*), and many others.

- **Speaking.** Bloggers can become rock stars in their field, and for those willing, there can be lucrative opportunities for speaking engagements. You can earn $2,500 to $10,000 for a one-hour speech, and if you have to travel, you'll be reimbursed for your airfare, hotel, and meals. Nervous about public speaking? Use part of the other 8 hours to learn the art and science of speaking by joining a local Toastmasters club (toastmasters.org). Once you feel comfortable, join the National Speakers Association (nsaspeaker.org) to get speaking gigs. And, of course, add a "Keynote Speaker" link to your blog. If you let your readers know you are available for speaking engagements, they will be more likely to contact you.

- **Paid reviews.** If you develop a loyal following, you may be hired by companies to write paid reviews of their products. Some bloggers post these reviews and hide that they are being paid to write them. I think this is a great way to piss off your readers and for them to lose all trust in you. If you decide to write a paid review, go for it, but tell your readers from the get-go that you are being paid. And write an objective review. Don't praise a crappy product. If you do, you might make a quick few bucks, but you will most certainly lose readers and tarnish your reputation.

TIPS

- **Build a complete Web site.** When you're just starting out, it's okay to ease into a blog and keep it simple, but as soon as you decide that blogging is the Cre8tor Channel for you, you need to think bigger. This is why I don't recommend the cookie-cutter free blog publishing services such as Blogger (blogger.com). Sure it's free, but guess who makes the ad revenue? Yup, Blogger (now part of Google). Do you want to pour your blood, sweat, and tears into your blog so that you can make Google more money? Come on now. Instead, choose a low-cost host that allows you to control the ads.

- **Newsletter.** You need a newsletter! Some bloggers may scoff at this suggestion and say there's no need. "Why have a monthly newsletter when I blog a few times a week anyway?" Two words . . . e-mail addresses. A newsletter gives you a legitimate reason to capture your visitors' e-mail addresses. And even if they aren't active visitors of your site, you can still communicate with them. Near the top of your home page and on every other page, add a "newsletter sign-up" form. Another strategy for newsletter sign-ups is to have a newsletter pop-up box appear after ten or fifteen seconds.

- **Blog carnivals.** This is a killer strategy for getting more traffic to your blog. A blog carnival, other than being a really lame name, is like a magazine with an editor, a theme, editions, authors, and articles. But this "magazine" contains a bunch of blog posts by different bloggers. For example, there are blog carnivals that focus on investing (just like there are magazines such as *Money* or *Fortune*). An investing blog carnival might have ten to twenty blog posts from various bloggers. If you're a money novice, you could check out this investment blog carnival and quickly learn what many bloggers are discussing about investing. If you have your own blog, your job is to submit your blog posts to the blog carnivals that match your subject. Go to blogcarnival.com to search blog carnivals and to submit your posts.

- **Have multiple blogs.** Monogamy is for marriage. It's okay to have several blogs on different topics. If you have the time to dedicate to them, I say do it. If you're just starting out, focus on one blog for a few months until you get the hang of it, but once you know the drill, you can start more blogs to make more money.

- **Be consistent and patient.** Successful blogs are not built in a day. They take time. Keep blogging and attracting readers. Don't expect miracles overnight. Some of the top bloggers started very slowly, but they kept at it and now they have popular blogs and are making six figures doing something they love.

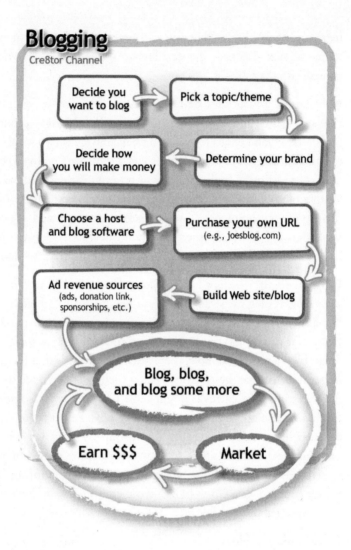

Blogging
Cre8tor Channel

Decide you want to blog → Pick a topic/theme →

Decide how you will make money ← Determine your brand

Choose a host and blog software → Purchase your own URL (e.g., joesblog.com) →

Ad revenue sources (ads, donation link, sponsorships, etc.) ← Build Web site/blog

Blog, blog, and blog some more

Earn $$$ — Market

RESOURCES

Anytime you're dealing with technology, it's bound to be out of date by the time the ink dries. And this is especially true when you're talking about Internet technology. The following list represents those services and resources that should stand the test of time, but do yourself a favor and check out the most up-to-date blogging resources at other8hours.com.

BLOGGING APPLICATIONS

- WordPress (wordpress.com)—Popular blogging platform. It's cheap and easy to use. They also offer inexpensive blog hosting.

- Typepad (typepad.com)—Another popular blogging platform. Users love it. They also offer inexpensive blog hosting.

BLOG WEB SITE HOSTING

- bluehost (bluehost.com)—Cheap hosting company that provides WordPress blogging platform.

- Go Daddy (godaddy.com)—Another cheap hosting company that provides several blogging platforms, including WordPress.

- Media Temple (mediatemple.net)—A robust Web hosting company. It will cost you more than the others (about $20 a month), but if your blog gets popular, you may need it.

BLOG MARKETING

- Blog Carnival (blogcarnival.com)—A great resource to spread the word about your blog.

- ProBlogger (problogger.net)—Tools and services that help bloggers "add income streams to their blogs."

- AddThis (addthis.com)—Ubiquitous little button at the bottom of articles and blogs that lets readers bookmark and share popular content. It's a must-have for your blog and it's free.

- FreeTellaFriend (freetellafriend.com)—Powerful application you can add to your blog to let readers easily e-mail your post to their friends.

MISCELLANEOUS

- copyblogger (copyblogger.com)—Tons of resources on blogging and how to write more effectively.

- ConstantContact (constantcontact.com)—One of the premiere e-mail marketing and newsletter services. Easily capture visitors' e-mail addresses and effortlessly send your newsletter to subscribers.

- FeedBurner (feedburner.com)—Free service that helps you publicize, optimize, analyze, and make money from your blog. I also love their tool that lets your readers get your blog via e-mail.

Blogging isn't for everybody, but if you like what you've heard, give it a shot. You've got nothing to lose and a lot to gain.

INVENTING

Inventing Channel Toolbar	
Start-up Time	🕐🕐🕐🕐🕐
Ongoing Time	🕐🕐🕐🕐🕐
Start-up Costs	$ $ $ $ $
Income Potential	$ $ $ $ $
Help Needed	🧍🧍🧍🧍🧍

Have you ever said, "I thought of that years ago" or "Why didn't I think of that?" If so, the Inventor Channel might be right for you. The Inventor Channel is one of the highest leverage Channels available—it is the reason the phrase "go nuclear" was coined. It's one of the only Cre8tor Channels or opportunities in the world where you can risk very little yet take your finances to a new level.

And the cool thing about inventing is that *anybody* can do it. Seriously. All it takes is an idea. Walk into any store, and what you see are products that began as ideas. Ideas are both priceless and worthless. All great things began as great ideas, but a great idea is just a starting point. The real secret is *action*—what you do with the idea.

This Cre8tor Channel is the cure for the frustration you feel when you see a new product at Target you thought of three years ago or the inspiration you feel when you discover a simple and silly invention that makes millions. One of the best examples of a ridiculously obvious and yet ingenious invention is the Jibbitz—those little rubber shoe decorations for Crocs. Every time I put on my daughter's Crocs, I look down at all the Jibbitz I've purchased for her and am reminded that the founders—stay-at-home mom Sheri Schmelzer and her husband, Rich—started the company in their basement and sold it to Crocs for $10 million in cash and an additional $10 million if the company meets certain projections.

The Invention Cre8tor Channel will show you what you need to do to go from idea to product. But you need to decide which route you want to take when creating a new product:

1. **New Product, Inc.**—You create the product, manufacture it, and sell it yourself. This involves a lot more work, but you don't have to share the profit with anyone else. If you like this idea, see the Starting Your Own Company Cre8tor Channel for more info.

2. **Sell your idea**—You come up with the idea, create a prototype, and sell the idea to a company for a one-time fee. You cash the check and move on and the company does whatever they want with your idea.

3. **License**—You come up with the idea, create a prototype, and license (rent) the idea to a company. The company, also called the

manufacturer, can be small and may produce a handful of products, or it can be huge, like Procter & Gamble or Hasbro. The company manufactures the product, applies for a patent, and sells the product. You typically get a cash advance and a royalty—usually 5 percent—on each sale.

Any of these options can work well, but I'll focus on licensing in this Cre8tor Channel because it provides the highest leverage, is the easiest to execute, and has the least risk.

RULES

1. **Don't fall in love with the idea.** Marry your spouse, not your invention. Of course, I want you to be optimistic and to think positively about your idea and its potential, but it shouldn't cloud your judgment. Keep your head clear. The minute you fall in love with your idea or product is the minute you've relinquished control. When you're in love, you do things you might not ever otherwise do (mix tapes, anyone?). You may dump more money into the product than you should. You may invest more time than you should. Love your idea. Love your product. Just don't fall *in* love with it.

2. **Research now, avoid pain later.** I know how it goes. You get a brilliant idea and you want to immediately work on it and bring it to life. The last thing you want to do is any stuffy old research. As difficult as it might be, though, you need to spend some time making sure your product is unique. That means investing some time on Google and in stores looking for existing products. It also means performing a patent search. Because even if you don't find any similar products for sale, someone might have a patent on it. You can waste a lot of time and money developing a product that has already been claimed.

3. **The manufacturer is your client.** Remember that scene from *Seinfeld* where Jerry and George are pitching the network execs

on an idea for a new TV show? One of the execs asks about the show, "Why am I watching it?" and George says, "Because it's on TV." The network guy says, "Not yet!" Your job is to sell it to the manufacturer. It's their job to sell it to the consumer. How do you sell to a manufacturer? They need to be convinced it is a big idea that has a large market of buyers and that they will make a lot of money on the product. Bottom line—sell them on making money.

4. **It must be a licensable idea.** This means it is thoroughly designed, proven to work, new, provides real advantages over existing products, and offers the manufacturer the potential for high profits.

5. **Get an independent analysis.** Your best friend and sister may love your new idea/product, but before you commit a lot of time or money, get an independent review by someone who knows what he's doing. There are many independent reviewers who will analyze your idea/product and provide you a written analysis for less than $200. Check out the Resources section for a list of these firms.

6. **Get an advance.** When you sign a licensing deal with a manufacturer, make sure you get a cash advance—a nonrefundable check that's an advance against future royalties. You want the manufacturer to have skin in the game. If you don't get an advance, they may sit on your idea. If they cut you a decent-sized check, they'll be more anxious to get the product to market.

7. **Get an NDA.** As mentioned earlier, an NDA is a nondisclosure agreement. Basically, it protects you from somebody stealing your idea. Most manufacturers will provide their own NDA, but in case they don't, make sure you have one of your own.

TIPS

- **First focus on problems.** This is key. If you're brainstorming for new ideas, think about problems. Some of the best products solve problems, so spend your time focused on solving aggravations—that's where you'll find gold.

- **Look for ideas at home, work, and in your hobbies.** Focus on what you know. You'll come up with the best ideas in these areas because when you're a consumer yourself, you know what works and what is needed.

- **Get an agent to represent you.** Want to go "supernuclear"? Use an agent. Without an agent, you have to come up with the idea, create the prototype, call on companies for appointments, make presentations, and negotiate deals. This is a whole lot easier than starting your own company and manufacturing and selling the product, but it still involves some work. If you hire an agent to represent you, the agent will call on prospective companies, fly out to visit them, make the presentation, and negotiate the deals. Of course, all of this comes at a cost. Most agents get 40 percent to 50 percent of your royalties. If you have an idea/product in an industry with little competition where you can easily call and get a meeting with a company, don't bother with an agent. On the other hand, if your idea/product is a new toy or a household consumer product, seriously consider an agent. These industries are supercompetitive and the buyers are used to working with agents. If an agent has contacts with these companies, it will save you a ton of time and aggravation. Check out the Resources section below for more information on how to find an agent.

- **Don't use an invention marketing company.** The ads you hear on radio and see on late night TV are for invention marketing companies—not agents! They encourage you to tell them about your idea and then promise to get you a patent and market your idea to companies. They don't mention the cost of their services—between $10,000 and $15,000. These companies make money on fees, not on royalties. Are there some decent ones? Probably. But as a general rule, avoid them.

- **Use a presentation prototype.** A prototype is a fancy word for a working model of your product. There are two types: presentation and preproduction. If you're going to build a company and

ANOTHER 8-HOUR SUCCESS

Sometimes the germ of a good idea is . . . a germ. Drew Oliver wanted to introduce small children to some of the inhabitants of the microscopic world to encourage them to wash their hands. He used some of his other 8 hours to build a company (giantmicrobes.com) that produces plush dolls of common cold viruses, stomachache bacteria, and many other miniscule creatures.

He spent two years working on the venture while working as an attorney. "I like learning how to do new things. Giantmicrobes began almost as a hobby research project on manufacturing and business, and became a challenge to see if I could really do it."

Like a true Cre8tor trying to limit his risk, he kept his day job. He didn't feel comfortable quitting his job at first. "It was much safer to start the business in my free time."

But while his microbes may be small, his success has been anything but. The company now distributes worldwide and is working on animated media starring the microbe characters.

What's he doing with the other 8 hours now? Now that running the company is his "real" job, he spends his free time brainstorming and looking for new ideas. "Running a business is a lot of work—like being an attorney. The fun of starting Giantmicrobes was that it was like playing, and I think I do my best work when I'm having fun."

manufacture the product yourself, you'll need a preproduction prototype. It's more detailed, refined, and expensive. If you're pitching the product to a company who may want to license your idea/product, it's always better if they can see and touch what you are talking about. For this route, your prototype doesn't have to be perfect or even fully functional, with all of the bells and whistles you hope the final production version will showcase. A less expensive presentation prototype is good enough for pitching the product to others.

- **Save money with a machinist instead of an engineer.** If you're handy, you might be able to create your own prototype, but if you're mechanically challenged like me, you should probably leave it to someone who knows what he's doing. This means hiring an engineer or a machinist. An engineer is more highly specialized and will cost more. If your idea isn't too complex, consider using a machinist. Often a machinist can create a great prototype for you for much less money than you'd pay an engineer to do the same work. For information on how to find a machinist, go to the Resources section below.

- **Use rapid prototyping.** The fastest way to go from idea to prototype is by using "rapid prototyping." Remember the *Jetsons* cartoon where George hits a button and the computer makes breakfast? Rapid prototyping is kind of like that. Using special software (CAD), you give the computer instructions for what you want. The computer reads the instructions and builds a real 3D physical model. (Where was rapid prototyping when I needed a date for the prom?)

- **Get face-to-face meetings with decisionmakers.** If you aren't going to use an agent to get the meetings and make the presentations, don't wimp out and e-mail or mail your idea/product to potential buyers. If you want to get a company to license your product, you're going to have to make an appointment to give them a presentation on your product.

- **Get a provisional patent.** A patent is a right granted to an inventor to exclude others from making, using, or selling a similar invention. Basically, it protects your idea from another company copying it and selling it without paying you a royalty. A typical patent can cost you $10,000, $15,000, or more. Obviously you want to protect your idea, but who's got $15,000 to burn? The

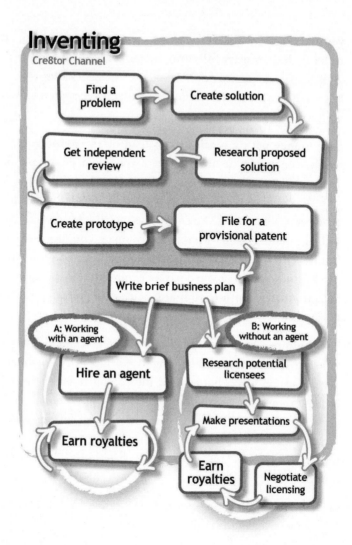

solution? A provisional patent. As mentioned before, for about $100 (if you file it yourself), you can protect your idea and claim that your product is "patent pending." Once you file a provisional patent, you have twelve months to file a "real" patent. You're basically buying yourself time while still protecting your invention.

- **Write a two-page business plan.** This doesn't need to be anything fancy. Just write a page or two about the product's features, benefits, market size, packaging ideas, production notes, cost to produce, and anticipated sales price. This is something you can give to your agent or discuss with potential companies.

RESOURCES

DEVELOPING A PROTOTYPE

- Elance (elance.com)—Easily find a technician skilled in CAD to help you create a digital version of your prototype, which can then be used to create the real deal.

- ThomasNet (thomasnet.com)—Comprehensive Web site that includes over 600,000 manufacturers, distributors, and service providers. Do you need a firm to create your plastic prototype? You'll find it here.

INDEPENDENT REVIEWERS

- Innovation Institute (wini2.com)—All these guys do is evaluate ideas and products using a system they developed called PIES. An evaluation will cost $200, which may sound like a lot of money, but if they can save you six months of your life (and possibly a lot of money), it is worth it.

- Harvey Reese Associates (money4ideas.com)—Harvey's a one-man show, and he's been around for years and has written extensively. He'll give you an honest assessment of your idea/product for $185, and if he really likes it, he will act as your agent (if you want him to).

LICENSING AGENTS

- Harvey Reese Associates (money4ideas.com)—You give him the idea, and if he loves it, he'll create the prototype, call on companies, make presentations, and negotiate the deal. For his work, he takes 40 percent on the first $100,000 per year in royalties and then 20 percent thereafter.

- International Licensing Industry Merchandisers' Association (licensing.org)—Contains a database of licensing agents and consultants.

MISCELLANEOUS

- United Inventors Association (uiausa.org)—Provides a wealth of information for inventors and entrepreneurs.

- InventNet (inventnet.com)—Inventor portal with lots of information and resources. Also has list of inventor's organizations by state so you can find a local group near you.

- United States Patent and Trademark Office (uspto.gov)—Here's where you can do a patent search and file a provisional patent.

- *Inventors Digest* (inventorsdigest.com)—Print magazine dedicated to inventors.

WRITING BOOKS, SCREENPLAYS, AND MUSIC

Writing Books, Screenplays, and Music Channel Toolbar		
Start-up Time	🕐🕐🕐🕐🕐	
Ongoing Time	🕐🕐🕐🕐🕐	
Start-up Costs	$ $ $ $ $	
Income Potential	$ $ $ $ $	
Help Needed	🚶🚶🚶🚶🚶	

Is there a best seller in you? Have you imagined hearing your song on the radio? Would you like to sell your screenplay to a Hollywood studio? With hard work, a little luck, and by following these rules, you'll be much closer to stardom . . .

RULES

1. **Avoid conmen.** There are leeches in every industry, but there seems to be an oversupply in this Cre8tor Channel (a very close second has to be the Inventor Channel). They prey on insecurities and promise fame and fortune. So how do you avoid their BS? Assume that everyone you meet is lying and out to separate you from your money. Too harsh? I know. I'm not usually such a downer, but please don't fall for their scams. Use Rule #2 (Network) to get a trusted friend who's been in the business (that is, who's been scammed himself) to help you navigate through the deception you're bound to face.

2. **Network.** If you're focused on this Cre8tor Channel, you must spend some of your time networking. Who you know can open doors faster than anything else. Once those doors are open, you have to have the goods, but sometimes it's a challenge just to get the doors open. This is why it is so important to dedicate some of your time to getting to know the players. Attend workshops, trade shows, and industry events. Make contacts and make friends. You may have written the next *Forrest Gump* or be the next Sarah McLachlan, but if your mother and your best friend are the only people who know it, you'll never make a dime. Get out there and meet some people who might be able to help you.

3. **Create a support team.** This Cre8tor Channel is highly competitive. No matter how talented you are, you will get rejected. In fact, you'll probably be rejected quite a bit. After a while, all this negativity can take a toll on your optimism and self-esteem. In order to keep going, you need to have some close friends, family, and contacts who are ready to inject you with support when you

need it. After your tenth rejection from an agent, it can be easy to give up. This is where you need your support team to prop you up and remind you how talented you are and why you are doing this.

4. **Get educated.** You may be able to sing in five octaves, but there's more (a lot more) to making money from your singing talent than singing well. Cre8tors are nimble. They are ninjas to a company's army. To perfect your different ninjalike moves, you can learn as much as you need to learn on pretty much any topic in a matter of hours. Don't know how to get an agent or write a book proposal? Buy a book (that's what I did!). Ten dollars and about two hours later, I knew everything I needed to know about writing a killer book proposal.

5. **Sell, sell, sell.** This is a "no-no" in artistic circles. If I'm talented, the thinking goes, people will buy my stuff. This kind of thinking is for people who are too chicken to risk rejection. Let me save you a boatload of time and frustration. If you don't plan on marketing and selling your product hard, don't even bother creating. I'm serious here. Do something else with your other 8 hours. Go have fun. Get a tan. Play Guitar Hero. Just don't waste your time creating if you aren't going to sell.

TIPS

- **Book publishing.** If you want to get a book published, you have two options. You can try to get a publishing deal from a publisher or you can self-publish. They are both valid methods for getting the book in your head to a book on a shelf. If you're writing on a narrow subject (best places to fish in the Pacific Northwest) or simply want to hand your book to potential clients and not sell it, self-publishing is a good solution. On the other hand, if you have the next great novel or a nonfiction book that could attract wide national audience, getting a publisher may be your best bet. The advantage to self-publishing is that anybody can do it, and you will make more on every book sold. The disadvantage is you won't get

ANOTHER 8-HOUR SUCCESS

Gabrielle de Cuir and Stefan Rudnicki follow the ABCs—Always Be Creating. They own and operate Skyboat Road Company, an audiobook recording and production company. They are used to putting in long days at the office but often pursue creative outlets during the other 8 hours, such as performing in or directing plays. One day Gabrielle had an idea . . . let's make a movie. And make a movie they did!

How did they make a film in a town where everyone talks about making one but few do? They got creative. Instead of going after private investors or studio money (like everyone else), they went to their largest corporate audiobook clients and pitched them on the idea of a corporate sponsorship. And then the checks rolled in, right? Not exactly. But that didn't faze them. They shortened the film and lowered the budget. Still no checks.

Going after corporate sponsors was brilliant, but what they did next was pure genius. They made their offer nearly risk-free. "Invest in us and we'll make a great film that will give you media exposure and educate people (i.e., your future customers) about audiobooks," and one more thing (this is the cool part) . . . Gabrielle and Stefan offered to donate their time and expertise to deliver their largest corporate sponsor a fully edited and mastered audiobook the company could easily sell to cover its investment. The checks came in.

Gabrielle and Stefan believe in taking risks. Stefan joked, "If you don't do scary things, you're dead. You might as well get your tombstone." But when you're trying to get investors or find partners, follow their lead and make your offer as risk-free as possible.

To watch the trailer for their festival award-winning film, *The Delivery*, go to their Web site at skyboatroad.com.

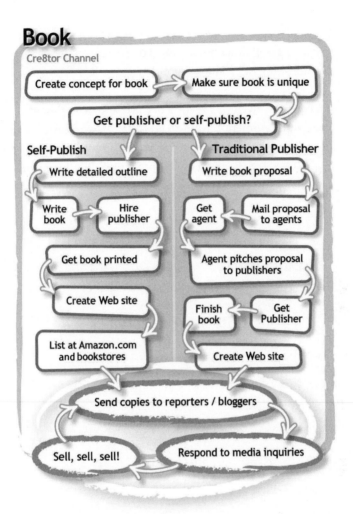

the distribution (that is, you probably won't see your book in your local Barnes & Noble) and you will have to pay between $2,500 and $5,000 to have the book published.

Getting a publishing contract ain't easy. You need an agent (and just getting an agent is hard), a thorough book proposal, a marketable book, and a lot of luck. If you do succeed, you'll get a cash advance and they'll pay for everything—editing, design, printing, and marketing. A good publisher will have connections with all the major bookstores, reviewers, and press contacts. Before you spend a lot of time (and maybe money) going down the wrong path, figure out which is best for you, self-publishing or getting a publisher.

- **Screenplay.** I lived in LA for a decade, and even though I wasn't in the entertainment business and didn't have an interest in writing a screenplay, I found myself reading them often. And most were B-O-R-I-N-G and a chore to get into. Not long ago I heard that when Quentin Tarantino was trying to pitch his first screen-

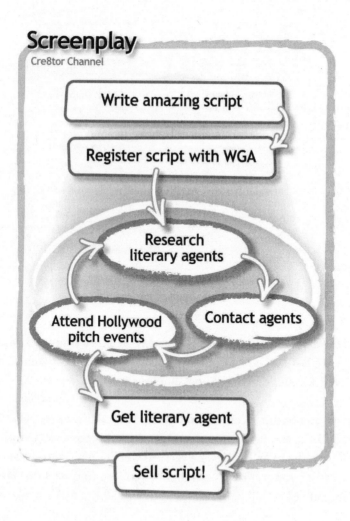

play, *True Romance*, he rearranged the story so one of the most exciting and clever scenes was at the very beginning in order to draw readers into the rest of the screenplay. If this story is true (and even if it's not), Quentin is a genius. He understood that his job as the writer was first to get people to read the script. If they don't make it past page three, it's over.

Hollywood is a chummy town. The only way you're going to get your script sold and turned into a movie is if it gets read by the right people. Write a page-turning script and get it in the hands of as many people as possible. This means that if you want success you'll have to network more, harder, and longer. Tap into your network and help them whenever possible. The more doors you can open for others, the more success you'll attain.

One more tip . . . don't send your script to an actor, director, or production company without first having an agent. They'll reject it and you'll look like an amateur. Your only job after writing a killer script is to get an agent.

- **Music.** It is the best of times, it is the worst of times. For old and crusty music executives trying to sell records the same way they have for the past fifty years, things aren't looking so good. But, for savvy musicians who know how to promote themselves both online and traditionally, this is a fantastic time to be in the music industry (remember Esmee Denters from the last chapter?). Music is such an integral part of media—new and old—that there are opportunities for musicians like never before.

Since anyone can (and seems like is) recording and promoting his or her own music, your music has to stand out. It has to be unique and exceptional enough that your fans love it and talk about it. Write the best songs you can and be sure to get them properly produced. But how do you find fans? Perform live as often as and wherever you can if you think the venue will help you reach your target demographic—even if you don't get paid. Just get out there and play, play, play. One of two things will happen. Either you will start to attract some fans or you won't.

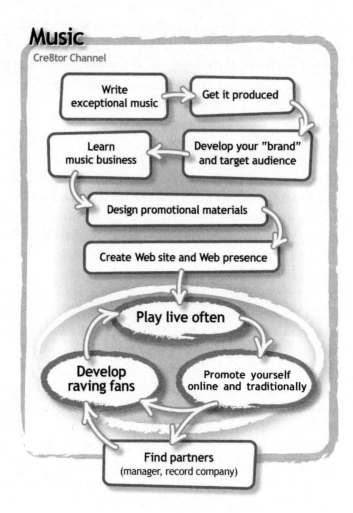

Spend some of the other 8 hours practicing your passion, but also invest some time learning the business side of the music industry. Network with others and learn from them. Read books on the business and take classes. Find a mentor, or, even better, get a well-connected and respected manager to help you navigate. Warning: Do NOT pay a manager anything up front! Managers should get a percentage (usually 15–20 percent) fee for only those business transactions for which they are responsible.

RESOURCES

- WGA West Registry (wgawregistry.org/webrss)—Register your screenplay before you send it out to agents. The cost is $20 per registration.

- Screenwriting.info (screenwriting.info)—Great resource to learn tips and rules for writing a screenplay.

- Script Frenzy (scriptfrenzy.org)—Need some motivation to start writing? Mark your calendars! For one month every year (April 1 through April 30), Script Frenzy holds an international "event" that challenges participants to write 100 pages of content (script, book) in just 30 days.

- Agent Query (agentquery.com)—Billed as the "Internet's largest and most current database of literary agents." Great resource to pinpoint the right agent for your work.

- Zhura (zhura.com)—Free online screenwriting software makes writing the next *Pulp Fiction* a little easier.

- Lulu (lulu.com)—Want to self-publish your book? Lulu offers an inexpensive print-on-demand service.

STARTING A COMPANY

Starting a Company Channel Toolbar	
Start-up Time	🕐 🕐 🕐 🕐 🕐
Ongoing Time	🕐 🕐 🕐 🕐 🕐
Start-up Costs	$ $ $ $ $
Income Potential	$ $ $ $ $
Help Needed	👤 👤 👤 👤 👤

This Cre8tor Channel is about starting a company. Maybe you have an idea for a clothing line, a Web site, or Facebook application. There's no doubt starting a company takes a lot of time and energy, but it can be exhilarating and life changing. The stakes are high, but to minimize your risk, follow these rules.

RULES

1. **Start small.** This is a common theme across all Cre8tor Channels. Why? I don't want you to risk too much. Remember Strike 4!? If you go all out on your first T-shirt design but nobody likes it, you're stuck. Make it a goal to start as small as you possibly can. Instead of twelve different necklace styles, focus on your best one or two designs. If you are successful with those, you'll have plenty of time and money to expand the collection.

2. **Research and test the product.** You have to develop a research mentality. But this is hard for most creative types for two reasons. First, they think they are betraying their creative integrity if they must get feedback. Second, when you're selling something you've created, you are exposing yourself. Most people feel vulnerable and want to avoid criticism. I totally get that. That's why it's important to get feedback from people you trust. I've got a friend who always ends his scathing criticism with, "I'm just keeping it real, man." You know what? Just keep it to yourself. Consult friends who will be honest about but *supportive* of your efforts.

   You can use Google AdWords to test any product in a day with just a couple hundred dollars. If you have a great idea for a new ab machine, create a digital image using Photoshop (you can sketch the design and then hire someone on elance.com to create a digital image), upload it to a Web site, buy a few targeted Google AdWords, and see how many people first click on your ad and then click on "buy." If you get a lot of clicks but little interest, you may want to make some changes. This strategy works great when you can create a sample product and take a picture of it, but it can also work for less tangible products.

Let's say you have an idea for how to lose weight doing aerobic water yoga. You want to do a sixty-minute workout video, workbook, and subscription-based Web site. Of course, you could spend six months and $25,000 creating all of these products, but that's too much risk to take on unless you know you can reach an interested audience. Instead, you could write a twenty-page e-book on the subject (or hire someone cheaply on elance.com to write it for you), put up a one-page Web site with information on the e-book, buy Google AdWords (such as "yoga, weight loss, aerobics, water exercise," etc.), and offer your e-book for free if the user provides his contact information. You'll learn a couple of things. First, are people interested enough to click through from the ad? Second, once they get to the Web site and see exactly what the book is about, are they willing to give you their e-mail address to get a free copy? If you get a hundred click-throughs but only three people want the free book, that's not a good sign. Third, for those who do provide their contact information, e-mail them. Ask them questions about what they are seeking. These are your customers and this is a great way to learn firsthand what they want in the product. Maybe it's a sixty-minute video on aerobic water yoga, but then again, maybe it's not. It's best to spend a couple hundred dollars to do this super-simple test and find out before you dump six months of your life and a lot of money into the project.

3. **Determine the best price point.** Play around with different pricing strategies. Look at what your competitors charge. Test to see what works.

4. **Get educated.** You may be an expert in fashion design, but there's more (a lot more) to creating a successful clothing line than design. You need to know about accounting, marketing, writing, networking, and more. Don't know about Internet marketing? Google it. Even if you have a partner or plan on hiring consultants, get educated enough so you can at least evaluate different marketing strategies.

A Cre8tor must have a PhD in resourcefulness. When my wife started her clothing line, we didn't know anything about the fashion industry. We went to one trade show and talked to a few people. Then we talked to a few more. A week later, we knew 95 percent of what we needed to know about sourcing—where to get blanks, which dye house to use, how to grind, where to get tags, who does the best screen-printing. We went from completely clueless to educated in about a week and all of this was done through trade shows and talking to people. There's a lot you can learn online through e-books, Web sites, and podcasts in even less time.

5. **Sell, sell, sell.** Put just as much time into thinking about how you are going to market and sell your product as you do into designing and creating the product. I'd take a mediocre product that is marketed well over a superior product that isn't marketed well. I know. It's not fair. The success of a product should be based on how good it is and not how well it is packaged and sold, but we live in America, folks (ever hear of the Snuggie?!). Develop a killer marketing strategy and get out there and sell, sell, sell.

TIPS

- **Ask the experts.** Get advice from experts in your industry by using informational interviews. Unlike a job interview, where the goal is to get a job, you use an informational interview to get advice. Research the movers and shakers in your industry (but don't stalk them), and ask them for ten minutes of their time. To get the interview, appeal to their ego. Tell them you are starting out and would be honored to ask them a couple of questions. Promise to be brief. Before the interview, make sure you have several insightful questions about your topic that can't be answered on Wikipedia. You have an expert in front of you; ask expert questions. Use this time to ask questions that relate to your product. Before the interview is over, ask them if there is anyone else they would recommend you speak to. Once you have those names, it's easy to call them and say, "I was just talking to Jill, and she suggested I call you for a quick meeting."

- **Remnant ads.** You don't need Nike's marketing budget to run print, TV, and radio ads. Instead, take advantage of remnant ads. This is advertising space that the magazine or radio/TV station has not been able to sell. Think of remnant ads as empty seats on a plane. The plane is taking off whether there are empty seats or not, so they might as well sell the seats for whatever they can get for them. Cre8tors can swoop in at the last minute and buy ad space for pennies on the dollar—sometimes 75 percent to 90 percent off regular rates. You have to be ready to buy, though, because you may only have a day or two's notice. Have several ads ready to go (print, TV, or radio). See the Resources section below for remnant ad companies.

- **Google AdWords.** Earlier I talked about how to use Google AdWords to test an idea or product, but once you've tested your idea and have a product that you want to sell, you can again use Google AdWords—this time to get customers. Google AdWords allows you to bid on search terms. For example, if you have a new machine that targets abs, you might be very interested in those people who Google "lose weight" or "six pack abs," because these are folks who are looking for precisely what you sell. You could place a small text ad next to the search results that says, "Lose belly fat and get rock hard abs by using new machine 10 minutes a day." How much does the ad cost? It depends, because you bid on search terms. Google has an easy-to-use tool that allows you to enter your search terms, and it will tell you approximately how much each click will cost and the number of clicks you can expect in a day. Go to adwords.google.com for more info.

- **Press releases.** You need to get the word out about your company or product. Targeted ads are fantastic for acquiring motivated customers—you display an ad and you might get a sale. Publicity, however, is great for generating bigger-scale interest—if you get in *USA Today* or on *Good Morning America*, you might get a few thousand customers. Your goal should be to distribute one press release a month (assuming you have something newsworthy to report!); or, if you are somewhat tech savvy, create and distribute one Social Media News Release (SMNR) a month. These are not your father's press releases—they are the next generation news release. SMNRs combine the best elements of new media, including photos, videos, podcasts, and RSS, which makes it easier for the media and bloggers to pull the parts they need. A traditional press release says read me. An SMNR says use me. Check out the Resources section below for more information on SMNRs.

- **Help a reporter out.** Reporters have tough jobs. They work long hours and are always under a deadline. They're in a never-ending search for experts and sources for their articles. One way they find these sources is by posting a media request on a newswire service such as ProfNet, which is viewed by public relations firms across the country. If the PR firm represents a client that would be a good fit for the reporter's article, they'll respond to the media request and try to get their client an interview with the reporter. This is all fine and good, but I'm guessing you don't have a PR firm on retainer (they cost at least $5,000 a month!). Savvy Cre8tors use HelpAReporter.com—a brilliant and free e-mail media service that connects them to reporters looking for sources on stories they are working on right now. Sign up and you'll get up to three e-mails a day, with fifteen to thirty reporter inquiries. All you have to do is read the e-mail, look for those inquiries that are related to what you're working on, and then e-mail the reporter. HelpaReporter.com founder Peter Shankman says that to have the best success getting noticed, you need "relevance and brevity." He suggests establishing your credibility and why you are the person to talk to in the first sentence. "Keep it short and keep your focus on helping the reporter," he adds. Here are a few more tips on how to respond to one of these reporters.

1. **Be fast**—A reporter writing for a big national publication like *Newsweek* or *USA Today* may get 100+ e-mail replies to an

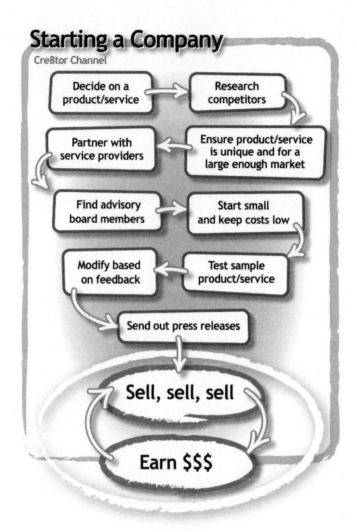

inquiry. If the reporter finds the source he needs on the third e-mail, he won't bother reading any more. Respond as quickly as you can.

2. Solve their problem—Reporters have a problem they are trying to solve. Show them at the beginning of the e-mail that you understand what they're looking for by giving them the tips or story they need. You don't have to write an article on the subject; a few bullet points will do. I've even had success writing, "I have a great deal of expertise on this subject. I can provide the top 5 tips your readers need to know to . . ."

3. Get their respect—Include a sentence or two about who you are and any of your professional accomplishments, press you've done, awards you've received.

4. Be brief—All of this has to be done in about two paragraphs.

5. Use boilerplate text—In order to speed up your response time and to eliminate extra work for you, craft a good paragraph that summarizes who you are, what your company does, what your product is, any press/awards you've received, and how the reporter should contact you. I strongly suggest you give them your cell phone number because they may need to reach you after-hours.

RESOURCES

START-UP RESOURCES

- Go BIG Network (gobignetwork.com)—Called the Craigslist of start-ups, this site brings together entrepreneurs, investors, advisors, and service providers.

- SCORE (score.org)—A nonprofit, associated with the SBA that helps entrepreneurs form and grow businesses. They have nearly 400 local chapters and over 10,000 volunteers throughout the United States. The best part? Working and retired executives and business owners become mentors—donating their time and expertise to small business owners.

PRESS RELEASES

- Press Release Grader (pressreleasegrader.com)—A cool application that evaluates your press release for free. Save time and money by uploading your press release to this site first.

- Your Pitch Sucks? (yourpitchsucks.com)—Based on the premise that most pitches suck (their words, not mine), they offer a free service that lets you submit your press release and get feedback from experts. It's a must-use!

- PR.com (pr.com)—A free service that allows you to upload your press release and get distribution.

- Associated Press (ap.org)—If your story has "national or international significance," they recommend you e-mail your release in the body of the e-mail (no attachments) to info@ap.org.

- SHIFT Communications (shiftcomm.com)—Todd Defren is a principal of SHIFT and invented the Social Media New Release. Go to their site to download a template.

MISCELLANEOUS

- Etsy (etsy.com)—Over 100,000 sellers from around the world put their handmade creations for sale on this Web site.

- LegalZoom (legalzoom.com)—They can help you form an LLC or corporation. I've used them. They do great work. Use code: **8HOURS** at checkout to receive $10 off any service they provide.

- The Company Corporation (incorporate.com)—They specialize in forming LLCs and corporations. Use code: **OTHER8** at checkout to receive $50 off their services.

RESELLING, AFFILIATING, AND LICENSING

Reselling, Affiliating, and Licensing Channel Toolbar					
Start-up Time	🕐	🕐	🕐	🕐	🕐
Ongoing Time	🕐	🕐	🕐	🕐	🕐
Start-up Costs	$	$	$	$	$
Income Potential	$	$	$	$	$
Help Needed	🧍	🧍	🧍	🧍	🧍

If you're not creative and don't have an interest in producing your own product, you can still make money by selling other people's products. You have three options:

1. **Affiliate.** When you affiliate, you become a middle person connecting a buyer with a seller, and you can do this for either a product or a service. For example, if you review books on your blog, you could provide a link to Amazon.com, where visitors could purchase the book. You don't have control over the price or markup. You simply get a commission—some percentage of the sales price. The nice thing is that you don't have to take inventory of anything, ship product, or deal with customer service or technical support issues— this is all handled by the company selling the service or product. You can become an affiliate in about three minutes—it's easy, and anybody with a pulse can do it.

2. **Resell.** As a reseller, you buy product, mark it up, and then sell it for a profit. For example, you could buy T-shirts from a manufacturer and sell them on your Web site. The advantage is that you control the markup and profit. But you have to take inventory and shell out cash for a product and possibly end up sitting on product that can't be sold. As a reseller, you are also responsible for shipping product, dealing with returns, credit card fraud, and customer service/technical support.

3. **License.** This is more sophisticated than reselling and affiliating. When you license a product, you are leasing a legally protected product—in other words, something protected by a trademark, patent, or copyright. In the Invention Channel section, I talked about licensing from the perspective of the inventor (licensor), but now we're looking at it from the licensee's perspective. Creating a licensing partnership takes time—especially if you want an exclusive agreement where you are the only person/company allowed to sell the product. This added effort can be well worth the results, because licensing has the ability to generate substantially more income for you than the other options.

RULES

1. **Stick to what you know.** If you're a techie geek, don't try to sell haute couture. Stick to what you know. You'll be able to determine what products are good and the right price point. You'll also know the market and what consumers want, since you are part of the market. Lastly, you can write about it and sell it better because you're an insider.

ANOTHER 8-HOUR SUCCESS

Nick Loper is twenty-six years old and runs an affiliate comparison shopping site for shoes (shoesrus.net). His Web site allows consumers to search for shoes and compare retail prices. He earns a percentage on any sales through the site.

He started the venture on a very small scale while going to college, but after graduating, he did what most people do . . . he got a job. He started at Ford, but didn't find the job fulfilling and had no urge to climb the corporate ladder. While working full time, he invested ten to twenty hours per week in the company during the evenings.

Nick is not a big risk taker. He says, "It wasn't until I was receiving enough monthly income on a consistent basis that I felt I could quit my job. I worked about eighteen months longer than I needed to, just to be safe."

His initial goal was to earn $200 to $300 a month. The company is projected to do $350,000 in sales in 2009. His advice for anyone who wants to work for themselves is: "If you have an idea, you owe it to yourself to go for it."

2. **Test market before you commit.** Before you buy a bunch of inventory, make sure you can sell the product. There are many entrepreneurs with a garage full of product because they didn't test the market first. Run a small Google AdWord campaign. Try to sell to local boutiques. What's the response? Any bites? If not, look for another product.

3. **Start small.** You might be inclined to buy a lot of product initially, but I don't care what kind of discount you get for ordering more product, start small. Order just enough and no more. If you immediately sell out, order a little more. If you are selling to fickle consumers for whom fads come and go or styles and interests change quickly, don't get stuck owning yesterday's hot product. The companies making the product aren't idiots. They've been in the game longer than you. If they're offering you a great deal on a boatload of product, be concerned that they are trying to dump it and move on to the next hot product.

4. **Negotiate.** The difference between a good deal and a great deal lies in your ability to negotiate. You'd be surprised how many people don't ask for a deal. Negotiate hard and negotiate until you get what you want. If you are dealing with a company that won't negotiate, find another product. Don't waste your time with stubborn companies that aren't willing to play the game.

5. **Get referrals.** Ask the company about the success of their resellers and licensees. How many do they have? How much product do they purchase? What does the average reseller/licensee buy? What's the median? The top 10 percent? How do the top 10 percent sell the product? Do they sell online? What's their distribution? What's their markup? You're trying to figure out how resellers/licensees are doing and what the top performers are doing. The company should gladly provide you with this information, since it will help you successfully sell their product.

6. **Build your reputation.** If you are negotiating an exclusive licensing deal, you'd better be able to sell yourself and your ability to

sell the product. Get a professional Web site and get some successes under your belt first.

7. **Target your buyer.** Put together a single product-focused Web site with information your target buyer wants to know before making a purchase. In other words, don't try to sell ten products on one Web site unless all the products are related.

TIPS

- **Get free test samples.** Don't buy a bunch of product without first inspecting the quality. Ask for several free samples. Tell the company your quality assurance division needs to review and test all product first. If you get enough samples, use them to test the market.

- **First order discount.** Negotiate for a substantial discount on your first order under the premise that you are testing a couple of competing products and that, before you commit a lot of resources to one product, you want to run some tests. Offer to pay cost for your first test run. If that test run is successful, you'll be back and will order more at normal prices. If you're not successful, they won't lose any money.

- **Review Web sites.** Review Web sites are a clever way to market an affiliate program. In a nutshell, these sites offer product or service reviews like *Consumer Reports*. They provide a great deal of information designed to help consumers determine what is best for their needs. The products are part of an affiliate program, so when a consumer clicks through to purchase, the affiliate gets a commission. For example, I am an expert in personal finance. I could become an Amazon.com affiliate and throw up a personal finance book review Web site where I talk about the ten best financial planning and investment books. Whenever a visitor clicks through and buys one of my top ten books from Amazon.com, I earn a commission. If you know your product and your target customer, review Web sites can be a good source of revenue, especially if you couple them with a blog.

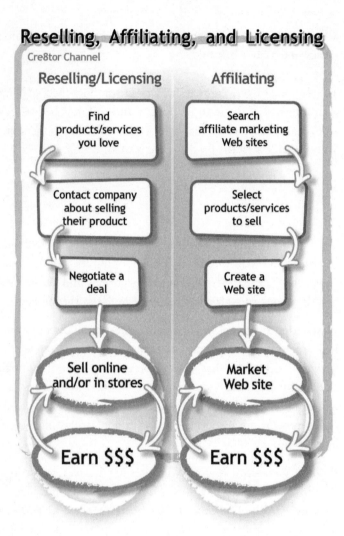

- **Market your product with an e-book.** Do you like to write? Can you put together a fifteen- or twenty-page e-book about the products or services you are selling? It shouldn't be fifteen pages of you hard selling them. That's a huge turn-off and won't generate any sales. You need to write it as someone who is passionate about the product and wants to share it with the world. Provide real information—both good and bad. Be objective. Nothing's perfect, so don't pretend your product is. Offer the book for free and point readers to your Web site for more up-to-date reviews or information.

- **Blog.** Bloggers have some of the best success stories using affiliate programs. Why? They've built a connection and relationship with their readers. When they discuss a product, their readers trust their opinion. Consider blogging and then using an affiliate program (see Blogging Channel for more info).

- **Partner with an expert.** For the right product, an expert endorsement can do wonders. Are you reselling a fat-loss supplement but you failed Biology 101? Google experts in the field and ask if they want to partner with you. Show them your marketing strategy and give them a split of your sales. Most will politely decline, but you only need one to agree to help. Even better, get them to write the e-book or blog while you focus on distribution and marketing.

RESOURCES

Finding Products to Sell:

- ClickBank (clickbank.com)—They list over 10,000 products you can immediately begin selling.

- Commission Junction (commissionjunction.com)—The name says it all. Use them to find products and earn commissions.

- LinkShare (linkshare.com)—A free service you can plug into to find products to sell.

- ShareASale (shareasale.com)—Another service that connects you to products to sell.

TAKING ADVANTAGE OF FADS/STUNTS

Taking Advantage of Fads/Stunts Channel Toolbar					
Start-up Time	🕐	🕐	🕐	🕐	🕐
Ongoing Time	🕐	🕐	🕐	🕐	🕐
Start-up Costs	$	$	$	$	$
Income Potential	$	$	$	$	$
Help Needed	🚶	🚶	🚶	🚶	🚶

This Cre8tor Channel is all about seizing the moment. If you're quick, you can have some fun and make money by taking advantage of the latest fad or quirky idea with virtually no risk. In a nutshell, this Channel is about coming up with an unusual idea or taking advantage of what's dominating the headlines by registering a Web site address, building a Web site, sending out a press release, and monetizing the traffic by selling products or ad space. You can do all of this for the grand investment of about ten bucks. I love America!

For example, do you remember, way back (it seems like ages ago) in the 2008 presidential election, when John McCain pointed to Barack Obama during a debate and referred to him as "that one"? The average viewer may not have noticed, but for the right Cre8tor this was an opportunity. Less than two hours after the debate ended, there were "that one" Web sites popping up all over the Internet, including That One08.com. The mystery owner of this Web site registered the domain name, built the Web site, and created several "that one" T-shirts and bumper stickers in less than twenty-four hours. He (or she) also got some kick-butt press, including the *New York Times, Politico,* NPR, *PC World*, and many others. Now that's a Cre8tor who knows how to jump on a fad.

Here's another example. The median income in the United States is about $30,000 per year. Jason Sadler made more than twice that amount ($66,795) last year by wearing T-shirts. Come again? He says, "I am always trying to think of things I do daily that I could promote and make some extra change from. I was lying in bed one late night and the idea popped in my head—why not charge people to have me wear their company's shirt?" With this thought, iwearyourshirt.com was born. Jason sold every day of the year at face value (January 1 was $1 and December 31 was $365) and promoted each shirt on You-Tube, Twitter, his blog, and elsewhere. And how much did this cost him? Next to nothing. "That's the beauty of this project. There are a few expenses here and there, like camera equipment, but I don't pay anything to wear a shirt every day and use social media to promote myself!"

If you want to use the other 8 hours to capitalize on the nation's latest fixation or to launch a crazy idea, follow these rules.

RULES

1. Be quick. This is rule numero uno for fads. Unlike an invention, a clothing line, or a screenplay, where you have a bunch of people coming up with original ideas, fads are just the opposite—you may have a bunch of people all focused on the same idea. You must be fast, because the first guy to get traction is the guy who will dominate. There is no time to write a business plan or to consult a team. You need to jump on these opportunities very quickly.

2. Be prepared. Hesitation is death for this Cre8tor Channel, so you should get as much set up as possible *before* you need it. I took my daughter on a tour of our local fire station recently. These guys know a thing or two about efficiency and being prepared. Everything is set up and ready to go—their boots, jacket, helmet, hoses, and trucks are all just waiting for the fire alarm to go off. If you want to succeed in this Channel, you have to get everything ready so that when it's time to pull the trigger, there is no delay. At a minimum, here's what you need to do:

   a. Register with a Web hosting and registration company so you can quickly purchase a Web site address and put up a Web site.

   b. Register for a PayPal merchant account so you can accept credit card payments online.

   c. Set up an account at a press release distribution company so you can quickly blast off a press release to let the world know what you are doing.

   d. Set up a Google AdWords account so you can purchase ads.

   e. Set up accounts with the companies listed in the Resources section.

3. Follow pop culture and the news. If you're going to take advantage of the latest fad, you need to keep your pulse on what's happening. If you're a news junkie, this should be pretty easy.

4. Be proactive. You can't sit back and wait for something to happen. You should actively seek opportunities. Be on the lookout for the next big and crazy thing. View the world and the news through a Cre8tor lens. Constantly ask yourself if this is an opportunity. At first, it may feel foreign and unnatural, but with time, you'll find that it's a lot of fun.

5. **Swing often.** Nobody can predict what will take off next, which is why you need to keep trying things.

6. **Take small risks.** Don't commit too much to any fad or stunt, because they have a limited life. There won't be another Million Dollar Homepage (milliondollarhomepage.com). That means you shouldn't buy 10,000 shirts thinking you'll sell them all. Today's hot idea that dominates the headlines can be forgotten (and often is) just a week or two later.

7. **Create a Web site quickly.** If you're a techie, this isn't a problem. If you're not, you have to partner with someone who is, find a firm that can act quickly, or use a do-it-yourself template Web site (most larger Web hosting companies offer templates and easy-to-use Web design software).

8. **Get out when the gettin's good.** No matter how great things are this moment, no matter how much you're selling, and no matter how much press you're getting, it is only temporary. Do not forget this. If you have the chance to sell the company, do it. Do not hesitate.

TIPS

- **Good enough is good enough.** You're not painting the Sistine Chapel. Don't kill yourself trying to be perfect. Get something— anything—up quickly. You can always go back and improve upon it later if you want.

- **Product on demand.** Instead of buying a lot of product and hoping you sell it all before the fad fades, consider product on

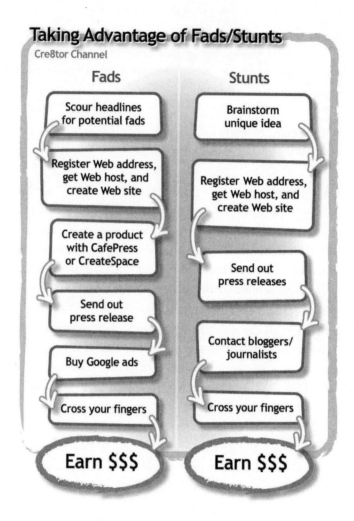

demand. This is where product is created only when ordered. This way there's no inventory and no cost or risk to you. The best resources for product on demand are CafePress (cafepress.com) and CreateSpace (createspace.com). Check out these sites—they are amazing resources if you are trying to take advantage of fads.

RESOURCES

Creating Products:

- CafePress (cafepress.com)—This is the biggest of the product-on-demand companies. It is brain-numbingly easy to create custom-designed T-shirts, hats, posters, stickers, coffee mugs, ornaments, and about a zillion other things on this site. If you sell something, CafePress gets a piece of the action. If you don't, it costs you nothing. There is NO risk at all.

- CreateSpace (createspace.com)—This site lets you create books, DVDs, CDs, e-books, and audiobooks quickly and easily. Like CafePress, there's no inventory, and it doesn't cost you a thing unless you sell product. And because it's an Amazon.com company, anything you create is made available on Amazon.com.

WORKING FOR STOCK IN A COMPANY

Working for Stock in a Company Channel Toolbar	
Start-up Time	🕐🕐🕐🕐🕐
Ongoing Time	🕐🕐🕐🕐🕐
Start-up Costs	💲💲💲💲💲
Income Potential	💲💲💲💲💲
Help Needed	🧍🧍🧍🧍🧍

How can you get rich with an IPO but not have to take the roller-coaster ride of working at a start-up? Most people get paid by the hour, with a flat salary, or by commission. These are all acceptable ways of earning an income during your work hours, but for the Cre8tor who wants maximum leverage, there's another way. Stock. It's simple and it can propel you into a whole new financial level.

Instead of getting paid cash for your work, you get paid in stock or in a share of future income. For example, let's say you work in the technology division of an insurance company by day and are an awesome graphic designer in your spare time. You like the security and stability of your job, but you want to make some more money with your other 8 hours. You decide to take on a few small projects for other companies after-hours (see the Freelancing Channel below) to make some extra money to pay off college loans. Getting out of debt would be good, but you have bigger dreams. So you decide you're going to offer your services to a select few start-ups for no up-front cash but instead will work for stock or a share of future income. If any of the start-ups get bought or become an IPO, your stock could be worth hundreds of thousands (if not millions) of dollars. Simple, right? Follow these rules to increase your chances of success.

RULES

1. **High-growth companies only.** In order to get the biggest bang for your buck, working for stock is effective only if you are providing services to companies with the potential for huge growth. Think high-tech, biotech, Internet, and the like. Stock in your local hardware store—no matter how much they are growing—isn't going to get you rich.

2. **Early stage start-ups only.** Get paid in dollars from mature companies and in stock or a share of future income from start-ups. You won't be able to get much stock from a mature company, but you can get it from a start-up with more stock than available cash. Also, the start-up stock you own could go up several thousand-fold. The stock of a mature company probably won't go up much.

3. Diversify. Would you dump all your money on black at the roulette wheel? Would you invest your entire 401(k) in one stock? In order to increase your odds of striking it big, you should get stock in several different companies. Most venture capitalists know that three out of ten companies will go under, four might be flat, two might do okay, but one will make up for all the rest. These are professional investors with years of experience, and they still get it wrong most of the time. So your job is to spread your stock across industries (for example, don't just focus on social networking ad-revenue applications) and across several companies (don't do twenty projects for the same company).

4. Pretend you are an investor. Don't jump into bed with any company willing to give you stock for your services. Be selective. Would you invest in the company? Analyze the industry. Is it growing or declining? How long has the company been around? What have they accomplished? Has the management had success in the past with other ventures?

5. Get stock (or income share). There are many ways to eat an Oreo, and there are just as many ways to get stock. Most companies will want to give you options or warrants instead of stock outright, and this is okay. Make sure the conversion is zero or low and that there is no vesting requirement. Some companies, especially young start-ups that aren't even yet incorporated, may not be able to give you stock (they don't have any). In these cases, you can instead get a piece of the revenue. It can work very well for both the company and you—just make sure your day job doesn't have a problem with your doing this.

6. Negotiate. If you are going to use your special talents and eat up part of your other 8 hours for no money but for the hope of some payoff in the distant future, you'd better make sure you are getting a sweet deal. Negotiate hard. Ask for more than you'd ever expect to get. A start-up has no value but a lot of potential. They need you. What's another 10,000 shares of a company worth nothing today? Help them understand that you believe in what they're doing, but that they need you. Make it clear you want to help them make it big, but when you do, you want a piece of their success.

7. **Get them to cover your out-of-pocket costs.** Make sure they cover any out-of-pocket expenses you incur (Web hosting, domain registration, materials). You'll contribute your time, but you shouldn't be expected to lose money. If they aren't willing to do this, they are greedy bastards and you shouldn't work with them.

8. **Use a bulletproof agreement.** The difference between a properly written agreement and a crappy one can mean hundreds of thousands of dollars in your pocket. Use a good agreement. In fact, it is always better to use your agreement than one the company puts together. Get a good template that is fair and protects you and use it over and over.

TIPS

- **Sell yourself.** As you are evaluating the company for its growth prospects and management team, they will be evaluating you, too. A smart start-up won't just give stock away to anyone. They will want to be sure they are getting a great service. In order to help them get comfortable with you, you need to act and look like a professional. That means you should have business cards, a great Web site, references, and a portfolio of work (if applicable). For example, if you want to offer your bookkeeping and accounting services for stock, you should put up a Web site that clearly shows your services with testimonials. If you are Web designer, make sure you have a Web site that shows off your skills and is accompanied by a link to other Web design you've done.

- **Get the gig.** You may have the skills, time, and desire, but how do you connect with start-ups looking for a work/stock partnership? There are two great resources:

  1) **Angel investing clubs.** Angel investing clubs are located across the country and are a place for high-net-worth investors to

learn about local companies looking for capital. Start-ups look-ing for funding will discuss their company and business plan, and investors will decide if they want to fund them (either as a club or individually). Contact local clubs and ask to participate in a meeting. Be prepared to explain what you do, who you can do it for, and that you wish to work for stock in any of their promising companies. Angel investors are looking for a great return on their money, and if you can save their portfolio com-panies cash, they will jump all over it. See the Resources section below for links to angel investor Web sites.

2) **Venture capitalists.** VCs are professional investors who fund high-growth start-ups as well as more mature companies. Like angels, they can be an excellent resource for finding work-for-stock gigs. Contact them and get involved with their clients. See the Resources section below for links to VC Web sites.

• **Work on advisory boards.** If you don't have an easily identifiable service you can sell, there is still an opportunity to provide huge value to start-ups and to get rich in the process. Start-ups are usu-ally short on cash, connections, and broad talent. Think about it. A couple of smart tech guys have an idea but no money, few con-nections, and little experience with management, sales, or build-ing a company. Start-ups need experienced people to give them direction and support. One of the best ways to get involved with a start-up and get stock is to be on their advisory board, which is like a board of directors but without the legal liability and head-ache. As an advisory board member, you might need to participate in a monthly or quarterly meeting, be involved in a few monthly phone calls, and introduce the start-up to people in your Rolodex. This is a great way to meet other board members and earn stock in a promising company.

• **Transition to F/T.** If you work as a service provider or advisory board member, there is the chance you can eventually transition into a full-time paid job for the company. It can be very natural. You start off working for stock on a few projects, the company starts doing well or gets some funding, and then they look to hire full-time staff. Who are they going to ask first? You.

- **Work for a start-up.** Okay, this isn't using your other 8 hours, but it is worth mentioning. If you don't mind the risk of a start-up, get a job at one. A good friend of mine lives in Seattle. She works as an office manager in a small mom and pop business. She has a lot of solid skills that almost any company would value. My advice to her almost a decade ago was to get a job as an office manager at a high-tech start-up. I told her she'd probably get about what she earned at her other job, but she could also negotiate to get stock, too. If the start-up goes under, she could easily get another job at another start-up, or, if she wanted security, she could get a job at a more stable and mature company. There is virtually no downside and a hell of a lot of upside. If you live in a high-tech area such as Silicon Valley, Seattle, Austin, or New York, this can be a terrific way to take very little risk but still get rich.

ANOTHER 8-HOUR SUCCESS

Shannon Hermes was the receptionist and office manager for YouTube. In addition to cash compensation, she received stock. After Google bought YouTube, her stock was worth a cool $1.3 million. She could have easily landed a job at Boresville, Inc., but she decided to work for a high-tech company, and it paid off handsomely. She's not alone. In fact, there were many others with "regular" positions at YouTube who did even better. YouTube's spokeswoman got $4.9 million of Google stock, their interface designer got $8.9 million of stock, and the community advocate got $1.63 million (I don't know what a community advocate is, but sign me up!).

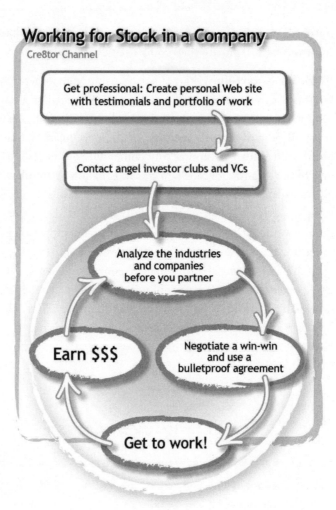

Working for Stock in a Company
Cre8tor Channel

Get professional: Create personal Web site with testimonials and portfolio of work

Contact angel investor clubs and VCs

Analyze the industries and companies before you partner

Negotiate a win-win and use a bulletproof agreement

Get to work!

Earn $$$

RESOURCES

ANGEL INVESTORS AND VENTURE CAPITALISTS

- Angel Capital Association (angelcapitalassociation.org)—Lists a ton of angel clubs across the United States.

- ActiveCapital (activecapital.org)—A government site that is run by the SBA.

- National Venture Capital Association (nvca.org)—A 35-plus-year-old trade organization for the venture capital industry.

CONNECTING TO START-UPS

- PartnerUp (partnerup.com)—A free Web site that lets you post a profile of your services or experience and who you are looking to work with. A great Web site if you are looking to become an advisory board member or if you want to contribute your services in exchange for stock.

- Go BIG Network (gobignetwork.com)—An online marketplace that connects start-ups with investors, advisors, and service providers.

ADVANCING OR JUMPING CAREERS

Advancing or Jumping Careers Channel Toolbar	
Start-up Time	🕐 🕐 🕐 🕐 🕐
Ongoing Time	🕐 🕐 🕐 🕐 🕐
Start-up Costs	$ $ $ $ $
Income Potential	$ $ $ $ $
Help Needed	♦ ♦ ♦ ♦ ♦

Maybe this Cre8tor thing isn't for you. Maybe you aren't entrepre-neurial or don't want to invent anything. That's fine. You can still use the other 8 hours to make more money. This Channel is about invest-ing time and money in yourself instead of in an idea/product. Whether you're happy with your career and want to move up or just can't stand your job, you can use this Channel to gain credibility, increase visibil-ity, improve skills, qualify for a new position or career, attract more clients, and get a bigger paycheck.

Want to be in the top 1 percent in your field? Don't do what the other 99 percent do, which is clock out at the end of their workday. The top 1 percent do things a little differently. They may stop work-ing, but they don't stop learning, networking, and building at the end of their "shift."

RULES

1. **Improve your skills.** The single best way to qualify for a new ca-reer or to get a raise is to boost your skills. Get that degree, desig-nation, or certification—if you sweet-talk your boss or HR person, your employer might even pay for this. Focus on a skill and dominate it. Become an expert in your field. Take night classes or sign up for distance learning. The underlying theme of this book is improving and getting better one day at a time. Use part of your other 8 hours to boost your skills so you are more valuable at your company or to help you qualify for a new career.

2. **Network.** Who you know has a major impact on your financial success. Invest part of the other 8 hours in meeting new people. Join a club or start one. Attend dinner meetings. Mix and mingle with the leaders in your industry. Spend at least a few hours every week meeting new people and going deeper with those you al-ready know. The secret to networking? Be a connector. Don't focus on what they can do for you, focus on how you can help them. Introduce them to your network and make connections. Use face-to-face networking with Web-based social networking for maximum impact.

ANOTHER 8-HOUR SUCCESS

How would you like to transform your business, shake up an entire industry, grow in influence, and get new clients just by creating a one-page PDF? That's exactly what Cre8tor Todd Defren did during his other 8 hours. "It elevated our agency and became quite controversial," he said. So, what's so important about that "one page with some colorful boxes," as he calls it?

Todd created the Social Media News Release—an updated, more usable press release—and it took the public relations world by storm. Some claimed it was genius, and others tried to dismiss it as nonsense. But at the end of the day, it catapulted his name and his company, SHIFT Communications (shiftcomm.com), into the spotlight. "We've always been a great company with great clients, but this definitely put us on the social media marketing map," said Todd.

With clients such as Virgin Mobile and Rhapsody, a wife, and two teenagers, how did he find the time? Get this. He spends two hours every morning, from 6:00 AM to 8:00 AM, in front of a fire, sipping coffee, thinking, and talking to his wife. He looks forward to this ritual. When I talked to him about it, it sounded less like a luxury and more like a necessity. "I can't imagine doing it a different way," he said. And when he's out of town, "It feels like something is missing."

So after a couple of weeks discussing the Social Media Release idea with his wife, she finally told him to stop talking and just do it. Todd is a real Cre8tor—he uses his other 8 hours to create value for his business and to nurture important relationships.

3. **Increase credibility/visibility.** If you want more responsibility at your company, a raise, or a promotion, you need credibility and visibility. Doing good work is not good enough. There's too much competition. Because of outsourcing and downsizing, you need to stand out from the crowd. Here are several ways to do just that.

TIPS

- **Articles, e-books, and blogs, oh my!** Want to increase your credibility to get a promotion or help close more clients? Want more visibility to get the attention of your boss's boss or to attract more clients? Take advantage of the fact that most of the people in your field are not actively marketing themselves. One of the best ways to get instant credibility and visibility is to write something—an article, a blog, or an e-book. When you've authored something, suddenly you've separated yourself from everyone else. Writers are authority figures. If you can write something unique or controversial, you will gain followers. Once you have followers, you can become a leader. Become the source that prospective clients learn from and that your peers look to for answers. Before you start banging away on the keyboard, check with your company to make sure you know any rules they have regarding employee writing.

- **Use PR.** With the right press, you can become a celebrity in your industry and get clients to call you. All it takes is a little time and a strategy. You can write a press release or, even better, an e-book, and then write a press release promoting your e-book. Contact local reporters and pitch them on new developments in your industry. Give them ideas for stories. Take them out to lunch. Get to know what they want. Respond to media inquiries in your field by signing up at Help a Reporter Out (helpareporter.com).

- **Negotiation training.** It's not what you deserve, it's what you negotiate. A single course in negotiation can save you hundreds of thousands of dollars over your life, and can help you get raises and move up the corporate ladder. Use a couple of your other 8 hours to learn to negotiate. You won't be disappointed.

- **Read.** For $15, you can have an expert teach you anything. Books are the single greatest source of knowledge and are a Cre8tor's best friend. You can learn anything in a few hours by reading a book. Take advantage of the knowledge and experience of others. Read. Learn. Grow. Advance.

- **Public speaking training.** Because most people would rather die a painful death than give a speech, that is an opportunity for you to take advantage of their fear. Like writing, those who give speeches are seen as leaders and experts. Public speaking gives you instant credibility and visibility, but you have to have the guts to get up there and do it. The best way to conquer that fear is to learn a few techniques and to practice. And, as mentioned earlier, the best way to do that is to join a local Toastmasters Club (toastmasters.org). Most of them meet once a week or twice a month for a few hours. You'll learn the "how" of public speaking and you'll get to practice in a supportive environment.

- **Create a personal Web site.** I don't care how pimped out your LinkedIn page is, you need your own Web site, where you can post your bio, add press clippings, and share your podcasts, articles, e-books, and blog entries. Regardless of how many times you change jobs, your Web site will always be yours. It doesn't have to be fancy, but it has to be yours. That means getting a personalized Web site address and a hosting account. This might set you back $5 a month, but it's worth it.

- **Write better.** Many people can't write very good enuf. Want to stand out? Write a sentence somebody can actually understand. Learn or relearn the basics. Trust me, you'll stand out.

- **Learn tomorrow's technology today.** If you really want to make a name for yourself, start learning tomorrow's technology today. You'll be one of the first to embrace it, and you will be positioned

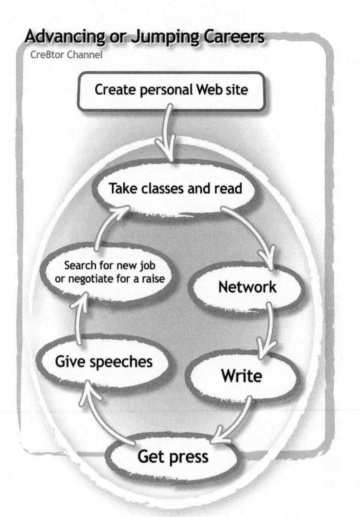

Advancing or Jumping Careers
Cre8tor Channel

Create personal Web site

Take classes and read

Search for new job or negotiate for a raise

Network

Give speeches

Write

Get press

to take a leadership role. The good thing is that you don't have to be ten steps ahead of everybody else, just one or two. In order to know and capitalize on tomorrow's technology, you need to identify what it's going to be. This is where you can tap into the early movers. The best source of cutting-edge information is written by bloggers in your field. Find out who they are and read everything they write. You can also read industry publications and talk to the industry's leaders for ideas.

RESOURCES

EDUCATION

- Local community college or university—Usually the best and cheapest way to increase existing skills or learn new ones. Many also offer online courses to make scheduling them during your other 8 hours easier.

NETWORKING

- Facebook (facebook.com), LinkedIn (linkedin.com), Twitter (twitter.com), and others—Social networking Web sites can increase your exposure and can be used as a tool to meet new people.

BLOGGING

- WordPress (wordpress.com)—Free blogging application. You can be up and running in about three minutes.

SPEAKING

- Toastmasters (toastmasters.org)—Find a group in your neighborhood and conquer your fear of public speaking.

FREELANCING

Freelancing Channel Toolbar	
Start-up Time	🕐 🕐 🕐 🕐 🕐
Ongoing Time	🕐 🕐 🕐 🕐 🕐
Start-up Costs	$ $ $ $ $
Income Potential	$ $ $ $ $
Help Needed	♟ ♟ ♟ ♟ ♟

A freelancer sells her services to companies without a long-term contract, sometimes getting paid by the hour or by the project. Freelancing can be an easy way to earn a few extra bucks to pay off debt or to save. It's a low-leverage venture, but it is easy to initiate and costs nothing to start. You could probably start earning money as a freelancer in about a day if you have the right skills. If you're not looking to jump to a new financial level and are content making a few extra hundred or thousand a month, free-lancing might be right for you, but you need to follow the rules.

RULES

1. **Specialized skills.** The best freelance jobs are those that require specialized skills. Here are just a few:

   a. Technology—Web programmer, application developer, Web master

   b. Design—Web design, logo design, brand management, user interface

   c. Sales and Marketing—advertising copy, public relations, e-mail marketing

   d. Finance—bookkeeping, accounting, bill paying

   e. Writing—editing, ghostwriting, article/Web writing, business plan writing

   f. Engineering—3D modeling, architecture, Autodesk

   g. Administrative—data entry, Internet research, virtual assistant

   h. Many others . . .

2. **Must be distance friendly.** Unless you have a lot of local companies vying for your services, stick to projects that you can work on remotely (that is, from home). It will save you gas and travel time and will allow you to work on your freelance projects when it is convenient for you.

3. **Need for good agreement.** Anytime you work for someone, make sure you nail the terms of the relationship with a good agreement.

Several of the freelance Web sites (see Resources section below) provide templates.

4. **Protect yourself (escrow).** An agreement will only take you so far. Use common sense. Don't work on a project for three months without getting paid. Before you send over your work (a logo, for example), use an escrow account. Many of the freelance sites offer these, so use them!

5. **Sell yourself.** It's always important to sell yourself, but when a company 3,000 miles away is thinking about hiring you sight unseen, you need to have a strong and professional appearance. That means a good Web site, maybe an e-brochure, and definitely testimonials or references. If you really want to get fancy, you can get an 800 number and professional phone service for a few bucks a month.

6. **Negotiate hard.** The beauty of freelancing is that your next job is only a mouse-click away. That means you can negotiate pretty hard. Make sure you are getting enough for it to make sense. If you are hot stuff but they are unsure, consider a lower initial fee with the expectation that it will increase once they see your genius.

7. **Upgrade continuously.** Great workers can toil for years at the same firm if their efforts aren't recognized or rewarded, but when you're a freelancer, your work speaks for itself. Regardless of your sex, race, age, or even experience, if you do exceptional work, you will be highly desired and you can charge commensurately. Freelancing is the ultimate meritocracy. When you can find a new job in hours, you don't have to be boxed into a role or job description. Good freelancers continuously upgrade themselves. They take on bigger projects. They increase their fees. They leverage their time more on each project.

TIPS

- **Be exceptional.** You can make decent money by doing decent work, but if you want to make exceptional money, you must be exceptional. What would it take for you to be one of the best? More training? Classes? Use the other 8 hours to do what it takes to stand out from the pack.

- **Build a portfolio.** What if you're just starting out and don't yet have a portfolio or references? In the traditional work world, this would be a deal killer, but in Freelanceville, this is a hurdle you can jump over pretty quickly. Your primary goal at this stage should be to build your portfolio, and your secondary goal should be to make money. That means you underbid on jobs you know are showcases for your talent and/or use Craigslist.com to get gigs. Sure, somebody's going to get a great deal, and you won't make much money, but you need to build your portfolio. Once you have a few examples of your work, then you can start charging what you're worth.

- **Review all online resources.** There are many Web sites (see Resources below) that help freelancers get gigs. Some are specialized, while others are more general. They each have a personality—some are chop shops where subpar freelancers do whatever it takes to get the job done, while others are more professional. Check them all out to see where you fit best. Look at the job requests posted in your field. What do the clients want? How much do they want to pay? Who won the project? How much did he bid? If possible, take a look at the finished work. Can you compete? Choose a site that works for you *after* you look at all of them.

    Once you review all of the freelance Web sites, choose one. Don't play the shotgun approach. You want to build a reputation and a presence. The Web sites allow prospective buyers to review your history and the feedback other buyers have left for you. Buyers want to see a good track record and positive feedback. If you spread your jobs around across a dozen sites, a buyer on each site won't see much of a track record. Unless you're doing so much business that you can build a reputation on more than one Web site, just focus on one.

- **Use Google AdWords.** Once again, this can be an awesome way to get targeted and qualified people to your site without its costing you much.

- **Create compelling profiles.** All of the freelance Web sites allow you to write about your services and your company. This is your chance to stand out. Don't just list all of the services you provide. Everyone does this. Get personal. Share something about yourself. Tell a story. Be funny. Put yourself in the shoes of a prospective buyer. What would make you feel comfortable? Make an oath on your profile. Hell, if airlines have a passenger bill of rights, you certainly can have a client bill of rights. Be unexpected.

    Also, if you do enough business and specialize in a few areas, create different profiles for the work you do. When I look for service providers, I always look for the specialists, not the ones that claim to do everything for everybody. If I need a logo, I want someone who specializes in logos. If I need an e-commerce Web site, I want someone who knows e-commerce inside and out. If you have a few areas of expertise, create different profiles, with each highlighting one service.

- **Be selective.** Again, the shotgun approach doesn't work. Rather than bid on everything, bid on just those projects that are right for you. I've posted many projects over the years, and about 90 percent of the bids I receive are generic "we can help you with anything you need, blah blah blah." I immediately delete these and focus on the bids where the providers have actually read my project description and have written a customized response.

- **Ask for good feedback.** You either have no reputation, a bad reputation, or a good reputation. The first two are fatal to your freelance business. In order to build a good reputation, you need to get others to leave you positive feedback after you complete a project for them. Ask them to leave feedback on the freelance

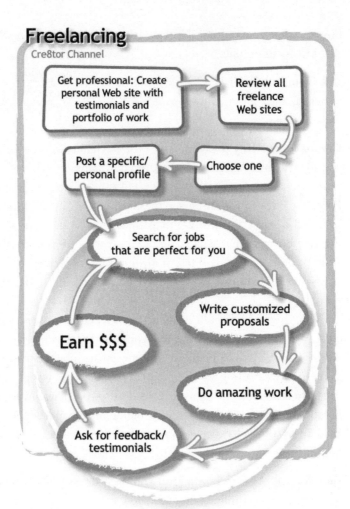

Web site you use and to e-mail you a testimonial immediately after the project is complete, when everyone is feeling good and still in communication.

- **Create your own Web site.** Many freelancers use the freelance Web sites exclusively, but I don't recommend this. Even if you get all of your business from these sites, you want to have your own Web site. When I am reviewing a service provider I have found on one of the freelance Web sites, I always check to see if they have their own site. I want to see that they are serious enough about their work and their business to put up their own site. And here's where the client testimonials come into play. You should have a link from your home page to your testimonial page. I can't tell you how important testimonials are for prospective buyers. We don't know you. Alleviate some of our concerns and fears by showing us others who have trusted you and were happy with your work.

- **Boost feedback with outside projects.** Chances are you'll get projects from friends or referrals outside of the freelance Web site. If you are still building your online reputation, ask the buyers to use the Web site. Not only will you build your reputation quicker, but you can use the site's escrow service. If your friends are anything like my friends, you'll be happy you did . . .

RESOURCES

FREELANCE WEB SITES

- Elance (elance.com)—This is the most popular of the bunch. It covers all jobs—everything from Web design to trademark services to proofreading. It has a large China/India freelance base, so buyers tend to have a low-cost expectation. It's definitely worth checking out, though.

- Guru (guru.com)—They claim to be the "world's largest online service marketplace." Like elance.com, they also cover all industries and offer many of the same services, such as escrow and filing of tax forms.

- oDesk (odesk.com)—Another service similar to the others that also covers many industries.

JOB SITES

- monster (monster.com)—The biggest job site. If you don't know it already, check it out.

- Dice (dice.com)—Job site for techies.

MISCELLANEOUS

- Freelancers Union (freelancersunion.org)—A nonprofit that provides benefits and services to freelancers.

- FreshBooks (freshbooks.com)—An online solution to track your time and invoice clients.

TURNING HOBBIES INTO INCOME

Turning Hobbies into Income Channel Toolbar	
Start-up Time	🕐🕐🕐🕐🕐
Ongoing Time	🕐🕐🕐🕐🕐
Start-up Costs	$ $ $ $ $
Income Potential	$ $ $ $ $
Help Needed	👤👤👤👤👤

This Cre8tor Channel is a little different from the others. The other nine focus on specific things you can do to make more money, but this Channel is more general. The goal here is to make a few extra bucks doing something you enjoy and are passionate about. You won't make enough to buy a château, but you might be able to make your monthly car payment or pay off some lingering debt by doing something you love.

RULES

1. **Inventory your interests.** Write down all of your hobbies, passions, and interests. This should be a fun exercise, but I've found that the biggest hurdle is that people don't think they have any interests. You might not have any hobbies, and that's fine, but you surely enjoy doing certain things. Come on. What do you like? Reading? Fine, write it down. Clubbing, shopping, talking on a CB? Write down everything and anything that gets your blood flowing, from animals and reducing your carbon footprint to playing poker and watching football to working with your hands and dancing. Everyone enjoys doing something.

2. **Narrow them down.** For each interest above, strip away as much as you can until you've identified one or two core reasons that explain why you enjoy each of your interests. You like to watch TV? What do you like to watch? Sports? Mostly football? Get specific.

3. **Focus.** Choose the interest you'd spend more time on if you won the lottery and never had to work another day in your life.

4. **Jump-start.** Spend ten minutes every morning brainstorming a product or a service you can provide others who are just as passionate about that interest as you are. Use the other Cre8tor Channels as a jumping-off point by matching your interest to each of the Channels. For example, if you love to garden, here's how you

can start thinking about how to make money doing what you love:

a. Blogging—You could quickly and easily start blogging about gardening and display garden-related ads to your highly focused group of readers.

b. Inventing—A wheelbarrow full of opportunities here. Having a hobby that you are passionate about makes you the ideal person to discover and create a new product. Remember, focus on the problems and frustrations you encounter and then create solutions.

c. Starting your own company—You could start a company that provides a service or sells products related to gardening.

d. Reselling, affiliating, licensing—Within minutes you could affiliate with several garden e-books or products and earn money every time one of your Web site, newsletter, or blog visitors clicks through and buys something.

e. Taking advantage of fads—No opportunities here.

f. Working for stock in a company—No opportunities here.

g. Advancing or jumping careers—No opportunities here.

h. Freelancing—Tons of opportunities for you to make money working for someone else. Even though it's not really "freelancing" per se, you could get a part-time job at a nursery or landscaper, or find one of a hundred other gardening-related jobs.

Do you see what we've done here? Take something you love to do and use the other Cre8tor Channels to get your mind thinking about how to make money from your interest.

Take another example—a friend of mine is into astronomy and astrology. When he narrowed down what he enjoys the most, he discovered he loves sharing his knowledge of astronomy with others. Once armed with this knowledge, it didn't take him long to create both products and services to capitalize on his passion. He does charts for people, has organized educational tours to the desert to view the stars, and is starting a blog and newsletter service. He makes pretty good money doing this part time and absolutely loves it.

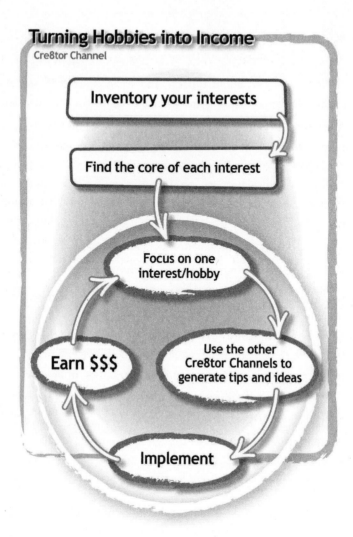

Turning Hobbies into Income

Cre8tor Channel

- Inventory your interests
- Find the core of each interest
- Focus on one interest/hobby
- Use the other Cre8tor Channels to generate tips and ideas
- Implement
- Earn $$$

TIPS

- **Keep it fun.** This is your hobby. Don't turn it into a job you hate. Keep it fun by focusing on what you enjoy and be proactive if your passion starts to feel more like a chore. If you find that your passion is feeling more and more like work and less like a hobby, cut the cord. You don't want to ruin something you enjoy by trying to make a few bucks from it.

- **Try several strategies.** Don't get bogged down on one strategy (blogging or affiliate marketing) if you don't enjoy it or if it's not profitable. Try several approaches until you find one or more that work best.

- **Try several hobbies.** Not all hobbies can make money. Start with one and then move on down your list until you get to one that works for you.

And there you have it. Ten Cre8tor Channels. It's a long list of opportunities, but I've only scratched the surface. There are hundreds of other Cre8tor Channels you can explore, including developing iPhone or Web applications, multilevel marketing, etc. Your homework assignment is to pick one that you want to pursue and do some more research into it. Don't be overwhelmed by all of the possibilities—focus on just one to start.

Remember, you want to focus on your strengths. The things we are usually most jazzed about are those that give us an edge. Once you have some success, you can take on two or three of these at the same time, but when you're getting started, don't take on too much. I'd rather you rock at one than suck at six. Remember, you may swing and miss a few times before you get a hit. Don't get discouraged, but do get started.

GET A LIFE

The previous section focused on how to make more money, but there's more to life than money. We want more money, but we also want a life. Unfortunately, these dual goals often turn into *dueling* goals, where the choice becomes living a rich life *or* being rich.

We want to make more money, but we also want to travel to Tuscany and watch the leaves turn in Vermont. We want to run a 5K and lose twenty pounds. We want to take our spouse on a date and play with our kids at a park. We want to speak French and cross-stitch a picture. We want to master the waltz and perfect squash-stuffed dumplings. We want to plant flowers and grow tomatoes. We want to read *The Grapes of Wrath* and play poker. And yes, we also want to just sit and relax.

The good news is that you can get rich *and* live a rich life, but you need to do something different with the other 8 hours. Too many of us feel stuck in a never-ending cycle. We've plugged into a routine that neither inspires nor enriches us. We get up, go to work, fight traffic on the way home, squeeze in a couple of hours of TV, go to bed, and do it all over again the next day. We've hit the "pause" button on our health, our relationships, and our dreams, thinking we'll get to them someday.

For many, that someday never comes. Years and even decades slip by. We survive and exist, but we don't thrive or truly live. For that someday to become today, you need to get clear on what "get a life" means to you, and you need to invest the other 8 hours in activities that enrich you and bring you closer to your ideal.

This section will show you the core principles for living a rich life. You will learn:

- How to identify your gaps—those areas in your life where you seek positive change.

- How to create IMPACT goals.

- How to identify potential problems and setbacks before they occur.

- How to use the other 8 hours to obtain your ideal life.

Enjoy a rewarding and fulfilling life by using your other 8 hours. This section will show you how.

CHAPTER NINE

COULD'VE, SHOULD'VE, WOULD'VE

What It Takes to Really Live

"I wasted the last eight years of my life," said the voice on the other end of the line. More shocking than that statement was the deep sorrow behind it. I was shocked. My friend is always happy, upbeat, and full of energy. I could not remember the last time I heard her cry. But on this day, she couldn't help herself. During the silence, as I tried to figure out what I should say to her, she blurted it out again, "I have wasted the last eight years of my life. I'm never going to get that time back."

I could tell that I had my work cut out for me, but I pressed on. "What are you talking about? You haven't wasted the last eight years . . ."

It turns out, she had. She was stuck at a job that was not fulfilling or challenging. Worse yet, she complained about it year after year after year and never looked for something different. She talked about traveling but never went anywhere. She wanted to connect with her friends more deeply but instead settled for surface-level relationships. She didn't grow or advance in any area of her life. Just so you don't think I'm a heartless jerk, these were *her* revelations, not mine.

I tried to focus on the positive, but I ultimately admitted she was right. She had wasted the last eight years of her life because she had failed to grasp the importance of the other 8 hours and had squandered them. When it was time to reap the harvest, there was nothing there.

Have you had a similar experience? Do you look back over the last month, year, or even decade and ask yourself what the hell happened? As I mentioned in the introduction, I've talked to hundreds of people, and this feeling of emptiness is prevalent.

If birthdays or New Year's celebrations are unhappy reminders of how little you have or have accomplished with your life, and if you're ready to take an honest look at yourself and your life, now's the time. It might not be pretty and it might not feel good, but I promise you that it's better than losing another decade to regret.

MONEY AND HAPPINESS

Even though the last few chapters have been about how to use the other 8 hours to get rich, getting a life has very little to do with making a lot of money and a lot to do with making enough money. Why? You need money to be happy.

But everyone says money can't buy happiness. For all the people who are living in poverty, who are wondering how they're going to pay rent this month, who are worried there isn't going to be enough food for dinner, who lie to their kids when they tell them the hole in their shoe is small and that nobody will notice, who can't afford medical insurance for their children, or who can't sleep because they are worried about losing their job, I say think again. If you are struggling to survive, you don't want to hear about how money can't buy happiness. It can buy food, pay the rent, and give you a little peace of mind.

When we are in survival mode, our dreams and goals go out the window. When you're scrambling to pay the bills each month, you probably aren't thinking about your higher purpose. Instead, you are swimming against the current and going nowhere. Picture a man floating in the water. You probably see his head bobbing along between the waves. He seems to be enjoying a nice swim. What you can't see are his arms and legs pumping under the water as he works to stay afloat.

When all of your energy is focused on surviving, you won't have the time, energy, or ability to have a rich or meaningful life. So if you're in debt or struggling financially, focus first on making some extra money. Get off the financial ledge. If you have no money concerns but are not satisfied with your life, skip the "getting rich" advice and focus the other 8 hours on getting a life. It's up to you how you invest the other 8 hours, but just know that you can "get rich" and "get a life" at the

ANOTHER 8-HOUR SUCCESS

Charla Muller is a social butterfly. She was always looking for a good time and she had the overscheduled life to prove it. In addition to working full time and raising two young children, she managed to squeeze in book club, social gatherings, parties, Bible study, and other commitments. All that changed during a Bible study group. After reading Galatians she thought about how she was spending her time. She admitted she was stressed and overwhelmed and that she wasn't spending time on what she cared the most about—her family.

Her husband's fortieth birthday was approaching, and she wanted to do something "crazy and over the top." She told me she wanted to give him something nobody else could. The gift? Sex. Not just birthday sex. But sex every day for a year.

Her husband was excited but incredulous. "How are you going to find time?" he asked. That's when Charla realized she'd have to completely reevaluate how she spent her time. She quickly learned that if she wanted to say yes at night, she'd have to say no more often during the day.

Through the "power of intention," she was able to focus her time and energy. She used the other 8 hours and now feels closer and more committed to her husband than ever before.

If that weren't enough, after the year was over, she decided to write a book during the other 8 hours about her experience called *365 Nights: A Memoir of Intimacy*. She's been on *Today*, *The View*, and *Oprah*. Sex, a deeper relationship with a spouse, a successful book, and national exposure. Is there anything Charla can't do with her other 8 hours?

same time. They are not mutually exclusive. It's not money vs. mean-ing. You can have both.

WHAT DOES IT MEAN TO "GET A LIFE"?

Getting a life is hard to define. It's kind of like determining if some-thing is obscene . . . you just know it when you see it (especially when it is wrapped in brown paper and the postman smirks when he hands it to you). In the end, you know you have a life when you are happy and fulfilled. The "how" of happiness is one of the most sought-after ques-tions. Nearly everyone, from the great philosophers to modern-day psychologists, has attempted to solve the puzzle of happiness.

What we know for sure is that nobody knows the answer. There is no formula for lifelong contentment and bliss. These issues have been debated by people a lot smarter than me. I've probably missed a great deal of what it takes to "get a life," but the following list will give you a solid foundation. It's about having more of some things and less of oth-ers. In the next chapter, we'll take your pulse—and discover the spe-cific things you need to accomplish and do to live a richer life.

A LITTLE LESS . . .

- **Regret.** There's a reason regret is at the top of this list. Regret has to be the single greatest buzz kill. What's worse than the plaguing thought of "Why did I?" There's only one thing worse, and it's "Why *didn't* I?" Regret sucks, but it's worse to regret not having done something than having done something you wish you didn't. The reason for this is because when you don't do some-thing, you never know what would have happened. You kill your-self with the "what if" game.

  In the real world, each of us regrets all kinds of things. No one is immune. Some things are small and trivial, while others may haunt you on your deathbed. There are a couple of strategies for minimizing and avoiding regret. The first is to get over the regret you are carrying. There's nothing you can do about it now. Every day you lug this mental weight around with you is another day you can't fully live or see the world as new. You must try to wipe the slate clean because, in doing so, you will gain a fresh view of the world. If you are experiencing significant regret, the best use of your other 8 hours may be to see a therapist. Now, I'm not usually quick to call in the professionals, but when it comes to regret, I've seen how it can eat at a person. I've seen how it can cloud every interaction and how it can debilitate. There's no way to fully "get a life" if you are beating yourself up over what you didn't do or what you did.

The second strategy for overcoming future regret is to prevent it from happening. Don't give yourself the chance to regret not taking action. Unless you're risking physical injury or bankruptcy, or violating some kind of ethical or moral code, the solution is to just do it. Even if it fails or you look like a complete moron, you'll probably feel better that you did it. You don't want to regret not having done it.

One trick to help you "just do it" more often is to start small. The beautiful thing about regret is that in the moment as you are deciding, you know you are going to feel regret if you don't do it. It's the damnedest thing. You're faced with a cognitive speed bump. In the split second before you say no, you can already feel the regret building. But it's this flash of the future that is our gift. We can use that to our advantage by taking small steps. Put yourself in safe situations where you are faced with a choice, feel the future regret forming, and then just do it. Again, you're taking small steps here at first. You're building your regret muscle until it is stronger, and it's going to take some work. It probably hasn't been exercised for a long time.

- **Fear.** If you're constantly worried and living in fear, you can't fully appreciate life. The more armor you wear, the less you will feel both pain and pleasure. In college, I dated a girl who suffered from minor depression (because she was dating me?). In an effort to feel better, she started taking an antidepressant. Almost immediately, the drug began "working." She wasn't feeling as low as she used to, but she said the things she used to enjoy didn't give her the same high, either. She stopped feeling the lows and the highs. She stopped feeling. Fear can have the same impact on our lives. It can reduce the frequency and severity of the lows, but it can also mute the highs. Fear can paralyze or it can rejuvenate. Too much fear or the wrong kind of fear is not healthy, but, as you'll see later in this chapter, some fear is good.

- **Laziness.** I don't believe people are lazy, I just think they are uninspired. I've seen people barely able to get out of bed because they hated their job look forward to Monday mornings once they found their calling. I've seen people who didn't want to get off the couch become full of life and ambition once they found their inspiration. Some people have the ambition bug. For whatever reason, they can't help but ooze positivity and action. These folks are inspired opening a bag of potato chips. For everyone else, it's a matter of finding your passion and your inspiration. This can take time and a whole lot of trial and error, but once you find it, look out!

- **LifeLeeches.** They'll suck your time and your life from you. Don't waste time doing things that don't enrich your life. This means identifying those things you absolutely hate doing and, as much as possible, not doing them. I despise fix-it projects. No matter how positive I pretend to be about them or how many affirmations I recite, I will immediately get in a horrible mood if I am forced into a fix-it project. Christmas has always been my favorite time of year, and now that I have a young daughter, it's even more fun. But I cannot stand putting her toys together on Christmas Eve. Normally I'm a pretty confident guy, but I turn into a jerk the minute I pull out my toolbox and try to assemble her toys. I butchered a little wagon last year. I put some washer thing on wrong and it took me about an hour and a half to cut, rip, and pry it off. In fact, just writing about fixing stuff makes me angry. You might be Ms. Fix It, but I'm sure you have your own private hell projects or activities. Whatever they are, the less you do them, the more satisfied you'll be.

A LITTLE MORE . . .

- **Growth.** Getting a life is about growing as a person. It's about being a better, fuller, and richer person today than you were yesterday. If you're stagnant, you are not fully living. You must be growing and advancing as a person.

- **Experiences.** Our lives are a collection of experiences. It's very easy to run through the motions day after day, but this is like recording and rerecording the same show over and over and over again. If you hired a film crew to record your life, how many tapes would they need? If you're doing the same thing over and over and over, they might need only a handful of tapes. Getting a life is about introducing new experiences. Your goal should be to use as many tapes as possible that reveal you living and experiencing new things. This is getting a life!

- **Change.** The worst compliment you could ever receive is "You haven't changed a bit!" If you're the same person you were last year or last decade, there's something wrong. I'm not saying you need to change your personality as often or dramatically as Sybil, but if we grow and experience, we cannot help but change. We might not change colors, but certainly we'll change shades. Our friends, experiences, challenges, setbacks, interactions, accomplishments all leave their mark on us—sometimes subtly and sometimes overtly. We've all experienced seeing someone after years and being shocked at just how much they haven't changed. They have the same vocabulary, interests, hobbies, dislikes, and taste in music and cars. They may even have the same style of clothes, haircut, and job. The world has changed around them while they continued living in a bubble that shielded them from development and experience, which ultimately prevented them from experiencing change and living.

- **Forward looking.** A popular concept nowadays is "living in the moment." I get this. If you're always living in the past or the future, you can't appreciate the reality of today. But if you are only living in the present, you cannot shape your future, you can only respond to it. If you do not look to the future, make plans, and create goals, you won't know what needs to be done in the present in order to create that future. To get a life means to be at peace with the past and the present but to radically and aggressively attempt to shape the future. The best way to avoid the glassy eyes of not living in the moment and the anxiety of always reacting to what comes at you is to schedule time where you give yourself permission and the gift of looking to the future.

- **Mistakes.** Yup. In fact, you should make a lot more mistakes! If you are not screwing up on a fairly regular basis, it means you are not doing enough. As we get older, wiser, more sophisticated, and more professional, we believe we shouldn't make as many mistakes. It would be embarrassing, right? So we stay in our safe little box and avoid the mess of making mistakes. The problem is that life is outside of that box. Growth and advancement are outside of that box, too. It's not about making the *same* mistakes over and over—that's not growth or getting a life, that's just dumb. It's about making new mistakes. Make them at home. Make them at the office. If we are messing up, it means we are doing something new and different, and that, my friends, is getting a life. You have to risk more in order to screw up more. I'm focusing on mistakes because if you risk enough and blow it enough, success will come. Success is a natural by-product of looking like a complete dummy over and over again.

- **Fear.** Remember when I said there is bad fear and good fear? Bad fear causes paralysis, but good fear can get you off your ass. Good fear can help you push through barriers and get more from yourself than you ever thought possible. Few people change because they want to or need to, but most will change when they must. Fear can be the motivation we need to take action. Good fear can be the spark that ignites your life. Good fear is the result of a challenge that we are confident we can handle, and bad fear is the result of a challenge we think we can't handle. Bad fear pervades our lives, and it can be hard to distinguish between the two, which is why it's important to start slowly. Take on small challenges. Accept a tiny dose of fear, and then a little more, and a little more.

Every time you accept and survive a challenge, you become stronger and more willing to take risks.

- **Hobbies.** When I was younger, I was called "phase boy," and now I'm called "phase guy" because I try a lot of different hobbies. Some I stick with, and some I don't. My wife thinks I'm nuts and uses the "phase guy" label as a dig, but I look at it differently. By trying a bunch of things, I know what I like and what I don't. Life is too short to continue doing something you don't enjoy, and life is too short to be ignorant about what you enjoy. Like the Cre8tor starting a new venture, it's okay to swing and miss and miss and miss.

- **Gratitude.** A sure-fire way to unhappiness, frustration, and bitterness is to take for granted what you have and what you've accomplished. It doesn't matter if you're broke, in a dead-end job, morbidly obese, alone, or depressed. There are things in your life you have the right to feel grateful for. If you're waiting for life to be perfect before you are grateful, you'll be missing out on a wonderful gift. Identifying and expressing gratitude can sometimes be difficult, especially if you don't think you have much to be grateful for. But if you want to get a life, gratitude has to be a big part of your persona and your day.

- **Purpose.** A meaningful life is what *The Other 8 Hours* is all about. Since most people don't get a lot of meaning from sleep or work, our last hope is to find meaning during the other 8 hours. If we can fill some of this time with identifying and reaching our purpose, our lives will be much more satisfying and full. But it is up to you to discover your purpose. That's where things get tricky. If you're too busy "living," it's hard to know what your purpose is, but if your goal is to get a life, that life must be filled with meaning and purpose.

- **Direction.** The most fulfilled people are those who can sleep soundly with what they've accomplished but are excited for the morning to come so they can continue their journey. Direction provides focus and inspiration and is the antidote to day-to-day monotony. In the real world, you achieve direction through

ANOTHER 8-HOUR SUCCESS

When you're faced with an unthinkable tragedy, it's easy to "check out" and become paralyzed with grief. But sometimes, in that deepest and darkest hour, someone makes the decision to turn darkness into light.

On February 10, 2005, Maddux Haggard died. He was six days old. His parents hired a professional photographer to take pictures of his last minutes and of them cradling him after he passed away. Looking back, his mother, Cheryl, says, "My world stopped, but the world around me kept moving. I knew how we dealt with the loss would shape my older children's future." She felt so grateful to have spent the time she did with her son and to have such beautiful photos of him. "When I look at those images, I'm reminded of the beauty and blessings he brought."

Cheryl didn't want other parents who lose a child to miss the opportunity and the joy of having professional photographs. She and her photographer friend partnered to found Now I Lay Me Down to Sleep Foundation (nilmdts.org)—a nonprofit that provides free professional portraits to families of babies who are stillborn or who are at risk of dying as newborns.

"I got up earlier than the kids and went to bed later," recalls Cheryl. "I still had to be a mom and run the kids around, but I put all of my free time into this. I answered calls twenty-four/seven. We recruited photographers, designed a brochure, and did what we could to spread the word."

Her success? They have photographed thousands of babies and have grown their network of volunteer photographers to over 7,000 in more than 28 countries. But it sounds like she is just getting started. "I want NILMDTS to be in every single hospital."

creating compelling goals. Concrete goals are great for uncovering what you want and for providing feedback along the way, and positive feedback can fuel even more motivation and inspiration.

- **Connection.** One of the greatest predictors of happiness is the number and depth of relationships we have. We need interaction with and connection to friends and/or family. We don't need a lot of friends, but we need those relationships we do have to be deep. Nowadays it's easy to have superficial relationships. E-mail, voicemail, text messaging, social networking Web sites, and the like make it effortless to connect with a ton of people, but this technology doesn't make it any easier to deepen relationships. The subtleties of a face-to-face talk are lost in 140-character messages.

- **Contribution.** One of the greatest opening lines in a book can be found in Rick Warren's *Purpose Driven Life*. The first line is "It's not about you." Rich lives are full of contribution. Giving back is what separates a superficial and selfish "me" existence from a richer, deeper, and more profound "we" existence. It's so easy to get caught up in our own little world that we can quickly lose focus of what's going on in the real world. But when we lose perspective, we lose a huge piece of our happiness, purpose, feeling of connection, and sense of meaning.

- **Learning.** This doesn't mean you need to register for classes at your local community college (although that's a great and inexpensive way to learn); it means you should know more today than you knew yesterday. If the last time you really learned anything was back in college, you're missing a big part of what it means to get a life. Whether you learn through books, articles, hobbies, friends, or whatever, learning is key to a richer and fuller life.

- **Action.** Wouldn't it be great to just think about what you wanted and then get it? Oh, whoops, that book has already been written! Unfortunately for us mortals, getting a life means getting off the couch. It's about thinking *and* doing. Not one or the other, but both.

As you can see, each of these characteristics can be accomplished, whether you make $30,000 or $3 million a year. Getting a life has nothing to do with getting rich and everything to do with living a richer, fuller, and more inspired life.

IT'S HARDER THAN WE THINK . . .

I believe that there are three options for just about everything—getting better, getting worse, or staying the same. So, when it comes to getting a life, are you getting ahead, staying the same, or falling behind?

If it feels like you are slipping behind or fighting to keep your ground, I'm not surprised. We all want more from life, but there's a huge gap between wanting more and getting it. Everyone has the desire to get in shape, eat better, earn more money, have better relationships, and be more fulfilled, but few actually achieve any of these goals. That's because

OTHER 8 EXPERT

Gretchen Rubin is the author of *The Happiness Project* and the blog of the same name (happiness-project.com). Here's how she answered the question, What one thing should readers do with their other 8 hours that will have the greatest positive impact on their lives?

Create an atmosphere of growth in your life: learn a new skill (Photoshop, Chinese cooking); master a subject (wine, the Civil War); help something grow (a child, the neighborhood thrift shop); make something better (clean your garage, pay your credit card debt). Novelty and challenge boost happiness, as does the sense that we are taking action to improve ourselves and the world.

it's harder than we think. In fact, it's a whole lot harder because it goes against our nature.

Life, and all of the things in it, are moving forward, progressing, and advancing or falling behind, stagnating, and dying. I think within each of us there is a burning desire to grow, advance, and excel, but we're fighting nature. It might not be popular to admit this, but our natural response is to decay.

A positive attitude is critical. You need to feel good about yourself and your future. Negativity and pessimism can sap your energy and drive. A positive attitude is just the first step, though. And you must balance that positive attitude with effort. If you think life is easy and things should come easily to you, you won't put forth energy because you won't think you need to. On the other hand, if you know that the real "secret" to success and life is that it is a struggle—a continuous challenge just to survive—you'll jump up and take action, and you won't count on the universe, karma, or fairness to bail you out. It is your life and your responsibility.

The Buddhists believe in reincarnation. We die and come back—each time trying to have a more perfect life until we reach the ideal state of nirvana. I don't think we have to die in order to start over. Each day is another opportunity to get it right and to create a better, more perfect life.

Now that you have a general idea of what characteristics it takes to live a richer life, you need to determine the specific things you want to do, experience, and accomplish that will enrich your life. What do you want from your life? We explore the answer in the next chapter . . .

CHAPTER TEN

FIND YOUR PULSE

Uncover Your Passions and Your Ideal Life

Growing up, my stepfather's mission was to teach me how to use tools and how to fix cars. I've spent a good deal of time under the hood and underneath cars. I listened. I watched. I had a great teacher, who was always patient and thoughtful, but I just never got it.

In a last-ditch effort to learn, I accepted a job at a local tire service station. I was fifteen or sixteen and eager to learn and make some money. I showed up the first day, and the owner showed me the ropes and then pointed to a pile of tires that needed to be patched and rebalanced. The work wasn't that strenuous, and it wasn't all that complicated, but I struggled all day. At the end of my shift, I walked to my uncle's house a couple of miles away. I was covered from head to toe in grease and grime. My hands were black; a dark substance was lodged beneath every fingernail. My face was caked with who knows what (probably asbestos!). The same black mystery substance under my nails also coated the inside of my nose.

Walking to my uncle's house, it hit me—this was not me. This was not my life. I saw the future and this was not the path I wanted for myself. I decided right then and there that I wanted something different. I had been so focused on doing what I thought was the right and safe thing to do—getting a job and learning a trade—that I hadn't stopped to think about what I really wanted that job to be or what I was really good at. I wasn't good at fixing cars (I was actually shocked the wheels didn't fall off as customers drove away), and I didn't want to be. I wasn't sure what I wanted out of life, but I was certain it was not this.

Standing on a rundown street corner blanketed with dirt and

ANOTHER 8-HOUR SUCCESS

Sometimes the best opportunity to start a venture is when you have absolutely nothing to lose. You can roll the dice and take bigger risks without consequences. That's the situation Michael Khalili faced when he was seventeen. He dropped out of high school and was living with his parents. He had few expenses and even fewer responsibilities. His mother told him he needed to get some kind of education, so he enrolled in a computer class, which helped him get a full-time programming job.

Most kids would be content making pretty good money at such a young age, but not Michael. After just a few months working for somebody else, he realized that "nine to five wasn't for me." True to the Cre8tor Rule of "swing often," he had been working during the other 8 hours on several Internet projects. Several had potential, but one was gaining traction more than the others. "I knew a few of them could be successful, but there was one that *was* successful, so that's the one I jumped on."

He was commuting an hour to and from work by subway, until one day on the train he made a fateful decision. "I didn't want to climb the ladder. I knew I could get what I wanted on my own, so I quit that day." When I asked him if he was worried, he laughed. "In the worst case, I'd have to take my car back and get a job."

There are a lot of high-school dropouts who quit their jobs but don't go on to make millions (his Internet company, Bradford & Reed, did over $30 million in revenue before he sold it to MySpace's parent company). What makes Michael different? He cherished his ideas. "I had all these ideas in my head, and I had to get them out. I couldn't sit still." He tested several ventures before committing to one. He found a partner—his brother Andrew Warner—who complemented his skills.

Fortunately, you don't need to move in with your parents so you can take risks. Follow the Strike 4! approach to reduce risks and create your own safety net.

grease, my future flashed before my eyes, and it wasn't pretty. Even at a young age, my life was already laid out in front of me—the path of least resistance was leading me to a life with the least. In that instant, I knew I couldn't sit back and let life happen. I didn't know what I wanted, but I knew the longer I stayed on the current course the harder it would be to change direction. I ran to my uncle's, picked up the phone, called my boss, and quit.

Can you relate to the way I felt on that street corner? Are you on the path of least resistance? Does your future look a lot like your present? Has the day-to-day grind sucked the life out of you? Do you long for the day when you are excited to get out of bed? In the land of the living dead, how do you find your pulse? How do you find the spark that ignites your imagination and lights a fire under you?

After working with a whole lot of people, here's what I found. Desire isn't enough. How many times have you started a diet or exercise program and then promptly quit? Desire may get you off your butt, but it's not enough to keep you on your feet. Clearly defined goals are not enough, either. They focus your attention and provide the "what," but they don't show you "how."

The cardiac shock paddles that will jump-start your life are the other 8 hours. It doesn't matter if you want to lose weight, run a marathon, learn a new language, find a (better!) spouse, get closer to God, earn more money, or get a promotion. But guess what? All of this requires desire and effort. Nothing great is found at the end of the path of least resistance.

As I stood on the street corner, I had no idea what I wanted, but

I knew exactly what I didn't want. Maybe you're unsure what you want. You might have a feeling of discontent and a glimmer of hope for something better. That's okay. If you want to close your gaps and are willing to create a new path, you've come to the right place! The next two chapters cover a six-step process that will help you find your pulse and figure out how to use the other 8 hours to achieve what you want.

1. Embrace the gap
2. Create a mantra
3. Identify priorities
4. Create goals
5. Expect setbacks
6. Habitualize

This chapter will tackle the first five steps, and the next chapter will focus on how to Habitualize, which is a strategy for creating automatic positive habits and rituals.

1. EMBRACE THE GAP

The gap is the divide between where you are and where you want to be. Don't be afraid of the gap. We've all got them across many areas of our lives. Your ideal weight and what your scale shows is evidence of the gap. Your butchering of the Spanish language is evidence of the gap. The car you drive versus the car you want to drive is evidence of the gap. The emotional distance between you and your family is evidence of the gap.

Your gaps are yours and yours alone. They are unique. Don't run from them or be embarrassed by them. In fact, you need to embrace them. That's right. I want you to feel the pain of the gap. Experience the sense of disappointment and frustration that accompanies them. Without emotion, there is no motion. If you disassociate and are too cerebral about your gaps, they won't provide the punch to get you moving.

You need to feel the disappointment and the desire for change in every fiber of your being.

Read through the questions below. If you feel a twinge of pain, you know you've found a gap.

CONNECTION

Feeling connection and a sense of belonging is critical to living a full and happy life. How connected do you feel?

FAMILY

- Are you happy with your marriage?

- Do you feel closer to or more distant from your spouse each year?

- Are your needs being met?

- Is there a disconnect between you and your parents or siblings?

- Are you thrilled with your relationship with your children?

FRIENDS

- Are you happy with the number of friends you have?

- Do you feel connected to your friends on a deep level?

COMMUNITY

- Do you feel like an important part of your community?

SPIRITUAL

- Are you satisfied with your religious/spiritual journey?

- Do you desire more spiritual knowledge?

- Are there organizations you want to help but haven't yet?

HEALTH

Ask a healthy guy what's important, and he'll tell you his job, making money, and his relationship with his family. Ask a sick guy what's important, and he'll tell you getting healthy is important. When we neglect our health for too long, it finds a way to get our attention. How healthy are you?

EXERCISE

- Do you get enough exercise?

- Do you recognize the guy staring back at you in the mirror?

- Are you as healthy as you want to be?

NUTRITION

- Do you get enough nutrients in your diet?

- Do you have enough energy throughout the day?

- Do you want to eat and look better?

FINANCES

Money problems can ruin marriages, split families, exacerbate ulcers, and generally wreck your life. Is there a gap between where you are and where you'd like to be?

MONEY

- Are you happy with the amount of money you make and have saved?

- Do you live in the house you want and drive the car you want?

- Do you wish you could provide more for your family?

- Do money problems cause you anxiety and keep you up at night?

CAREER

- Do you want to move up within your company?

- Are you sick of your job and what you do?

- Do you feel your employer doesn't recognize your talents?

- How happy would you be if you could quit tomorrow?

GROWTH

If you're not growing, you're dying. It's that simple. In order to have a full and rich life, you need to be advancing, experiencing, and learning. Does it feel like you are stuck in quicksand?

HOBBIES

- Are you happy with the hobbies and interests you have?

- Do you get bored often?

DEVELOPMENT

- When is the last time you read a book?

- Do you feel up to speed on current events?

- Have you been able to travel as much as you like?

- Are there classes you've wanted to take but haven't?

How are you feeling? If you're feeling fine, you're either taking too much Lithium or are quite happy with your life. These questions were designed to help you find your gaps. If you're feeling a little frustrated or uneasy, that's a good thing. Use that discomfort. If you stopped at this step and didn't read on, you might curse your life and this book. I don't want you to live in the gap. You'd get too depressed. I just want you to visit it. Remember, you need to feel it before you can get the motivation to change it.

2. CREATE A MANTRA

A powerful mantra is a short phrase that immediately connects you to your core values. And one mantra isn't going to do it. You need a mantra for each area of our life that is important to you. Use the general list above (connection, health, financial, growth), or drill down further (family, friends, career, exercise, nutrition) as a starting point, or create your own categories.

Here are a few tips on creating your own mantras:

- **Short.** The phrase should be short—just four to six words. Anything longer is going to be too specific, and you won't be able to remember it.

- **Core values.** The phrase should encapsulate your core beliefs and values.

- **Controllable.** Your mantra should be something you can personally control.

- **Inspiring.** When you read your mantra, it should inspire you. That's when you know you've got a phrase that moves you.

- **Realistic.** My "friends" mantra could be "Tons of deep friendships." It sounds good and it looks good, but it is not me. With a spouse, child, and many projects, I only have time for a few deep friends. Don't create a mantra that sounds good but that isn't realistic or true to you.

Here are a few examples:

FAMILY

- *To be there and engaged.* It's not enough to be present. You need to be actively engaged.

- *To make my children independent.* This mantra is specific to parenting. Although you want your children to be happy, successful, and fulfilled, your most important objective—and one that will guide their decisions—will be to help your children learn to be independent.

- *To give them what they need.* Simple and, for the right person, inspiring.

FRIENDS

- *Depth, not breadth.* Are you interested in attending a social networking event? Probably not.

- *Have many close friends.* If this is your mantra, having a lot of close friends is very important to you, even if that means sacrificing alone time or time with family.

- *Support them in times of need.* You would do whatever it takes to help your friends when they're down but wouldn't come running to them when they have just any problem. Friend catches his girlfriend cheating and needs a place to stay? You wouldn't hesitate. Friend wants a ride to the airport? Tell him to call a cab.

SPIRITUAL

- *A little closer each day.* This mantra might encourage constant growth through a weekly church group and nightly Bible reading.

- *What would Jesus do?* Regardless of the situation, this quick but powerful question can immediately help you make a decision that is true to your values.

CHARITABLE

- *Support those who can't help themselves.* You might focus your charitable efforts on helping the homeless or animal shelters before donating to your local museum.

DEVELOPMENT

- *To know more today than I did yesterday.* This mantra focuses on knowledge and the never-ending pursuit of learning and growing.

- *To experience something new.* When faced with two choices, you would opt for the new experience—whether it's a restaurant or vacation.

CAREER

- *Always seek more responsibility.* A promotion without more responsibility? No, thank you. Volunteering for a side project? Absolutely.

- *To do what I love.* You might sacrifice money, success, and promotions if asked to do something you didn't love.

HEALTH

- *Be proud in a bathing suit.* This mantra is simple, but certainly not easy. It can inspire, and it can help you make day-to-day decisions about fitness and health.

- *Have enough energy to play with my grandkids.* Being in good health is good enough. It's okay if you don't want abs of steel.

The goal of a mantra is to keep you inspired and to help you quickly make decisions, but it has to jibe with your values. For example, I've been toying with the idea of producing a TV show. After talking to a production company, I learned they were excited about either a weekly or a daily show. A daily show would mean less free time, more travel, and a lot less time with my family. Because of my mantra ("to be there and engaged"), I immediately shot down the daily show format. It wouldn't have meshed with my core values.

Now it's your turn! Come up with a meaningful mantra for each important area of your life. You'll turn to this mantra when you're faced with decisions, and you'll incorporate them into your daily habits in the next chapter.

3. IDENTIFY PRIORITIES

There's too much to do and too little time, which is why we need to focus. Software companies do this instinctively. They dream up a killer application but release the bare-bones version. When they launch version 1.0, they are already planning version 6.0 in their heads. Then, over time, they develop more features and add the bells and whistles, but they had to first get 1.0 out the door. This requires focus.

Even though you may have uncovered many gaps in your life, you

OTHER 8 EXPERT

Dr. Sonja Lyubomirsky is a pioneer in the study of happiness and the author of *The How of Happiness*. Here's how she answered the question, What one thing should readers do with their other 8 hours that will have the greatest positive impact on their lives?

For the past two decades, I have been conducting research on the science of happiness—what causes it, what benefits does it have, and how can people obtain more of it. The conclusion of this work is that becoming lastingly happier is possible, but that, like any worthwhile goal in life, calls for vast investments of effort and commitment. So, spend your time, energy, and resources on practicing those activities that have been shown empirically to bolster happiness. Engage in random and systematic acts of kindness, express gratitude and forgiveness, savor the present, nurture your relationships, take baby steps toward your life dreams, look on the bright side, and strive to become fully absorbed in your work, family, and hobbies. However, not everyone will benefit from every positive activity, so choose just one (for now) that fits your personality and lifestyle best.

need to focus on those gaps that bother you the most. They may not be the widest gaps, but they are the ones you want to close as quickly as possible. For example, if you're working at a dead-end job and hate what you do but are also fifteen pounds overweight, your focus may be on losing the weight, even though, to the objective observer, it might make more sense to focus on your career.

Priorities are personal. They don't have to make sense to anyone else. But how many gaps should you focus on at any one time? There is no right answer. For some, it might be one at a time, and for others, it is ten. It depends on you, the amount of time you have, and what it takes to close the gaps.

As you go through your gaps, highlight the priorities—those you get a knot in your stomach just thinking about. Start with three or four. When we get to the next chapter, you'll be able to determine how many you can work on closing at any one time.

4. CREATE GOALS

I love goals. I love creating them, talking about them, and achieving them, but I also know not everybody shares my enthusiasm. Before your eyes glaze over, let me tell you why setting goals is so important. The latest research indicates that the simple act of setting goals improves our experience and our performance. It also shows that we are happier when we are progressing toward our goals. Setting goals helps us focus on what we want.

Even if you set mediocre goals, it's better than nothing. But if you really want to set goals with the most opportunity for impact, you need to set IMPACT goals:

Inspiring—Your goal might not inspire me, but it had better light a fire under you. If it doesn't, get a new goal.

Measurable—Your goals must be measurable. In other words, there usually is a number involved—dollars, days, times per week, weight.

When you create a goal that is measurable, it's easy to determine if you are getting closer (you weigh 152 but your goal is to weigh 135) or if you've reached your goal.

Purposeful—Your goal must support your values and your mantra. If there's a conflict between your goals, you won't achieve them.

Active—Nothing happens without action. Your goal must promote action. In the next chapter, we'll take the goals and break them down into actionable tasks.

Controllable—If you can't control the outcome of your goal (I want Nickelback to stop recording music), it's not a real goal. It's a wish and a dream. Your goals must be something you can control (I want to run my first marathon by this time next year).

Time-specific—Anybody who starts a goal with "someday I want to . . ." will never achieve the goal. It is too vague, and there is no time frame. The best goals have a deadline.

Unlike hopes and wishes, IMPACT goals are targeted. They provide the greatest motivation and opportunity for success.

Go through your gaps. Are you better off than you were a year ago in each of these areas? What would it take for you to look back a year from now and be thrilled with your progress? The answer to that question becomes your goals. Now start creating IMPACT goals that bridge where you are and where you want to be.

5. EXPECT SETBACKS

Think positively. We've all been told that, but it's bad advice. A little negativity can be a good thing. In fact, a little negativity can help us reach our goals.

Does this story sounds familiar? You're amped about achieving a new goal. It sounds good and it's inspiring. You think about how wonderful it will feel when you've accomplished it. You daydream of success. Things go well for a while, but then, for whatever reason, you get derailed. Maybe you have a bad day, feel a little under the weather, or just don't have the same spark you had the day earlier. Sometimes it's easy to get back on track after a setback, but more often than not, you never do. The dream evaporates and you lose the goal forever.

I've been there, and I know you have too. You want to get in shape, so you decide you will run every morning. A week into it, you wake up tired. It seems colder and darker outside. The bed seems warmer and softer. In that split second—when you decide whether you will push through the resistance or succumb to the soft bed—you decide your fate. If you skip it that one morning, chances are you will skip it tomorrow morning and so on.

The rush we get when we set the goal quickly disappears. The power we feel when we think of accomplishing the goal in the future is met only with the reality of the moment—I'm tired and it's warm in bed. All the feel-good affirmations won't help us get out of bed.

So let's be honest with ourselves from the start. We will face setbacks. We will want to give up. We will become negative and pessimistic. We will rationalize our desire to quit. We will experience all of these at some point on our way to reaching our goals. It might be on day two or month two, but, sooner or later, we will get discouraged and want to quit.

Even the most enthusiastic among us will get discouraged when stepping on the scale after weeks of exercise and seeing no improvement. The person who studies Spanish like crazy for several months but forgets how to tell the waiter "please" the first chance he gets may want to give up. The ambitious executive who wants more recognition may feel like throwing in the towel after working two months on an article that gets passed over by her industry's trade publication.

Any goal will face challenges and disappointments. Not only do you have to know this going in, but you need to inoculate yourself from these setbacks if you want to reach your goals. The best way to inoculate yourself from them is to come up with as many hurdles, problems, challenges, and reasons why you will quit as you can and then find solutions for each of them.

Your own challenges and potential setbacks will be unique, but here's a few of the most common reasons you might quit and what you can do about it.

1. **No time.** I like to load on goals like I load on food at a buffet. My eyes are always bigger than my stomach, and my ambitions are always bigger than my available free time can support.

   The best solution is proper scheduling, which the next chapter addresses, but you can also start by clearing your plate. Get rid of those commitments that are not important or that are not getting you closer to your goals. Can you resign from the PTA board to free up more time to learn sculpting? You can also prioritize your responsibilities. Instead of watching TV first, put it last.

   Plan around problems. For example, if you want to go to the gym every day, but you work for a boss who always keeps you late, you'd better plan to make that trip to the gym happen by scheduling your gym time before work or after the kids go to bed.

   Reread chapter three. Get as efficient and productive as you can. Become a chunk master! Use other people's time. Create more time so you can accomplish more of what's important to you.

2. **Lose motivation.** I did a financial makeover for a couple on *20/20* a couple of years ago. I asked them if, after the cameras stopped rolling and the lights dimmed, when it was just the two of them, they would be willing to make the changes they needed. You need to ask yourself the same thing. Setting goals is easy. Achieving goals is hard. What happens when you lose your motivation?

   a. Use a DreamBoard. A DreamBoard is a photo collage of your goals. What is more effective, reading your goal about taking a trip to Fiji or looking at a picture of a Fijian beach with crystal clear water and palm trees? Which one gets you more excited? Which one will move you closer to accomplishing the goal? Which one will get AND keep you motivated? When you're having a tough day, a photo can inspire you better than words.

      For each of your goals, cut out two or three pictures from magazines that get your juices flowing. If you want to earn a

PhD, cut out a picture of a diploma. If you want to learn how to play the piano, cut out a picture of a baby grand or Billy Joel. If you want to work fewer hours, take a picture of your empty office with a clock at 3:30 PM.

Once you've cut out all of the pictures, paste them on poster board and hang your DreamBoard where you'll see it several times a day. Or, if you know you'll have trouble getting out of bed to jog in the morning, put a picture of yourself when you were in shape on your nightstand.

b. Find a partner. My wife wakes up at 5:30 many mornings to jog. Why? She conned a few friends into running with her at 6:00 AM. She doesn't want to get out of bed at that time, but she knows her friends are counting on her. Getting others involved may force you to stay on track even if you lose your motivation.

c. Reward yourself for progress. Take a day off. Get your boyfriend to give you a massage. Buy a martini. What can you do to stay motivated?

3. **Get distracted.** Maybe you're the type to bounce from one unfinished project to another. You enjoy setting goals, but once it comes time to do the work, you are ready to bounce to the next goal. If bouncing is part of your nature, you need to break the cycle. One way to do this is to get clear on what you want and to build up the benefit of achieving the goal as much as you can. The grander the finish line, the more likely you'll stick to it. Also, the bigger the gap and the more pain you feel about the gap, the more likely you'll stick with it. Focus on those gaps where you feel the most pain and where you'll feel the most pleasure from achieving the goal.

4. **Fear of failure.** The best way not to fail is not to try. If you're scared about not achieving your goal and/or looking like a failure, you may sabotage your success. You may quit too soon so you won't suffer disappointment.

Fear of failure can stop the strongest person in his tracks. If this is something you struggle with, get a partner. Often the fear is intensified if you feel like you are alone. If you have a partner who is also struggling, it can diffuse your fear as you support him.

Reread the section on failure in the FAQ chapter. Start with some easy-to-reach goals to build your confidence, or pair a challenging goal with an easy one. If you're struggling with all of your goals, it can quickly deflate your motivation.

Achieving a goal is like going to battle. Hopes are high, but there are many obstacles. You need to go into battle with a plan and plenty of armor because the enemy will be shooting at you.

Now it's your turn. Ask yourself, "Why would I quit?" What would have to happen for me to quit? You know yourself. Do you get discouraged easily? Do you put a lot of stock in what others say? Do you jump from one thing to the next—never completing anything? Get a pen and pad and make a list of all the possible things that could go wrong and setbacks you could face in pursuit of your goals.

6. HABITUALIZE

Let's stop talking and start getting! You have a bunch of goals you're itching to accomplish and ventures you want to start. In the next chapter you're going to take everything you've learned through the book and put it into action . . .

CHAPTER ELEVEN

STOP TALKING AND START GETTING

How to Use the Other 8 Hours to Create the Life You Want

A newly married couple was in the kitchen one Sunday. The wife was preparing a pot roast and cut two inches off both ends before putting it in the oven. The husband asks, "Sweetie, why did you cut off the ends and throw them away?" The wife replied, "Oh, well, that's how my mother always did it."

The following Sunday they visited her mother's for her Sunday roast and the husband asked, "Your daughter tells me you taught her to cook pot roast by first cutting two inches off each end. Does this make the roast better?" Her mother hesitated, and then said, "I honestly don't know. I've always done it that way, just like my mother taught me."

The husband was intrigued. He patiently waited for Thanksgiving dinner to ask his wife's grandmother why it was so important to cut the ends off the roast. Laughing, the grandmother said, "I haven't done that for fifty years! You see, when my daughter was growing up we didn't have much money. The apartment we lived in had a little oven with a tiny door. The only way the roast would fit through the door was if I cut off the ends."

What's to blame for the watered-down version of a life we lead? Habits. We all have habits. In fact, we spend much of our day bouncing from one habit to another; we get up at the same time, brush our teeth, shower the same way (don't you have an almost subconscious routine?). We drive to work and then home again using the same route, plop down in front of the TV and watch the same shows, go to bed, and start the process all over again the next day.

Do you ever catch yourself doing something really dumb and realize that you've been doing it for years without ever thinking about it? That, my friends, is habit creep. Habit creep is when we get stuck in a rut doing the same things the same ways—not because they are the most efficient or because they help us grow or advance, but because we did it once that way a long time ago and nothing immediately bad happened. So we did it again and again and again until it became part of our daily routine.

Habit creep can squeeze the life from us. It can drain our time and cause one day to bleed into another and another. Habit creep can prevent us from closing the gaps and achieving the life we want. And some bad habits, like smoking, driving without wearing a seatbelt, or exposing our skin to the sun, can even kill us.

But not all habits are bad . . .

HABITUALIZE

Habits and rituals can be powerful tools that help us squeeze the most from the day and close the gap, but only if we consciously create them. How can you kill habit creep and replace negative and unconscious habits with positive habits that will move you forward? You need to habitualize. A habit is an acquired behavior that is performed over and over until it becomes almost involuntary. A ritual is any pattern of behavior regularly performed in a set manner.

When we Habitualize, we dump our negative and mediocre habits and replace them with positive habits and rituals that enrich our lives and bring us closer to our goals. When we Habitualize, we get the most from each day. We pack it full of positive action. Instead of one unfulfilled day bleeding into a week that bleeds into a year and then into a decade when we Habitualize, we can't help but move forward and close our gaps. There are nine steps to Habitualize:

1. Block out fixed commitments on your schedule
2. Replace your "mourning" routine

3. Bracket your day

4. Block other commitments

5. Find open areas

6. Schedule your goals

7. Create tasks

8. Chunk multiple tasks

9. Create energy

Before you can Habitualize, you need to download the Goal Action Plan (GAP) template at other8hours.com. The GAP is a scheduling system that will help you Habitualize and will, quite literally, help you close your gaps.

Even if you already use a calendar or scheduling system such as Outlook or Day Planner, I've found using this template is the best way to Habitualize. Once you've gone through this process, you can easily migrate your results into your own calendar/scheduling system. But I recommend you use the template now to get started.

1. BLOCK OUT FIXED COMMITMENTS ON YOUR CALENDAR

Wouldn't it be great if we completely controlled our schedules? If it weren't for commitments and responsibilities, we'd have a lot more free time to pursue our goals and dreams. But, alas, we have places to be and people to answer to.

So, the first task you need to do is list all those things that must absolutely be done. For example, drop the kids off at school at 7:45, start work at 9:00, and pick the kids up from soccer practice at 5:30. But don't add these to your calendar quite yet. Watch out for false start times. Even though you may start work at 9:00, you must include the time it takes you to drive there. Or, even though you may want to go to bed at 11:00, you must include the time it takes to floss, brush your teeth, wash your face, etc. So, instead of trying to figure out what time the commitment starts (for example, starting work at 9:00), determine the trigger time— the time you must start doing something in order for something else to

GAP – Goal Achievement Plan

Start Time	Action	Chunk
8:30 AM	Drive to work	
9:00 AM	Work	
5:15 PM	Leave work	
5:30 PM	Pick up kids	

happen (the trigger time for work is 8:30 because if you get in the car at that time you will get to work at 9:00).

Think about all of your fixed commitments, and then add them as well as the trigger times to your GAP.

2. REPLACE YOUR "MOURNING" ROUTINE

Does your morning routine feel more like a "mourning" routine? The first thirty minutes of your day has a powerful grip over the rest of your day—your morning behaviors and attitudes can influence how you feel and what you do for the rest of the day. Instead of smashing the alarm clock, kicking the cat, and cursing your life every morning, you can do a couple of simple things that will start your day off on a better note.

- **Kill the kryptonite.** You are no longer allowed to hit the snooze button. This is coming from a guy who had a bad habit of abusing the snooze button. I'd set my alarm an hour early (yes, an hour early!) just so I could hit the snooze button six times. I found that this little and seemingly innocuous button made me weaker and

ANOTHER 8-HOUR SUCCESS

Concerned you won't have the energy to pursue your passions during the other 8 hours? Hogwash! I'm not sure what they say "down under," but Australian superblogger Darren Rowse doesn't agree.

After reading an article about blogging in 2002, he started his own blog within twenty-four hours. His first blog recorded the journey of his church and he wrote it for the church's congregation. When I asked him if it was an overnight sensation, he laughed and said, "Nobody from church read it!" But that didn't dissuade him.

Even though he had a full-time and a part-time job, a wife, and children, he invested thirty minutes to an hour each day in writing and ultimately founded ProBlogger (problogger.net). This is a superpopular blog that "is dedicated to helping other bloggers learn the skills of blogging, share their own experiences and promote the blogging medium."

When asked how he was able to juggle so many commitments early on, he said he had to free up time on his calendar. TV was first to go and then his part-time job. But Darren was quick to point out that pursuing his passion during the other 8 hours didn't feel like a third job. In fact, it was just the opposite. After a long day of work, he looked forward to blogging. He said it gave him energy.

By using the other 8 hours to focus on his hobby, Darren has been able to quit his jobs and do something he loves, giving him freedom, flexibility, and more time with his family.

weaker every day. Every time I hit it, I was unconsciously reinforcing the belief that I was weak and that I couldn't get out of bed
when I was supposed to. Break this habit and replace it with a much
better one. Set your alarm for when you want to get up, and when
it goes off, make yourself stronger by doing the shocking thing—
getting up. Do this every day and you will grow in confidence.

- **First five seconds.** When it's dark and cold out, you need a
  burst of inspiration to get your juices flowing. The first thing
  you should do is feed your mind. Read your mantras, look at
  your DreamBoard, read an inspirational quote or Bible passage,
  etc. Do this first—before you reach for your Blackberry, remote,
  or toothbrush.

- **Get the blood flowing.** While your mind has been active all
  night, your body has not. The best way to get the mind engaged
  and primed is to get the body moving. Immediately after you feed
  your mind, do a few minutes of light stretching or yoga to get the
  blood flowing to your muscles and to get your joints loosened.
  You don't need to be Richard Simmons on crack—slow and steady
  is good.

- **PowerJournal.** For fifteen or twenty minutes every day, I want
  you to write, brainstorm, and just think. Here are some ideas for
  PowerJournaling:

  Gratitude—One of the best ways to increase your happiness and
  sense of well-being is to express gratitude. A powerful and easy
  way to do this is by writing about those things that you are grateful for.

  New Business Ideas—The Cre8tor should always be thinking
  about the next project. Setting some time aside every day to brainstorm new products or businesses is a great way to get and keep
  your mind focused and to discover new ventures to start.

  Future—Spending a few minutes daydreaming about your future is a wonderful way to start your morning. Instead of immediately getting sucked into the day's pressures, responsibilities,

and problems, take a few minutes of quiet time to focus on your perfect future. This can provide you with a sense of calm and peace that can last the whole day.

Spirituality—For some, getting grounded in scripture is the perfect way to inoculate against the stress and anxiety of the day. Read a random Bible passage or say a prayer.

$1 Million in 1 Year—This is a fun game that will get your juices flowing. If you absolutely, positively had to create $1 million within 365 days, what would you have to do? It's fun and you might just come up with a great business idea.

I've found that the best approach is to combine several of these ideas each day. Maybe start the session by reading your mantras, write what you're grateful for, think about your future, and then end in a prayer. The next day you can start by reading an inspirational quote; then, brainstorm business ideas and end in a peaceful personal meditation. I like the idea of starting the routine the same every day—it becomes more of a ritual.

- **Breakfast.** I know. You've heard it before. But I'll risk repeating it because studies show about 40 percent of us still skip breakfast. The benefits of eating a nutritious breakfast are well known. Avoid bacon, sausage, pastries, and processed cereals, and go for something simple, like a bowl of whole grain cereal with nonfat milk— and add a banana and raisins.

    If you don't have time for breakfast or want a little something extra, you can chug down a power shake. My shake takes about three minutes to make and about two minutes to drink. The cool thing is that you can load it up with just about anything. I use protein and vitamin powder, green tea, physillium husk, brewer's yeast, omega-3 oil, cinnamon (great for lowering blood sugar levels), and liquid glucosamine for joint health. This shake was created with my needs in mind, so find out what you need and build your shake around it.

    If you did all of these things, it would add maybe twenty or thirty minutes to your morning schedule. I know a half hour in

GAP — Goal Achievement Plan

Start Time	Action	Chunk
8:00 AM	Morning routine (breakfast, PowerJournal, etc.)	
8:30 AM	Drive to work	
9:00 AM	Work	
5:15 PM	Leave work	
5:30 PM	Pick up kids	

the morning is huge, but look at this time as an investment in your day and in you. Doing these things will make you healthier, give you a more positive attitude, provide a much greater feeling of control, and grant you a sense of peace and calmness.

Add a morning routine to your GAP.

GAP — Goal Achievement Plan

Start Time	Action	Chunk
7:00 AM	Wake up and get ready	
8:00 AM	Morning routine (breakfast, PowerJournal, etc.)	
8:30 AM	Drive to work	
9:00 AM	Work	
5:15 PM	Leave work	
5:30 PM	Pick up kids	
10:30 PM	Get ready for bed	
11:00 PM	Get into bed	

3. BRACKET YOUR DAY

How much sleep do you want to get at night? Once you know this, you can bracket your day and fill in more of your GAP. Since you've added your new morning routine and you know what time you need to leave the house to get to work on time, you can now determine what time you must wake up. Write that on your GAP. Now that you know when you need to wake up and how much sleep you want, add when you need to go to sleep to your GAP. Remember, use the trigger time—don't just add "go to sleep" but also add "get ready for bed," since this requires time.

4. BLOCK OTHER COMMITMENTS

Hanging out with family, making dinner, cleaning the house, paying bills, taking the garbage out, watering the lawn, watching TV, and going to the post office all take time that we need to account for on our

GAP – Goal Achievement Plan

Start Time	Action	Chunk
7:00 AM	Wake up & get ready	
8:00 AM	Morning routine (breakfast, PowerJournal, etc.)	
8:30 AM	Drive to work	
9:00 AM	Work	
12:00 PM	Lunch	
1:00 PM	Work	
5:15 PM	Leave work	
5:30 PM	Pick up kids	
5:45 PM	Family time (dinner, kids, household, etc.)	
7:45 PM	Kids to bed	
10:30 PM	Get ready for bed	
11:00 PM	Get into bed	

GAP. Otherwise, we'll make the mistake of thinking we have a lot more time to focus on our goals and ventures.

Give yourself time each day for these activities. You don't have to schedule specific activities, but you should block out chunks of time for these on your GAP.

5. FIND OPEN AREAS

Take a look at your GAP. All the empty space (I hope you have some) is open time in which you can focus on your goals and your ventures.

6. SCHEDULE YOUR GOALS

Focus on your higher-priority goals and decide how much of your open time you want to dedicate to each of them. For example, if getting in better shape is one of your priority goals, schedule thirty minutes or an hour each day to exercise. Research shows the best results are achieved when you can schedule activities at the same time each day, or, for things you don't do every day, that you schedule them at the same time and on the same days each week. Doing this helps create positive habits and rituals that will become automatic for you. So instead of mentally debating about going to the gym, your autopilot will take over and you will get to the gym.

When you're placing your goals on your GAP, consider these issues:

- **Energy.** Your energy ebbs and flows throughout the day. You might be most alert and able to tackle mental tasks early in the day or late at night. Optimize your natural energy cycle by scheduling your goals when it makes the most sense to do them. For example, if you're mentally exhausted after work, that might be a bad time to schedule work on your Cre8tor venture, but it might be a great time to work up a sweat.

- **Flow.** Be conscious of how your day flows from one activity to another, and schedule activities that flow together best. For example, after I write for a few hours, I need a break. I wouldn't schedule

GAP – Goal Achievement Plan

Start Time	Action	Chunk
7:00 AM	Wake up and get ready	
8:00 AM	Morning routine (breakfast, PowerJournal, etc.)	
8:30 AM	Drive to work	
9:00 AM	Work	
12:00 PM	Lunch	
1:00 PM	Work	
5:15 PM	Leave work	
5:30 PM	Pick up kids	
5:45 PM	Family time (dinner, kids, household, etc.)	
7:45 PM	Kids to bed	
8:00 PM	Exercise/treadmill at home	
8:30 PM	Goal #1: Start blog	
9:30 PM	Goal #2: Learn Spanish	
10:00 PM	Goal #3: Get closer to spouse	
10:30 PM	Get ready for bed	
11:00 PM	Get into bed	

another "brain" activity immediately after I write. Instead, I'd schedule reading, exercise, dinner, or even TV for that time.

- **Surroundings.** If you need peace and privacy to work on a goal, you shouldn't schedule this goal for when the kids get home from school. It might make more sense to schedule this goal time later at night or first thing in the morning, when the kids are sleeping.

  Insert your goal times on your GAP. Don't forget to add the trigger times. For example, in addition to "exercise" at 5:30, you might need to add "leave work" at 5:15 in order to get to the gym by 5:30.

7. CREATE TASKS

I love really big, life-changing goals, such as to lose sixty pounds, to buy a cottage in Aspen, and to make $2 million from the sale of an

Internet company. These big goals can get you pumped up like nothing else. The problem is that they can feel daunting and unattainable. As I said before, setting goals is easy. Achieving them is hard. The bigger the goal, the harder it can feel to achieve.

To make goals much more manageable, you need to break them down into smaller tasks. Each task—like a rung on a ladder—builds on the other until you've reached your goal. For example, let's say your goal is to lose twenty-five pounds by next Christmas. That's a nice goal, and I'm sure it would look great laminated and attached to your bathroom mirror, but how are you going to achieve it? In other words, what subgoals or tasks would you need to complete in order to reach it? A very cool and effective way to brainstorm and document the tasks is by mind mapping. This is a technique for creating a visual diagram around a central theme, and it is ideal for breaking down goals into tasks.

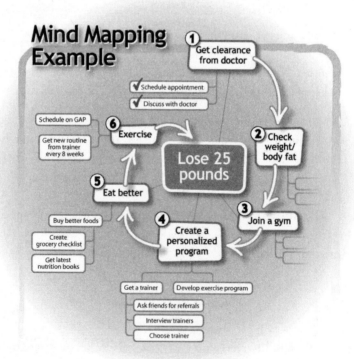

Even though we started with one goal of losing twenty-five pounds, we need to complete a lot of steps/tasks to achieve it.

Your job is to break down each of your goals into smaller tasks. If you like mind mapping, you can create one by hand or you can use a program to help. For a list of free and proprietary programs, search for "mind mapping software" on Wikipedia. My favorites are mindmeister (mindmeister.com) and MindManager (mindjet.com).

The time you've blocked for your goal on your GAP is stable—it won't change until you've reached your goal. But the tasks you need to do to reach the goal are flexible—sometimes changing every day. For example, when I was writing this book, I blocked out two hours a night to work on it. I always knew that from 9:00 to 11:00, I'd be working on

GAP – Goal Achievement Plan

For October 5th

Start Time	Action	Chunk
7:00 AM	Wake up and get ready	
8:00 AM	Morning routine (breakfast, PowerJournal, etc.)	
8:30 AM	Drive to work	
9:00 AM	Work	
12:00 PM	Lunch	
1:00 PM	Work	
5:15 PM	Leave work	
5:30 PM	Pick up kids	
5:45 PM	Family time (dinner, kids, household, etc.)	
7:45 PM	Kids to bed	
8:00 PM	Exercise/treadmill at home	
8:30 PM	Goal #1: Start blog 1. Research trademark 2. Talk to Web designer 3. Write Web site text	
9:30 PM	Goal #2: Learn Spanish 1. Read chapter 4 2. Complete workbook 3. Learn 10 new words	
10:00 PM	Goal #3: Get closer to spouse 1. Go over DreamBoard together 2. Give 15-minute massage	
10:30 PM	Get ready for bed	
11:00 PM	Get into bed	

my book goal—on my GAP I wrote, "Work on book." Even though "Work on book" didn't change on my GAP, my tasks would change all the time. Sometimes I'd write, but other times I'd research or brainstorm or pray to the writing gods for inspiration all during the "Work on book" time.

To get maximum accountability and a more active calendar system, update your GAP every day to reflect your top three individual tasks that will move you closer to your goal. By doing this, you'll always know exactly what you need to do to move forward—it eliminates all the "what should I work on right now" guesswork.

Your turn. Break down all of your goals into smaller tasks and add the top three tasks for each goal to your GAP.

8. CHUNK MULTIPLE TASKS

If you stopped here, you'd be ridiculously far ahead of where you were. But if you want to get a little nutty, keep reading. Remember way back in chapter 3 when we talked about chunking—combining head activities with body activities? It's back! Even though you've packed your GAP with life-changing action, there's still probably some dead time (driving to work, getting ready in the morning). Let's take advantage of this time.

Look at your list of tasks and determine if you could add another activity. If so, add these chunk activities into your GAP in the chunk column. You can have new chunk activities every day or, even better, you can do the same ones at the same time every day— again, we want to create a ritual as much as possible. So when you sit down for your hour lunch, you know that for the first half hour, you'll eat and read everything in your "to read" folder, and the next half hour, you'll go for a brisk walk and listen to a business-related podcast.

Go through your GAP and add chunk activities. Of course, you'll also want to add positivity throughout the day, but you don't have to add your sparking activities to your GAP.

GAP – Goal Achievement Plan

For October 5th

Start Time	Action	Chunk
7:00 AM	Wake up and get ready	Review DreamBoard Go over goals Read mantras
8:00 AM	Morning routine (breakfast, PowerJournal, etc.)	
8:30 AM	Drive to work	Listen to *New York Times* on iPod
9:00 AM	Work	
12:00 PM	Lunch	Read "to read" folder Take brisk walk and call family
1:00 PM	Work	
5:15 PM	Leave work	Listen to Spanish lessons on iPod
5:30 PM	Pick up kids	
5:45 PM	Family time (dinner, kids, household, etc.)	
7:45 PM	Kids to bed	
8:00 PM	Exercise/treadmill at home	Watch TV
8:30 PM	Goal #1: Start blog 1. Research trademark 2. Talk to Web designer 3. Write Web site text	
9:30 PM	Goal #2: Learn Spanish 1. Read chapter 4 2. Complete workbook 3. Learn 10 new words	
10:00 PM	Goal #3: Get closer to spouse 1. Go over DreamBoard together 2. Give 15-minute massage	
10:30 PM	Get ready for bed	Go over goals Read mantras
11:00 PM	Get into bed	Pray

MINI FAQ

Q—*My GAP looks a little blah. How can I spruce it up a bit?*

A—I'm a visual guy, so I use a lot of colors on my GAP. I use a light green for that time that isn't goal oriented (waking up, eating breakfast, work, dinner, getting my daughter ready for bed, sleep). I then use a light yellow for all the time I use to achieve my goals (PowerJournal, exercise, working on my Cre8tor venture, reading the Bible). For those primary actions where I can't chunk another activity, I use a dark gray, but for those where I can chunk, I'll also color-code it light yellow.

Lastly, I use big red blocks for trigger times. I know these are critical times when I must do something specific or the rest of the day will be thrown off. You can even set an alarm in Outlook, on your watch, or on your cell phone at these trigger times to remind you.

Q—*Should I create a GAP for each day or just use one?*

A—Chances are you will need at least a few different versions for different days of the week. For example, if you want to exercise three days a week at 5:30 PM, you'd need a GAP that reflects this. But for the other two workdays, you'd need another GAP that shows a different activity at 5:30 PM.

Q—*Do I need a GAP for the weekend?*

A—It's best if you can wake up at or near the same time each day and that you keep your morning routine consistent. Your gaps don't take the weekends off, so if you're serious about closing them and/or starting a Cre8tor venture, the weekend is a great time.

Q—*You talk about a morning routine, but what about a night routine?*

A—Adding a ritualized night routine can be a nice way to end the day, but if you have trouble falling asleep, you need to be careful not to overload yourself right before bed. Consider some light stretching or meditation. Follow this by writing what you're grateful for in your PowerJournal (nobody says you have to do this in the morning).

Q—*It looks like every second of the day is scheduled. What about spontaneity and having time to do nothing?*

A—Research shows that we are most creative when we schedule time for creativity, but this doesn't mean you have to work every waking moment and chunk at every opportunity. This is your schedule. Make it work for you. If you want to add just a couple of activities to your day, that's fine. If you want to schedule TV time every night, go for it! The other 8 hours are your life. Use them as you want. Just be aware of how you are using them. Make choices about your life, so life just doesn't happen to you.

9. CREATE ENERGY

Whew! If you've completed your GAP, you probably feel excited but also a little intimidated about your new schedule. Even though you're taking action to close your gaps and improve your life, it takes a lot more effort than watching TV and munching on chips. You have a full-time job, a long commute, a family, and countless other responsibilities. You're probably tired and overwhelmed (but still anxious to improve your life). This is why it's critical for you to know how to boost your energy:

- **Working on your gaps.** You will get a boost of energy just by thinking about and working on your goals and Cre8tor ventures.

- **Success.** One of the cool by-products of breaking down distant goals into tasks is that you can see immediate and continuous success as you complete each of the smaller tasks and achieve small pieces of your goal.

- **Exercise.** This is one of the best ways to create energy (research shows it may be the best solution for depression, too). If it's not already on your GAP, include some form of exercise every day. Also, consider adding pockets of exercise into your schedule, such as riding your bike to work, walking at lunch, or taking the stairs. Even a little movement throughout the day can help boost your energy.

- **Nutrition.** To get the most out of your body, you need to put the best in your body. If you eat crap, you'll feel like crap. Focus on eating whole grains and lowering your consumption of fat, sugar,

AN**OTHER 8-HOUR SUCCESS**

Allison Hagendorf considers herself a professional multitasker and thrives on being busy. She blogs, is the voice of Oxygen TV, does voiceovers for MTV, Jergens, and Verizon, and is the VJ for Steve Madden Music.

She wanted to find another way to challenge herself personally. Playing sports has always been a part of her life, but since her schedule was erratic, participating in an organized sport would be difficult, so she decided to run a marathon. She began training 5–7 days a week a few hours a day. As the date of the marathon came closer, she was running 3–4 hours a day.

She managed to complete the training successfully by working the training sessions into her daily schedule. She said it was easier to complete the runs first thing in the morning, so it was done and out of the way and she could fulfill her work commitments. She said, "Training just became a part of my day after a while. Establishing a schedule for the sessions made it easier to succeed."

So how did she do? She completed the New York Marathon in 4 hours, 7 minutes. Allison says, "It isn't luck that I'm professionally successful or able to complete a twenty-six-mile marathon. To me, luck is when your own preparation and opportunity meet. Anyone that has the physical capabilities to walk and move their bodies can run a marathon. I loved the experience and challenge of pushing myself to achieve this goal and would definitely do it again!"

and processed junk. Schedule nutritious snacks on your GAP. Try the power shake in the AM. Add a midmorning snack and an afternoon snack. My energy booster in the afternoon (when my energy level is low) includes prunes, dark chocolate, and a slice of whole grain bread. If you want to learn more about nutrition, check out RealAge (realage.com)—it's the site run by Dr. Mehmet Oz and Dr. Michael Roizen.

- **Juicing.** No, not the Barry Bonds kind of juicing, I'm talking about fruits and vegetables. I started doing it recently and I'm addicted. Now everything I look at I want to juice. It's a fast and nutritious snack—especially in the late afternoon. Also, there's something cathartic about grinding the hell out of a bunch of stuff.

- **Music.** I don't care how tired I feel, if I crank up Nirvana's live "Drain You" (actually, anything by Nirvana), I can't help but get a boost of energy. Make a playlist of your best energy-creating music and play it at certain times during the day to get a boost (during your lunch walk, driving home, while working out).

- **Reality TV.** Whenever I need a burst of inspiration, I flip on *COPS* and suddenly I feel better about myself and my life. Maybe for you, watching *Intervention* or tryouts for *American Idol* make you feel better about yourself. Reality TV is better and cheaper than therapy. Try it.

- **Get some sun.** Take a break and get outside. The fresh air and sunlight can relax and rejuvenate you. If you live in a sun-challenged climate or just have a long winter, consider shifting your schedule to wake up earlier and go to bed earlier or getting a sunlamp. This can help those who suffer from SAD (seasonal affective disorder) and anyone who craves the sun after the 120th day of dreary clouds.

Add these energy boosters to your day so you have the energy to close the gaps and get the life you want.

You did it! How does it feel to Habitualize? Going through this process and completing the GAP form may feel unnatural at first. That's to be expected. Creating new positive habits takes time and faith that the new habits—even though they might not feel comfortable at first—are better in the long run. If you complete the GAP form and stick with it for a couple of weeks, it will become automatic and you'll wonder how you ever lived without it.

To help you stick with it, it's important to keep in mind that the objective is not to fill your day with tasks and activities—remember, a full calendar doesn't equal a full life. Don't get caught up trying to *do* more. Instead, focus on those things that provide meaning and help you *become* more. The less this process feels like work and the more it feels like pursuing your purpose the easier it will be to implement and the more transformational it will be.

Don't be like the woman in the story at the beginning of this chapter. Don't get stuck doing the same things over and over without a direction and without purpose. When you Habitualize, you create an environment where purposeful action becomes part of your life and where each day is another opportunity to get a little closer to reaching your goals.

CONCLUSION

It had been raining for several days in southern Mississippi and another huge storm was expected. The local sheriff was going door to door telling residents to evacuate. An old woman who had been faithfully following God all her life told the sheriff that God would take care of her.

The rain was relentless. The water now was nearly up to her porch. A man in a rowboat paddled by. As he rowed by the house, he noticed the woman sitting in a rocking chair. The man yelled out, "Ma'am! Please get in my boat. I will row you to dry land." The old woman politely declined, "No, thank you. God will save me." "Whatever," the man mumbled as he paddled off to help others. The floodwaters kept rising and the woman had to go to the second floor of her house. A man in a motorboat came by and told the woman in the house to get in because he had come to rescue her. Again, the woman in the house politely declined. She had faith and would wait for God to save her.

The floodwaters continued rising. Just the very top of the roof was above water. Perched on top of the house, the woman sat still and calmly. A FEMA rescue helicopter buzzed overhead (now you know this story is fiction). Through a bullhorn, the rescuer pleaded with the woman to grab the rope so they could fly her to safety. The woman yelled back, "I don't need your help. God will save me!"

The floodwaters kept rising and the woman in the house drowned. When she got to heaven, she was flabbergasted. How could God have allowed this to happen? She stormed into God's office and asked him why he didn't save her. "What more could I have done?" asked God. "I sent the sheriff, two boats, and a helicopter!"

Like the old woman, we can't idly sit back and expect great things to happen. Faith and optimism are powerful forces, but at the end of the day, we have to get off our asses and make something happen. Too many of us pick up a book or attend a workshop and expect a miracle. The truth is that we don't need a miracle to save us. We just need to get clear on what we want and go after it.

Again and again and again, I've worked with people who are fed up and desperately want change in their lives but, ultimately, do not want to change themselves. They think it is too hard or takes too long. But the truth is change can happen in an instant.

Change starts the moment you decide to lose weight after you look in the mirror and don't recognize yourself. Change starts the moment you decide to stop working seventy hours a week after surviving a heart attack. Change starts the moment you ask Jesus to come into your life after attending a church service. Change starts the moment you commit to making more money after your rent check bounces.

Change happens the moment you realize good enough isn't good enough. When you realize there are gaps in your life you want to close. When you realize where you are right now doesn't have to be where you are tomorrow. Change begins when you dream of a more rich and inspired life.

If you're not sure about what changes are necessary, then you're not to blame. I can imagine many a caveman clubbing his woman over the head for having yet another baby. But, and this is a big "but," the moment you have knowledge, you have no excuse. As soon as you know what needs to change, the burden is on you to make the change.

Guess what? Now you know. You can create a life with more meaning, more money, and deeper relationships with your family and friends by using the other 8 hours. The woman in the story drowned because she failed to take action. It's easy to say you want more from life, but it takes great courage to throw down the gauntlet and go after it.

That ticking sound? That's your life. That's the other 8 hours. Put the book down and go use them . . .

RESOURCES

This book is full of resources you should look into further, but I wanted to showcase a few of them here. I've even been able to negotiate some pretty good discounts with some of them for you. They were nice enough to provide a discount, but I can't guarantee how long it will be valid—the discount and terms of the offer can be changed by them at any time.

Elance (elance.com)—This is *the* site I use to find designers, assistants, developers, and just about anything else I'm looking for. I highly recommend them.

LegalZoom (legalzoom.com)—They can help you form an LLC or corporation. I've used them. They do great work. Use code: **8HOURS** at checkout to get $10 off any service they provide.

The Company Corporation (incorporate.com)—They specialize in forming LLCs and corporations. Use code: **OTHER8** at checkout to get $50 off their services.

Grasshopper (grasshopper.com)—They provide an inexpensive virtual phone solution for small businesses starting at $9.95 a month. I've used them and highly recommend them. Go to grasshopper.com/other8hours to get the activation fee waived and 400 free minutes.

TimeSvr (timesvr.com)—Outsource your tasks on the cheap. They offer a unique "all you can eat" approach for $69 a month plus a free trial period to test it out. You have nothing to lose by trying it—except for a bunch of tasks you want to offload! Use code: **OTHER8** at checkout to get 15 percent off their Personal or Dedicated plan for the first three months.

Logoworks (logoworks.com)—It's hard to get that perfect logo, but it's a lot easier when you use these guys. They create unique and eye-catching logos that won't cost you a fortune. Use code: **other8discount** at checkout to receive a 15 percent discount on logo design projects.

FINAL NOTE TO READER

The goal of this book is to provide accurate and useful information to you about personal financial planning. It is designed to help you focus on goals and actions that are important to address in the financial planning process. The book provides general guidelines that are for informational purposes only. The guidelines are provided with the understanding that the author is not engaged in rendering professional services or in providing specific investment advice.

The application of general guidelines involving regulatory, accounting, and legal practices, which may differ from locality to locality and which are constantly changing, is highly dependent on an evaluation of individual facts and specific circumstances. With regard to any decisions that can potentially have significant financial, legal, tax, or other consequences, no book can take the place of individual professional advice. You should not regard this book as a substitute for consulting with a competent lawyer, accountant, or other financial professional, as appropriate to the nature of your particular situation.

The book presents various investment strategies that may or may not be appropriate for your specific situation. It is also important to keep in mind that different types of investments involve varying degrees of risk, and there can be no assurance that the future performance of any specific investment, investment strategy, or idea discussed in this book will be profitable or suitable for you. If you have any questions regarding the applicability of any investment strategy discussed in this book to your particular financial situation, you should consult with a professional advisor.

With regard to references to products, service providers, and potential sources of additional information, the author cannot vouch for such products or services or the information or recommendations in those sources. Neither the publisher nor the author is responsible for any third-party product or service or content over which they do not have control.

ENDNOTES

CHAPTER TWO

1. Joe Napsha, "American Workers are Laboring Longer Hours," *Pittsburgh Tribune-Review*, January 2, 2008, http://www.pittsburghlive.com/x/pittsburghtrib/business/s_545439.html.

2. Chuck Salter, "Solving the Real Productivity Crisis," *Fast Company*, December 19, 2007, http://www.fastcompany.com/magazine/78/sanity.html.

3. Keith Naughton, "The Long and Grinding Road," *Newsweek*, October 16, 2007, http://www.newsweek.com/ (accessed June 9, 2008).

4. Ibid.

5. American Psychological Association, "Stress a Major Health Problem in the U.S., Warns APA," *APA Online*, October 24, 2007, http://www.apa.org/releases/stressproblem.html.

6. Anxiety Disorders Association of America, "Americans Report Stress and Anxiety On-the-Job Affects Work Performance, Home Life," *Anxiety Disorders Association of America Online*, November 8, 2006, http://www.adaa.org/aboutadaa/PressRoom/newsreleaseDoc/11_8_06pressrelease.asp.

7. Anxiety Disorders Association of America, "Statistics and Facts about Anxiety Disorders," *Anxiety Disorders Association of America Online*, http://www.adaa.org/AboutADAA/PressRoom/Stats&Facts.asp (accessed June 22, 2008).

8. Associated Press, "Many Americans Fear Another Terrorist Attack," MSNBC.com, August 31, 2006, http://www.msnbc.msn.com/id/14598506/.

9. M. McPherson, Lynn Smith-Lovin, and Matthew E. Brashears, "Social Isolation in America: Changes in Core Discussion Networks Over Two Decades," *American Sociological Review* 71 (June 2007): 353–75.

10. Durex Global Sex Survey 2007, http://yesboleh.blogspot.com/2007/04/durex-global-sex-survey-2007.html.

11. Leslie Goldman, "Surprising Reasons You're Not Having Sex," CNN.com, February 12, 2008, http://www.cnn.com/2008/HEALTH/02/12/healthmag.no.sex/index.html 4/.

12. Diane Smith, "Study: 75% of Americans Overweight by 2015," Johns Hopkins Bloomberg School of Public Health's Center for Human Nutrition, Efluxmedia.com, July 12, 2007, http://www.efluxmedia.com/news _Study_75_of_Adults_in_US_Overweight_by_2015_06990.html.

13. MetLife, The 2008 MetLife Study of the American Dream, 6.

14. US Census Bureau 2007 data.

15. Russell Goldman, "Wages Through the Ages: Men Earn Less Than Fathers at Same Age," ABCNews.com, May 25, 2007, http://abcnews.go.com/ Business/LifeStages/story?id=3213731&page=1.

16. Peter S. Goodman, "Economy Fitful, Americans Start to Pay as They Go." *New York Times,* February 5, 2008, http://www.nytimes.com/2008/02/05/ business/05spend.html?_r=1&scp=1&sq=economy%20fitful&st=cse.

    There are flaws to the calculation. It doesn't include some things that really are savings, but, as Laura Rowly pointed out in her Yahoo! Finance column titled "Americans' Debt: Worse Than You Think," the calculation may exaggerate our savings rate because it considers housing expenses as an investment, even though many may be expenses.

17. Shannon Buggs, "Time to Make Outsaving the Joneses a Reality," *Houston Chronicle,* January 12, 2008, http://www.newthrift.org/articles/buggs.htm.

18. Commission on Thrift, "For a New Thrift: Confronting the Debt Culture," 2008, http://www.newthrift.org/.

19. Employee Benefit Research Institute, "Americans Much More Worried About Retirement, Health Costs a Big Concern," 2008 Retirement Confidence Survey, http://www.ebri.org/publications/ib/index.cfm?fa=ibDisp& content_id=3903.

20. Dennis Jacobe, "Many Americans Fear They'll Outlive Their Money," Gallup.com, February 27, 2008, http://www.gallup.com/poll/104605/ Many-Americans-Fear-Theyll-Outlive-Their-Money.aspx?version=p.

21. Employee Benefit Research Institute, "Americans Much More Worried."

22. Ibid.

23. Rome Neal, "Postponing Retirement," CBSNews.com, January 6, 2004, http://www.cbsnews.com/stories/2004/01/05/earlyshow/living/main591475 .shtml?source=search_story.

24. Ibid.

25. Sandra Block, "Rising Costs Make Climb to Higher Education Steeper," USAToday.com, January 12, 2007, http://usatoday.com/.

26. The Project on Student Debt, *Quick Facts on Student Debt,* 2006.

CHAPTER THREE

1. Ivan Berger, "The Virtues of a Second Screen," New York Times.com, April 20, 2006, http://www.nytimes.com/2006/04/20/technology/20basics. html?scp=2&sq=virtues+of+a+second+screen&st=nyt.

CHAPTER FOUR

1. Barry Schwartz et al., "Maximizing Versus Satisficing: Happiness Is a Matter of Choice," *Journal of Personality and Social Psychology—American Psychological Association* 83, no. 5(2002):1178–97.

CHAPTER SEVEN

1. Here's the calculation: One gallon of uranium weighs approximately 150 pounds. One pound of uranium-235 has the energy of about 1 million gallons of gasoline. So, 150 pounds × 1,000,000 = the energy of 150,000,000 gallons of gasoline. A Prius gets 40 miles per gallon, so 150,000,000 gallons of gas in a Prius would allow you to drive 6,000,000,000 miles.

   Distance from earth to the sun = 93,020,000 (93,020,000 × 2 × 19 = 3,534,760,000 miles to go from the Earth to the sun and back 19 times).

   Distance from Earth to moon = 238,857 (238,857 × 2 × 2,619 = 1,251, 132,966 miles to go from the Earth to the moon and back 2,619 times).

   Distance around the Earth at the equator = 24,901 (24,901 × 41,016 = 1,021,339,416 miles to go around the Earth at the equator 41,016 times).

   Distance from Los Angeles to New York = 2,780 (2,780 × 2 × 34,670 = 192,765,200 miles to go from LA to NY and back 34,670 times).

   So, 3,534,760,000 + 1,251,132,966 + 1,021,339,416 + 192,765,200 = 5,999,997,582 miles.

CHAPTER EIGHT

1. Mark Penn, "America's Newest Profession: Bloggers for Hire," *Wall Street Journal*, April 21, 2009, http://online.wsj.com/article/SB1240264158086 36575.html.

INDEX

ABOUT THE AUTHOR

I'm obsessed with improvement and making the most of the other 8 hours to create an ideal life. I'm also obsessed with sharing what I know, inspiring others to achieve their ideal life, and learning from others who are improving their lives. I've always, consciously or subconsciously, placed great importance on the other 8 hours.

For a guy who hated English class, I'm thrilled to have written the personal finance book *The Six-Day Financial Makeover: Transform Your Financial Life in Less Than a Week!* as well as the counterintuitive financial how-to book *Plan Z: How to Survive the 2009 Financial Crisis (and even live a little better)* during the other 8 hours.

I also write a weekly column for CBS MoneyWatch (yourother8hours .com), have appeared on national TV, cofounded a hip and upscale clothing line, have taken Spanish language classes, attended Toastmasters, helped start a nonprofit to aid underprivileged children, earned my Certified Financial Planner designation and master's degree, served as a deacon, founded Internet companies and a Facebook application, and, of course, wrote this book you are holding in your hands during the other 8 hours.

I'm proud to say that some of my (ad)ventures were successful and not embarrassed to say others crashed and burned. But that's kind of the point. Improvement and growth means taking risks. Sometimes you win and sometimes you learn.

I am the president and owner of Pacifica Wealth Advisors, Inc., (pacificawealth.com) a boutique wealth management firm recently ranked one of the top firms in the country. I've worked with a wide range of clients over the years, including stay-at-home moms, schoolteachers, lawyers, widows, self-made millionaires, business owners, entrepreneurs, and doctors, and specialize in serving "sudden money" recipients.

I love sharing my ideas with the media. I've appeared as a financial expert on *20/20, Good Morning America, Dr. Phil, ABC Morning News*, and NPR's *Marketplace*, and in the *Wall Street Journal, Newsweek, BusinessWeek, Money Magazine*, and many others.

I live with my beautiful wife, Elizabeth (who is at least twice as smart as me), and my four-year-old daughter, Alexandra "Bean" (who is way smarter than my wife and me combined), in Orange County, California. On most Sundays you'll find us at Saddleback Church and occasionally at Disneyland.